Robert M. La Follette, Sr.

Robert M. La Follette, Los Angeles, California. April, 1907. Photo used to illustrate campaign pamphlet for 1908. Photo provided by the State Historical Society of Wisconsin.

ROBERT M. LA FOLLETTE, SR.
The Voice of Conscience

Carl R. Burgchardt

Foreword by Bernard K. Duffy

Great American Orators, Number 14

Bernard K. Duffy and Halford R. Ryan,
Series Advisers

Greenwood Press
New York • Westport, Connecticut • London

Library of Congress Cataloging-in-Publication Data

Burgchardt, Carl R.
  Robert M. La Follette, Sr. : the voice of conscience / Carl R.
Burgchardt ; foreword by Bernard K. Duffy.
      p.   cm.—(Great American orators, ISSN 0898-8277 ; no. 14)
  Includes bibliographical references and index.
  ISBN 0-313-25842-2 (alk. paper)
  1. La Follette, Robert M. (Robert Marion), 1855-1925—Oratory.
  I. Title.   II. Series.
  E664.L16B87   1992
  973.91'092—dc20   91-32194

British Library Cataloguing in Publication Data is available.

Copyright © 1992 by Carl R. Burgchardt

All rights reserved. No portion of this book may be
reproduced, by any process or technique, without the
express written consent of the publisher.

Library of Congress Catalog Card Number: 91-32194
ISBN: 0-313-25842-2
ISSN: 0898-8277

First published in 1992

Greenwood Press, 88 Post Road West, Westport, CT 06881
An imprint of Greenwood Publishing Group, Inc.

Printed in the United States of America

∞™

The paper used in this book complies with the
Permanent Paper Standard issued by the National
Information Standards Organization (Z39.48-1984).

10 9 8 7 6 5 4 3 2 1

Copyright Acknowledgments

The author and publisher are grateful to the following for granting permission to reprint excerpts from copyrighted material:

Reprinted with permission of Macmillan Publishing Company from *Robert M. La Follette, June 14, 1855-June 18, 1925, Volume I and Volume II* by Belle Case and Fola La Follette. Copyright 1953, renewed 1981, by Fola La Follette.

Reprinted by permission of Speech Communication Association from Carl R. Burgchardt, "Discovering Rhetorical Imprints: La Follette, 'Iago,' and the Melodramatic Scenario." *Quarterly Journal of Speech* 71 (1985): 441-56.

Reprinted by permission of Greenwood Publishing Group, Inc., Westport, CT, from *Oratorical Encounters: Selected Studies and Sources of Twentieth-Century Political Accusations and Apologies*, edited by Halford Ross Ryan. Copyright by Halford Ross Ryan and published in 1988 by Greenwood Press.

To my daughters,
Jane and Lucy

Contents

Series Foreword ix
Foreword xiii
Acknowledgments xvii

PART I: CRITICAL ANALYSIS

1. Introduction 3
2. "Iago" and the Evil Principle 11
3. Congressman La Follette 23
4. The Menacing Machine 35
5. Governor La Follette 53
6. Senator La Follette 73
7. "Willful Men" 85
8. "Forward, Progressives!" 101
9. Conclusion 117

Notes 125

PART II: SELECTED SPEECHES

Iago	153
Oleomargarine	159
The Menace of the Political Machine	171
Governor La Follette's Speech of Acceptance	185
Free Speech and the Right of Congress to Declare the Objects of the War	191
Labor Day Address	207
Chronology of Major Speeches	217
Selected Bibliography	227
Index	233

Series Foreword

The idea for a series of books on great American orators grew out of the recognition that there is a paucity of book-length studies on individual orators and their speeches. Apart from a few notable exceptions, the study of American public address has been pursued in scores of articles published in professional journals. As helpful as these studies have been, none has or can provide a complete analysis of a speaker's rhetoric. Book-length studies, such as those in this series, will help fill the void that has existed in the study of American public address and its related disciplines of politics and history, theology and sociology, communication and law. In books, the critic can explicate a broader range of a speaker's persuasive discourse than reasonably could be treated in articles. The comprehensive research and sustained reflection that books require will undoubtedly yield many original and enduring insights concerning the nation's most important voices.

Public address has been a fertile ground for scholarly investigation. No matter how insightful their intellectual forebears, each generation of scholars must reexamine its universe of discourse, while expanding the compass of its researches and redefining its purpose and methods. To avoid intellectual torpor new scholars cannot be content simply to see through the eyes of those who have come before them. We hope that this series of books will stimulate important new understandings of the nature of persuasive discourse and provide additional opportunities for scholarship in the history and criticism of American public address.

This series examines the role of rhetoric in the United States. American speakers shaped the destiny of the colonies, the young republic, and the mature nation. During each stage of the intellectual, political, and religious development of the United States, great orators, standing at the rostrum, on the stump, and in the pulpit, used words and gestures to influence their audiences. Usually striving for the noble, sometimes achieving the base, they urged their fellow citizens toward a more perfect Union. The books in this series chronicle and explain the accomplishments of representative American leaders as orators.

A series of book-length studies on American persuaders honors the role men and women have played in U.S. history. Previously, if one desired to assess the impact of a speaker or a speech upon history, the path was, at best, not well marked and, at worst, littered with obstacles. To be sure, one might turn to biographies and general histories to learn about an orator, but for the public address scholar these sources often prove unhelpful. Rhetorical topics, such as speech invention, style, delivery, organizational strategies, and persuasive effect, are often treated in passing, if mentioned at all. Authoritative speech texts are often difficult to locate, and the problem of textual accuracy is frequently encountered. This is especially true for those figures who spoke one or two hundred years ago, or for those whose persuasive role, though significant, was secondary to other leading lights of the age.

Each book in this series is organized to meet the needs of scholars and students of the history and criticism of American public address. Part I is a critical analysis of the orator and his or her speeches. Within the format of a case study, one may expect considerable latitude. For instance, in a given chapter an author might explicate a single speech or a group of related speeches, or examine orations that comprise a genre of rhetoric such as forensic speaking. But the critic's focus remains on the rhetorical considerations of speaker, speech, occasion, and effect. Part II contains the texts of the important addresses that are discussed in the critical analysis that precedes it. To the extent possible, each author has endeavored to collect authoritative speech texts, which have often been found through original research in collections of primary source material. In a few instances, because of the extreme length of a speech, texts have been edited, but the authors have been careful to delete material that is least important to the speech, and these deletions have been held to a minimum.

In each book there is a chronology of major speeches that serves more purposes than may be apparent at first. Pragmatically, it lists all of the orator's known speeches and addresses. Places and dates of the speeches are also listed, although this is information that is sometimes difficult to determine precisely. But in a wider sense, the chronology attests to the scope of rhetoric in the United States. Certainly in quantity, if not always in quality, Americans are historically talkers and listeners.

Because of the disparate nature of the speakers examined in the series, there is some latitude in the nature of the bibliographical materials that have been included in each book. But in every instance, authors have carefully described original historical materials and collections and gathered critical studies, biographies and autobiographies, and a variety of secondary sources that bear on the speaker and the oratory. By combining in each book bibliographical materials, speech texts, and critical chapters, this series notes that text and research sources are interwoven in the act of rhetorical criticism.

May the books in this series serve to memorialize the nation's greatest orators.

Bernard K. Duffy
Halford R. Ryan

Foreword

In his introduction Professor Carl R. Burgchardt comments that his book is a "rhetorical biography." It is an apt term to describe this work whose approach embodies our idea for the series; I have used the term "oratorical biography" in the same sense. Rhetorical or oratorical biography seems a particularly appropriate means to consider the life of Robert La Follette, who was an orator in the nineteenth-century conception of one who influenced the *polis* by marshalling language on behalf of the public good. La Follette attended college at a time when an education in oratory possessed a level of importance that it has lost today. Literary and debating societies sponsored declamation contests and gave oratory a cachet that attracted the best and brightest students. La Follette learned early the thrill of moving an audience through "perspicuous speech." As with protégés who exhibit skill in musical or artistic pursuits, La Follette's precocity as an orator predicted his later accomplishment. What is more, Burgchardt shows that resonances of the rhetoric of the young La Follette's prizewinning oration on Iago's consummate evil are revealed in his later addresses. The youthful products of intellect and imagination preserved in La Follette's oration provide a window to the rhetoric that would lead him to be one of Wisconsin's most celebrated governors, a controversial United States senator, and a leader in the progressive movement in American politics.

The Iago speech was a work of literary criticism, expressed in the spacious rhetoric admired in nineteenth-century America. Burgchardt reveals that the representations of evil that made the Iago speech successful found their way into speeches against large corporations and combinations, political machines, and railroad rates, all of which were common objects of progressivist scorn. Burgchardt even helps us hear the rhetoric of the Iago speech in a political oration La Follette made against oleomargarine, which for Wisconsin dairy farmers was a palpable manifestation of the evils of the meat-packing industry that produced it. This is not to say that La Follette's speeches never evolved or responded to changing circumstances. His nascent Iago oration demonstrated his rhetorical talent and proclivities, particularly his ability to use language to create vivid imagery that could inspire and move his audiences. But his later political speeches made heavy use of statistical evidence and authority as well as strategic moral propositions.

La Follette had the orator's gift of interpreting and adapting to the needs of his audience. His political philosophy was perfectly attuned to his commitment to oratory as a means of communicating with the people. He claimed the democratic virtue of trusting in the opinions of the people, a fitting viewpoint for a politician whose career was animated by his public speeches. La Follette's highmindedness and confident moral stance made him immensely appealing to a culture ready for reforms in business and government. He rose to a role of leadership because his oratory put into words the beliefs and sentiments of his audiences. La Follette's generation was affected by a Civil War remembered as a spiritual quest and was interested in civic-mindedness and social betterment in the face of corruption and inefficiency in government, anti-democratic tendencies in party politics, and the moral callousness of big business. Among the reforms La Follette proposed while he was Wisconsin's governor were the graduated income tax, legislative restraints on lobbying, and the regulation of telephone and telegraph industries and the railroads. Railroad freight rates were an especially potent issue for the electorate, both because they had a significant effect upon the price of goods and the cost of commerce, and because they seemed capricious, since there was no consistency or recognizable rationale for the setting of individual rates for different commodities. Although La Follette's tack in arguing for the regulation of railroad rates was to expose the evils of the railroad's monopolistic practices, his text was thick with statistical evidence.

As an indication of his skill and popularity as an orator, in 1903 alone, La Follette spoke on fifty-seven occasions on the Chautauqua circuit. One of his often-repeated speeches was a literary interpretation of Hamlet, which attempted to assess Hamlet's motivations and to render a moral judgment about him. Although this might seem an unusual rhetorical undertaking for a practical politician, La Follette's career was built on judging the moral conduct of others in the interests of protecting the citizenry. La Follette followed Cicero's prescription that it is the orator's place to influence ethical thought and conduct. Whether he was bent on assessing the reasons for Hamlet's brooding, Iago's singular malevolence, or the misdeeds of politicians in both political parties, his rhetoric rang with ethical pronouncements couched in moving and memorable language.

La Follette, the *vox populi*, who had capitalized on the people's faith in him as one who claimed ultimate faith in them, enjoyed less success on the national political scene than in Wisconsin. In the Senate his orations won ovations from the gallery, for he continued to speak on behalf of progressive themes and later against conscription and United States involvement in World War I without the explicit consent of the people. His colleagues in the Senate, however, greeted La Follette with less enthusiasm. In one fateful speech delivered in St. Paul, La Follette expressed doubt about the legitimacy of the sinking of the munitions-laden *Lusitania* as a justification for United States entry into the war. As a result, he found himself misinterpreted by a hostile press and excoriated in the Senate as a traitor. His apologia included not only an indictment against Wilson for attempting to intimidate the Congress into supporting the war, but also a plea for the importance of free speech even in times of war. Nevertheless, La Follette found himself the subject of a Senate investigation that for a time mitigated against his political effectiveness. La Follette was also among those senators who defeated the passage of the Treaty of Versailles and the League of Nations on the argument that the treaty was a boon to British imperialism and an impediment to future peace. Later he pleaded for the repeal of the Alien and Sedition Act and helped to disclose the Teapot Dome scandal. La Follette capped his political career by running for president as an independent in 1924. Although he lost to Coolidge, he was able to disseminate his progressive ideas more widely than as either governor or senator. By the time of his death, few in the United States denied the importance of his leadership in the progressive movement, his success in articulating a philosophy of popular government, or his tenacity in fighting for the cause of labor, small farmers, and the common man oppressed by large corporations and by a government insensitive to the popular will.

La Follette used oratory to assert moral as well as political leadership. His rhetoric was shaped by a confluence of idealism and faith that political action could correct social evils. The skein of thought that runs throughout all of La Follette's speeches was that truly representative government could rectify civil society with its highest ideals. Whether his topic was oleomargarine, Hamlet, or the League of Nations, La Follette had a clear vision of moral right.

Burgchardt was the first person invited to write a book in this series and his project has born fruit in proportion to the considerable effort he has expended to complete it. His carefully researched and lucidly written monograph is one whose contribution to rhetorical biography should be apparent to all who read it.

Bernard K. Duffy

Acknowledgments

My interest in Robert M. La Follette began as a graduate student at the University of Wisconsin-Madison in the late 1970s. A series of seminar papers on La Follette's oratory evolved into a Ph.D. dissertation: "The Will, the People, and the Law: A Rhetorical Biography of Robert M. La Follette, Sr." My dissertation formed the foundation for subsequent publications concerning La Follette, including this book. Because of its lineage, the current volume owes a special debt to several faculty members I encountered in graduate school. Historians John Milton Cooper and Daniel T. Rodgers guided my study of the progressive era in the United States and encouraged my efforts to analyze La Follette's career from an oratorical perspective. In the Communication Arts Department, Lloyd F. Bitzer honed my understanding of rhetorical theory, while Donald K. Smith molded my perceptions of great speakers and speeches in society. Anyone familiar with the writings of Edwin Black will recognize his salutary influence in my work. Stephen E. Lucas directed my Ph.D. dissertation and served as a model of superb scholarship in public address studies.

Colorado State University also had a significant role in the production of this book. A Professional Development Grant from the College of Arts, Humanities, and Social Sciences supported research at the State Historical Society of Wisconsin and the Library of Congress. Speech Communication Department Chairs Ann M. Gill and G. Jack Gravlee provided me with advantageous teaching schedules, financial help, and moral support. As well, Professor Gravlee saved me from numerous errors by providing a very close reading of my manuscript. During numerous lunchtime conversations, my colleague David Vancil helped me clarify concepts. Linda Kidder of the Speech

Department did an outstanding job of transcribing La Follette's orations into the computer.

Bernard K. Duffy, one of the editors for the Great American Orators series, improved the manuscript conceptually and stylistically, while he guided me through the obstacle course of book writing. I owe special thanks to my editor from Greenwood Press, Mildred Vasan, who exhibited extraordinary patience and flexibility in working with me. Although Halford R. Ryan was not assigned to edit my manuscript, I am grateful for his unceasing efforts to create publishing opportunities for historical and critical studies in American public address and for his willingness to take chances on struggling assistant professors.

I would have been lost without the support of my wife, Jill C. Burgchardt, who contributed materially to the completion of the manuscript through her expert editing, proofreading, and knowledge of computers. As always, I thank my parents, Carl and Elva Burgchardt, for their unfaltering encouragement and sage advice over the years.

I
CRITICAL ANALYSIS

1
Introduction

Robert M. La Follette was one of the most significant politicians of his age. Historians have recognized him as an outstanding leader of the progressive era, both at the state and national levels. He also won notoriety because of his opposition to World War I and his defense of free speech. Despite many episodes of conflict, he enjoyed a public career that lasted, with few interruptions, for forty-five years. At the heart of his political success was his skill in oratory. Indeed, more than most politicians, rhetoric was the driving force in La Follette's career. He relied on public speaking to capture the public's attention, to promulgate his reform ideology, to overcome formidable political obstructions, and to maintain his popularity during periods of fierce public controversy. Moreover, La Follette was conscious of the vital role of rhetoric in society: "It is the orator . . . who . . . directs the destinies of states."[1]

I maintain that La Follette's thought and contributions cannot be understood properly apart from his public discourse. For one thing, he was unusually preoccupied with the preparation and presentation of speeches. For another, his ideas were almost always framed in strategic language and directed toward an audience. Such language cannot be interpreted accurately without understanding its persuasive purposes, the social and political contexts that called it forth, and its influence on society.

By themselves, conventional biographical or historical methods are inadequate to analyze properly La Follette's political oratory. Instead, this book uses the method of "rhetorical biography," which focuses on the creation, transmission, and reception of persuasive, public discourse. Ordinarily, the term "rhetoric" implies written, as well as oral, persuasive messages, but this book confines itself to analysis of La Follette's public speaking. Although La Follette generated enormous amounts of essays, editorials, and pamphlets, these written materials either preceded, or derived from, his oratory. Thus, this study is safe in limiting itself to criticism of La Follette's speeches because his oral discourse is representative of the entire corpus of his rhetoric.

The narrative of this rhetorical biography is guided by the progression of important public speeches. The relative weight assigned to each speech is determined by the internal and external significance of the rhetoric. Internal significance concerns the evolution of major themes, arguments, and images across time. External significance concerns the social and political impact of particular speeches. As a result of following this method, I place more emphasis on the early portions of La Follette's oratorical career, 1879-1905. His Wisconsin campaigns were rhetorically more interesting from the standpoint of innovation and political success. After 1905 La Follette's rhetoric played out well-established strategies and themes, and his victories were limited. The exception is La Follette's rhetorical response to the extraordinary events surrounding World War I. Even in this case, however, most of his discourse is still governed by rhetorical patterns established at the beginning of his career.

The purpose of this book is not to write a conventional history. Indeed, I include just enough historical context to make the analysis of La Follette's oratory understandable. I do not discuss La Follette's private life or inside political dealings except insofar as they became part of the public debate. I focus on the creation and consequences of ideas manifested in arguments, metaphors, images, and strategies. In doing so, I strive to accomplish two interrelated objectives: to describe the development over time of La Follette's political ideology and to understand the processes by which his ideas were popularized in Wisconsin and the nation.

The analysis of why an orator's discourse was persuasive is a central function of rhetorical biography, but there are other yields, as well. First, rhetorical biography can increase our understanding of social, intellectual, or cultural history. La Follette became involved in many of the major political debates of American life from the 1880s to the 1920s. By examining La Follette's political rhetoric, one can partially reconstruct the temper of the times in which he lived. Political discourse invariably represents one facet of the competing ideas and values that exist simultaneously in society. Politicians, through their rhetoric, seek to respond to constituencies; hence, they often are sensitive barometers of public opinion. As Ernest Wrage observed,

because speeches are instruments of utility designed in the main for the popular mind, conversely and in significant ways they bear the impress of the popular mind. It is because they are pitched to levels of information, to take account of prevalent beliefs, and to mirror the tone and temper of audiences that they serve as useful indices to the popular mind.

In other words, La Follette's orations provide historical insights into audience values, beliefs, and attitudes. Moreover, through the analysis of discourse, rhetorical biography may reconstruct the public persona of an orator. La Follette's popular image, which he cultivated through rhetoric, is a version of himself that is probably similar to the way he was actually perceived by his contemporaries. In short, according to Wrage, "To adopt the rhetorical perspective is actually to approximate more closely a genuinely historical point of view when analyzing and interpreting speeches as documents of ideas in social history."[2]

Another critical yield of rhetorical biography is to provide insight into an orator's motives, values, and attitudes. As Edwin Black has commented, rhetorical criticism may consider "the relationship between a man's deepest motives and his discourses." It is possible to probe, through rhetoric, an orator's psychological state because

language has a symptomatic function. Discourses contain tokens of their authors. Discourses are, directly or in a transmuted form, the external signs of internal states. In short, we accept it as true that a discourse implies an author, and we mean by that more than the tautology that an act entails an agent. We mean, more specifically, that certain features of a linguistic act entail certain characteristics of the language user.[3]

Contained within La Follette's discourse are characteristics that reflect the distinctive mental faculties of the rhetor. Therefore, an analysis of La Follette's oratory can contribute toward a better understanding of the basic motives, beliefs, and *Weltanschauung* of the orator. Particularly since La Follette produced a limited amount of introspective, private writings, his public discourse is a primary source for revealing his personal beliefs and political ideology. La Follette's oratory was the fruit of his intellectual life. As such, it was the highest expression of his spirit and conviction.

The remainder of this book is divided into eight chapters. The first seven each deal with a major chronological unit of La Follette's rhetoric, and the final chapter summarizes and concludes the study. In each chronological chapter I provide an overview of the major speeches, the exigencies that called them forth, and the impacts that they had on La Follette and society. Exceptional or seminal speeches are analyzed in depth, and some of these texts are reproduced in the Part II of this book. Other speeches are grouped together and evaluated topically. In analyzing La Follette's orations, I have not attempted to catalog the contents of each document. Instead, I have focused on its most salient features. I have highlighted the underlying values, attitudes, and strategies that most clearly express La Follette's distinct personality as an orator. At the same time, I have tried to maintain an accurate balance, so that the reader experiences the true texture of La Follette's rhetoric.

Chapter 2 covers the period 1855-1879. Robert M. La Follette won the Inter-State Oratorical Contest on May 7, 1879, while completing his senior year at the University of Wisconsin. This was obviously a personal triumph for young La Follette, and it is an interesting biographical note. But one would hardly expect a student's speech to be very significant. Yet La Follette's speech, titled "Iago," is very important. It is the earliest full text we have of La Follette's oratory, and it was the major source for his early reputation as a powerful and eloquent speaker. La Follette used this renown as a springboard for obtaining political office two years later. In addition, "Iago" provides an opportunity to scrutinize a rhetorical archetype. Several of La Follette's most deep-seated oratorical traits were present in "Iago," albeit in immature form. Most notably, "Iago" contained La Follette's first use of what I call the "melodramatic scenario"—a pattern of discourse in which a speaker condemns an evil villain who gradually ensnares unsuspecting victims. Before taking up the text of "Iago," however, I will consider the elements in La Follette's upbringing that predisposed him to participate in the Inter-State Oratorical Contest and that helped shape the speech he presented there.

La Follette spoke on a variety of issues and in different settings between 1879 and 1890. These speeches are the subject of Chapter 3. Throughout this time, La Follette's political fortunes were intimately linked with his skill as an orator and campaigner. Because of his victory at the Inter-State Oratorical Contest, he was in demand as a speaker after graduating from college in 1879. During the next two years he improved his reputation for eloquence by addressing local patriotic celebrations, and in 1880 he was elected district attorney of Dane County largely because of his popularity as an orator. His nomination and election as a U.S. Representative in 1884 was similarly prompted by his public speaking skills. While in Congress, La Follette won further plaudits for his oratory, but in 1890 he misjudged the mood of his constituents and was defeated for reelection to the House.

Since La Follette did not advocate a unified program of political reform from 1879 to 1890, some observers have minimized the significance of these years by dismissing La Follette as a "more or less typical politician whose main distinguishing quality was his receptivity to the mood and feelings of the voters." Such a perspective implies that La Follette's early rhetoric was not integrally connected with his later attempts to enact progressive legislation. While there is a measure of truth to that view, it obscures the fact that the years 1879-1890 were crucial to the development of La Follette's rhetoric. Although the subjects of his speeches at first seem unrelated, La Follette's discourse from this time is thematically unified and linked to his past and future rhetoric. Significantly, La Follette continued to use the themes and strategies of "Iago" in his political rhetoric, even during congressional debates on taxation and tariffs. Equally important, he began to define concepts and develop techniques that he would later modify and expand during his famous reform crusades.[4]

Chapter 4 covers 1891-1900, the period in La Follette's career between his terms in Congress and the governorship. It is divided into two sections: 1891-1896 and 1897-1900. The years from 1891 to 1896 were, from a political and personal perspective, highly significant for La Follette. From a rhetorical perspective, however, these years were relatively less important. He gave few notable speeches, and his discourse did not evolve or break new ground. The major reason for this comparatively dormant period in La Follette's rhetoric was an unbroken string of political setbacks that constricted opportunities for innovative discourse. Six months after losing his seat in Congress, he became involved in a feud with Philetus Sawyer, the leader of the Republican Party in Wisconsin. La Follette charged that Sawyer attempted to bribe him to influence the outcome of a court case. This accusation, and the attendant public outcry, brought about negative political consequences for La Follette. Indeed, his career was seemingly ruined. In order to revive his influence, in 1894 La Follette backed an attempt to wrest political power from the Sawyer faction, but the campaign failed. Two years later, he ran unsuccessfully for the governorship.

While La Follette's rhetoric from 1891 to 1896 was uninspired, it was nevertheless important to the revival of his political fortunes. Throughout this period La Follette struggled to maintain contact with the voters through public appearances and speeches. Moreover, he campaigned energetically and effectively for Republicans during national campaigns. Consequently, by 1896 La Follette had largely repaired his public reputation and had reestablished influence within the national Republican Party.

From a rhetorical perspective, the next three years (1897-1900) were probably the most crucial of La Follette's career, for during this time he defined and popularized the reform issues he needed to win the governorship of Wisconsin. "The Menace of the Political Machine," a speech La Follette delivered at the University of Chicago in 1897, marked the beginning of a twenty-eight-year crusade against the influence of concentrated wealth on the American political system. In this speech La Follette developed his well-established concern with representative elections into a specific and compelling issue—the direct primary. He advocated replacing the caucus and convention method of nominating candidates with the primary election.

Four months later La Follette expanded the ideas from "The Menace of the Political Machine" into another speech, "The Dangers Threatening Representative Government." In addition to advocating the direct primary, La Follette now proposed more equitable taxation of corporations. During the summer and fall of 1897, he repeated "The Dangers Threatening Representative Government" at county fairs all across Wisconsin. These speeches articulated the discontent of many people in Wisconsin, made La Follette the dominant spokesman for reform in the state, and marked the opening of La Follette's try for the 1898 Republican gubernatorial nomination. Significantly, the melodramatic scenario continued to be the major persuasive technique La Follette used in his reform discourse.

Despite his growing popular appeal, however, La Follette's attempt to capture the nomination in 1898 fell short because the Republican state convention was dominated by his opponents. During the next two years, La Follette assembled a powerful coalition that allowed him to take control of the nominating process, and in 1900 he became the Republican nominee for governor. After conducting an intensive public speaking campaign in the general election, La Follette's six-year struggle was finally rewarded with victory.

Chapter 5 covers La Follette's years as governor, 1901-1905. La Follette was inaugurated governor of Wisconsin on January 7, 1901, he expected the state legislature to enact promptly the reform program he had advocated for the past three years. It soon became evident, however, that conservative legislators were not about to pass serious reform measures. Faced with staunch opposition in both the Senate and the Assembly, La Follette abandoned his conciliatory strategy and returned to the campaign trail, where he resumed his familiar rhetoric of uncompromising attack. Moreover, his oratory continued to be guided by the melodramatic scenario, which resulted in polarized, moralistic discourse. For the next four years La Follette directed his appeals beyond the legislature to arouse the public and pressure his political opponents into complying with his proposals. He became, in effect, an agitator in the statehouse.

At the same time, La Follette adapted the resources of the statehouse to his combative, melodramatic style. He devised new methods for sustaining public interest, keeping his opponents off guard and making his proposals the center of political debate in Wisconsin. He pioneered the practice of converting official addresses, vetoes, and special messages into personal opportunities for condemning the legislature and appealing to the public. When his reform crusade began to lose momentum, La Follette unveiled a new issue—regulation of railroad rates—that allowed him once again to dominate public discussion. He took his message directly to the people through extensive speaking engagements on the county fair and Chautauqua circuits. While on these speaking tours, he popularized an unorthodox rhetorical tactic called "reading the freight rates," which consisted of presenting detailed statistical proof that railroads overcharged the citizens of Wisconsin. In addition, La Follette invented the technique of reading to audiences the roll call votes of his opponents to expose their subservience to the corporations. By doing this, he integrated the official legislative record of Wisconsin with his partisan rhetoric.

Wisconsin voters responded favorably to La Follette's appeals, and he was reelected as governor twice, a nearly unprecedented achievement in the state. By 1904 he had complete control of the legislature, and he guided his reform program into law. His legislative triumphs included passage of a direct primary law, tax reform, and railroad regulation. By the time he left Wisconsin in 1906 to become a U.S. senator, La Follette had instituted all of the major reform measures he had campaigned for since 1897.

In Chapter 6, I discuss La Follette's early years as a U.S. senator, 1906-1913. When La Follette entered the Senate on January 4, 1906, he was a man with a mission. La Follette thought of his new office as an opportunity to carry

Wisconsin's message of reform into the wider field of national legislation. La Follette's rhetorical methods had been strongly shaped by his experiences in Wisconsin, and he now brought to the Senate the same message, tactics, and sense of urgency he had used so effectively in his home state. During the next eight years he conducted a topically and strategically unified crusade to enact progressive domestic legislation on the national level.

While in the Senate, La Follette participated in major debates concerning railroads, banking, and tariffs. In each case he advocated measures to discipline organized monopoly, special privilege, and concentrated wealth. The Senate frustrated his reform efforts, so La Follette went to the hustings to "educate" the voters, to popularize reform measures, and to remove Senate conservatives from office, much as he had done in Wisconsin against conservative legislators. By 1911 La Follette believed that his progressive causes could only be adopted at the national level with the strong support of the chief executive. Since La Follette distrusted the motives of William Howard Taft and Theodore Roosevelt, he decided to run for president himself; but he failed to win the Republican nomination. Although La Follette's immediate goals were frequently blocked between 1906 and 1913, his rhetoric helped make him leader of the Republican insurgent faction in the Senate and an important voice for progressive reform throughout the nation.

Chapter 7 covers La Follette's senatorial career through the war years, 1914-1919. Although La Follette and the Senate continued to consider domestic legislation after the outbreak of war in Europe in 1914, the attention of the country turned increasingly toward foreign affairs. In La Follette's case, the topics of war and peace dominated his rhetoric from 1914 to 1919. Throughout his career, La Follette was frequently at odds with establishment figures and policies. Never was he more controversial, however, than during the period of his opposition to Woodrow Wilson's wartime program. La Follette earned the wrath of Wilson and a significant part of the public for his opposition to the war, to conscription, to financing measures, and especially to censorship.

During this period, there was widespread public questioning of his motives—even of his loyalty. In response, La Follette delivered one of the most important speeches of his career. On October 6, 1917, he defended himself in the Senate against charges of disloyalty and sedition, and this oration proved to be a classic argument for free speech during time of war. In the face of unprecedented condemnation, La Follette did not moderate his positions, and in the end he was exonerated. Despite the vituperation directed at La Follette by many at the national level, his rhetoric was generally well-suited to his native constituency. He remained strong in Wisconsin and survived another determined attempt to remove him from office.

With the limited exception of the free speech issue, La Follette's rhetoric continued to use substantially the same techniques, ideas, and arguments that had characterized his public speaking since entering the Senate. Even though the subject of his rhetoric shifted to foreign affairs, he argued, largely through the melodramatic scenario, that the money trusts controlled the lives and destinies of Americans. He maintained that the great corporations, particularly the munitions industry, encouraged war solely for the sake of profit and special privilege.

With the conclusion of the war controversies, La Follette devoted the remaining six and one-half years of his life (1919-1925) to reviving national interest in domestic reform. These speeches are the subject of Chapter 8. Although public demand for progressive reform had waned, La Follette refused to alter the form or content of his rhetorical appeals against corporate control of society. In the Senate he blamed organized monopoly for the severe problems facing postwar America. To solve these problems he advocated stricter control of special privilege and concentrated wealth, but his proposals were usually rejected. He remained popular in Wisconsin, though, and in 1922 won a fourth term in the Senate.

The 1922 campaign was La Follette's last as a Republican. Since the GOP had repeatedly rejected his political ideology, La Follette ran for president as an independent in 1924. Although his rhetoric did not capture the dominant public mood of 1924, it presented the views of a substantial number of Americans and stood as a monument to his fighting spirit. By the time he died in 1925, La Follette had become the sage of radical progressivism.

2
"Iago" and the Evil Principle

Like many children in the nineteenth century, La Follette dreamed of becoming a famous orator. As a four-year-old boy, he supposedly entertained family and friends by mounting a table and reciting the poem "Lines Written for a School Declamation."

Public speaking was a major part of La Follette's social and educational life in rural Wisconsin. Frank Higgins, one of La Follette's elementary school teachers, remembered him as a "natural orator." Although La Follette "wasn't anything above the average as a pupil," recalled Higgins, he "took naturally to speaking. Even down town in the evenings, the men would get him up on a drygoods box and have him make speeches." At school picnics, exhibitions, and spelling bees, La Follette often had a star role as a speaker and entertainer. His recitation of the poem "The Polish Boy" was especially memorable.[1]

In 1873 the La Follette family moved to Madison, and Robert enrolled in a private preparatory school called the Wisconsin Academy. The school placed major emphasis on oratory, and the students sharpened their debating skills on current social and political issues. Christopher Gorham, a classmate, remarked that La Follette was not an exceptional debater, "But we had no one who could compare with him as a declaimer—he was the feature of every program."[2]

In 1874 La Follette enrolled as a "sub-freshman" at the University of Wisconsin, where an important part of the curriculum for all students was the study of rhetoric and public speaking. Students were expected to deliver orations during regularly scheduled chapel "rhetoricals." More important, though, was the extracurricular training received in the literary societies, which were campus groups devoted to the study of letters and the practice of rhetoric. Membership in one of the seven societies was prized because students and faculty alike viewed skill in rhetoric as an important measure of competence. A majority of the student body belonged to these societies, and there was intense competition for the most talented students. Societies met on Friday evenings to listen to a program of debates, essays, declamations, and recitations. In his freshman year La Follette joined the Athena Literary Society, one of the oldest and most prestigious societies on campus. He was immediately recognized by his fellow members as a brilliant elocutionist and declaimer, but only a fair debater.[3]

At the end of his freshman year, La Follette borrowed enough money to purchase part ownership of the unofficial student newspaper, *The University Press*. At that time, the student paper was a private business opportunity, and La Follette became a publishing partner with the hope of defraying his educational expenses. Because of his managerial ability, energy, and talent for selling advertising, the newspaper made a healthy profit each year he operated it.[4]

As part owner of *The University Press*, La Follette considered himself a professional journalist. Charles Van Hise, a classmate, believed that La Follette was the best essay writer in their class, but it is difficult to substantiate Van Hise's judgment by reading issues of *The University Press*. For one thing, La Follette shared editorial responsibilities with several other students, and the editorials were invariably unsigned. For another, La Follette's newspaper colleagues, such as Alexander Berger, testified that he "did very little if any of the editorial work. . . . I think he devoted his time toward securing advertisements and subscriptions." According to A.N. Hitchcock, La Follette's journalistic contributions centered on "short paragraphs and newsy items pertaining to persons and 'doings' about the University."[5]

Perhaps La Follette's influence can be seen in the tone and philosophy of his paper. He undoubtedly took part in drafting the publisher's statement of October 3, 1876: "In selecting the present corps we have endeavored to be entirely independent of all classes, parties and societies. . . . We wish the students to feel that the PRESS is theirs, that its columns are always open to them." This desire to be free of outside control and to provide equal opportunity are two ideas that would come to dominate La Follette's rhetoric in later years. Interestingly, La Follette made good on his promise to provide an open forum for student opinion. His paper featured articles on contemporary campus issues, including stories on the importance of intercollegiate competition in oratory. Moreover, *The University Press* printed the texts of prize-winning student orations, such as O.A. Curtis's "Satan and Mephistopheles."[6]

Despite the lack of direct evidence, La Follette's tenure as a newspaper publisher probably contributed to his later development as a political essayist, and in conjunction with his oratorical work, it honed his facility with language. In any event, La Follette's wife, Belle, believed that "this experience created a longing to own a paper that was not satisfied until he started *La Follette's Magazine* some thirty years later."[7]

Another central element of La Follette's college days was his intense interest and participation in theater. He appeared in several dramatic productions in his sophomore and junior years. Reportedly, he never missed an opportunity to attend a theatrical event in the area, and, according to Belle, he was known to "take the time and spend the money to go to Milwaukee or Chicago to hear a good play" even though he might be penalized for missing classes. La Follette was very likely in the Madison audience when the Shakespearean actor Lawrence Barrett appeared in the role of Iago on April 14, 1877.

For a time La Follette even considered an acting career, but he was discouraged because of the uncertain financial security of the profession and also because he was too short for leading roles. As one famous story goes, the acclaimed Shakespearean actor John McCullough appeared in Madison in 1879, and La Follette obtained an interview with him. La Follette performed some lines of Iago in a short reading from *Othello*. According to Alexander Berger, McCullough was impressed with La Follette's delivery but advised him to pursue a political career because of his diminutive stature: "if you were then taking the role of Iago and I Othello, . . . I am expected to take hold of your throat, and when I did so the boys in the gallery would say 'Oh, leave the little fellow alone.'" This remark may have influenced La Follette to abandon his ambition to be a professional tragedian, but it did not curtail his strong love for oral reading. Throughout his life, a favorite pastime was to read aloud passages of Shakespeare and Robert Burns to family and friends.[8]

As one would expect, La Follette also idolized the leading public speakers of the day, especially Robert G. Ingersoll. As a student, La Follette reportedly studied Ingersoll's works in order to become more eloquent. Years later La Follette recalled that Ingersoll "was the greatest orator, I think, that I have ever heard; . . . Ingersoll had a tremendous influence upon me, as indeed he had upon many young men of that time." Examining the writings of Ingersoll available to La Follette reveals several possible points of influence. Stylistically, La Follette probably attempted to imitate Ingersoll's rich use of metaphors, rhythmic phrases, and vivid imagery, as well as the technique of bringing dramatic scenes before the eyes of the audience. In later years La Follette's rhetoric also had many thematic commonalities with Ingersoll (as well as many other orators of the day). Both men glorified the past, especially the founding of the Republic and the Civil War. Both believed in the sovereignty of the individual, the importance of the ballot in representative government, and the necessity for exercising responsibility in public affairs. Both attacked the Democratic Party and praised the Republicans. Both decried the outrages of slavery, and both believed in the importance of agriculture and the home to national prosperity. Both shared a spirit of reform and sense of moral earnestness. "It was not that he [Ingersoll] changed my beliefs," said La

Follette, "but that he liberated my mind. Freedom was what he preached: he wanted the shackles off everywhere."[9]

La Follette's reputation as a student orator built steadily from 1875 and climaxed in 1879. When La Follette was still a freshman, the Athena society elected him to deliver "a few appropriate words" in tribute to a recently deceased professor, Dr. I.A. Lapham. Interestingly enough, this occasion marked the first time the future governor addressed an audience in the state capitol building. As a sophomore, La Follette represented his society at its anniversary celebration, where he read poetry. During the "Junior Exhibition," La Follette presented a speech titled "The Stage." We do not have the exact text of this speech, but according to newspaper accounts it was "an able and logical refutation of the prejudice against the drama, which prevails in too many minds." La Follette used "historical illustrations" to show the "great good which had been accomplished" by the theater. Perhaps the use of historical illustrations in this address foreshadowed La Follette's later practice of tracing the evolution of a problem through time. In any event, "The Stage" was yet another confirmation of La Follette's interest in drama, an interest that surely influenced his selection of Iago as a topic for the Inter-State Oratorical Contest in 1879.[10]

At the end of his junior year, La Follette became a traveling "elocutionist" with a group of Athenaeans who presented public showings for money in local villages and towns. La Follette electrified audiences with his reading of "The Raven." According to Kemper Knapp, La Follette "could make your hair stand on end. He put more in it than Poe ever did." The local press opined that La Follette had the talent of a professional actor. Everyone agreed that his skills of delivery and interpretation were remarkable.[11]

Despite La Follette's success in a wide range of endeavors at the university, the outstanding event of his college years was winning the Inter-State Oratorical Contest in May, 1879. The Inter-State Oratorical Contest was begun in 1874, and the state of Wisconsin had participated since 1875, although the University of Wisconsin had never won. At the end of La Follette's junior year, the Oratorical Association of Madison chose four men to participate in the local contest, and La Follette was one of them. The winner of the Madison contest would advance to Beloit, where the state champion would be determined. The best student orator of the Midwest would then be crowned at the final event, held in Iowa City.[12]

Honored by his selection, La Follette was highly conscious of his responsibility to his classmates. After choosing his topic, a literary analysis of the Shakespearean character Iago, La Follette labored many hours on his manuscript, polishing phrases and rehearsing his delivery. In addition, he checked the accuracy of his analysis with Judge A.B. Braley, a local authority on Shakespeare. He also sought the advice of former rhetoric professor John M. Olin and received coaching from his current rhetoric teacher, David B.

Frankenburger. Belle Case, then La Follette's fiancée, observed that as he struggled with revisions, La Follette was

moved . . . by a very practical ambition. . . . He saw in the Interstate Oratorical Contest a chance to achieve in a field where he knew he excelled, which at the same time he greatly enjoyed. With characteristic determination he concentrated on winning the contest.

And win he did, at Madison, Beloit, and Iowa City.[13]

The central message of La Follette's prize-winning speech was an indictment of Iago as a disloyal, insidious, inhuman villain: "Shakespeare's conception of the 'Evil Principle.'" While appearing to serve Othello, La Follette maintained, Iago actually destroyed him. Iago was "artful," "cunning," "sly," and "crafty," using "carefully perfected schemes" to ruin the marital bliss of Othello and Desdemona. In addition, La Follette characterized Iago as an unseen foe—one who could fade into the background, "changing like the chameleon." Iago's method for destroying Othello was insidious and slow-acting, like poison, cunningly administered: "with every dose of poison," said La Follette, Iago "gives just a little antidote." Furthermore, La Follette argued that Iago's power became so complete that he controlled the fates of all the characters in *Othello*, who were "but puppets, moving at the will of this master."

La Follette used the device of contrast to underscore Iago's inhumanity. Iago was "cold intellect," while those around him were "warm life." The relationship between Iago and Desdemona was a "moral antithesis." Iago was the "sneer," Desdemona the "smile." Iago was grossness, Desdemona purity. Yet another comparison occurred between Richard III and Iago. Richard was human, flawed, while Iago was cold, perfect. Richard was "fire, Iago ice." Moreover, to amplify the wickedness of Iago, La Follette took pains to demonstrate the innocence of Othello and Desdemona. He maintained that Othello's house was not brought down by "some unguarded vice, but through its very virtues." Desdemona's "goodness" was made "the instrument of the infernal," La Follette insisted; and "The strength of the Moor's affection is made a fatal weakness." In sum, La Follette's analysis made Iago entirely culpable for the tragic events of *Othello*.[14]

La Follette based his interpretation of Iago on Samuel Coleridge, who argued in his *Shakespearean Criticism* that Iago should be regarded as a character of "motiveless malignity."[15] La Follette quoted that phrase in the text of his speech and identified its source, but he amplified the notion of motiveless malignity far beyond Coleridge's probable intent. In La Follette's view, *Othello* was really a play about the destruction wrought by Iago, the satanic incarnation of evil. Thus, he represented Iago as a truly supernatural character. According to La Follette, Iago "betrays never a weakness"; he was "perfect" in the "elegant symmetry of his fiendishness." Iago was "pitiless" and showed "devilish cruelty." Indeed, at various times La Follette called Iago a "sarcastic devil," a "scoffing demon," and a "goblin." He possessed "Stygian skill" and performed "diabolisms." The tragedy of *Othello*, according to this view, stemmed from the supernatural wickedness of Iago, not the human failings of Othello and Desdemona. In short, La Follette conceived of *Othello* as a kind of melodrama, with the devilish Iago menacing the innocent characters.

In La Follette's mind, the character Iago was profoundly disturbing because he defied immutable moral laws, disrupted cosmic order, and escaped unpunished: "Iago would like to reverse the order of things" and "turn cosmos into chaos." "By all the principles of dramatic tragedy," La Follette reasoned, Othello should execute Iago on the stage, but that does not happen. Indeed, La Follette was not satisfied by Shakespeare's promise that Iago's "punishment shall torment him much and hold him long" because La Follette claimed that "Iago is just beyond the reach of death and we can fancy him disappearing in the darkness of which he is a part." The fate of Richard III, on the other hand, was fulfilling because he was "scourged by the invisible lash of violated conscience," and "his death satisfie[d] the equation of right." What appealed to La Follette in this instance was that *Richard III* conformed to a law of drama: the logical and the right outcome was for Richard to suffer and pay for his sins with death on the stage. This formula was so precise that it could be described as an "equation of right." *Othello*, however, violated the just laws of the universe. What was appalling about Iago, yet fascinating in a literary sense, was the concept of unpunished wickedness, the "Evil Principle" that La Follette believed was the dominant theme of "Iago."

While such an analysis may appear simplistic or misguided in light of subsequent Shakespearean scholarship, audiences in 1879 marvelled that La Follette's speech disclosed the hidden meanings of *Othello*. Indeed, one listener praised the clarity of La Follette's "study of that strange Shakespearean character, Iago, that impersonation of crafty, slinking, covert evil." Charles Van Hise, a classmate of La Follette's, said, "It happens that I have studied *Othello* and *Richard III* more than any other plays of Shakespeare, but this oration shows a study of their characters of which I never had a tithe. Upon reading this production, many points which were obscure became clear."[16]

Without doubt "Iago" impressed audiences, but, specifically, why did La Follette win the Inter-State Oratorical Contest of 1879? In retrospect, we can see a number of possible explanations. First, La Follette chose a literary topic. In previous years, successful orations had considered "Dante," "Satan and Mephistopheles," and "Beatrice and Margaret." The analysis of literary figures avoided the controversy created by addressing political or social issues. La Follette's topic was a fictive character, yet he was familiar, concrete, and specific. By contrast, La Follette's competitors at Iowa City had abstract topics such as "Unsolved Problems," "Science Not the Soul's Teacher," "The Decay of Institutions," "Unlimited Culture," and "Mahometanism and Its Enemies."[17]

In addition, as I have demonstrated, La Follette chose to organize his speech around a set of contrasts, most notably the contrast between Iago and Richard III. Interestingly, previous contestants had been successful with comparisons of "Satan and Mephistopheles" and "Beatrice and Margaret."[18] The device of contrast provided a strong sense of organization and created a framework for sharp analysis, both desirable attributes for a speech contest.

Another significant factor concerns La Follette's preoccupation with evil in "Iago." Two previous prize-winning orations focused on evil, devils, and hell. Perhaps "Dante" and "Satan and Mephistopheles" served as models for La Follette's oration. According to J.B. Simpson, a classmate and close friend, La Follette had originally planned to call his speech "Shakespeare's Devil." La Follette was certainly familiar with O.A. Curtis's "Satan and Mephistopheles" because it was printed in La Follette's newspaper on May 25, 1877. La Follette may have borrowed from Curtis the formula of amplifying the wickedness of a devil-figure through a series of stylistic devices. Consider this passage from Curtis' oration:

This is Mephistopheles. Satan—revengeful, willful, haughty, intrepid, ambitious Satan; an archangel fallen yet still resplendent with a lingering ray of his original glory, like the Coliseum [,] magnificent even as a ruin—Satan seems worthy of the crown of sainthood in contrast with this mean, jeering, sarcastic doubter; this confident sophist; this cool, artful, cautious strategist, this malignant destroyer, grinning calmly at the damnation of souls; the "abortion of dirt and fire"; this counterpart of the real devil, who has already crowded our lives with anguish and filled this beautiful world with the bitter, bitter pangs of hell.

La Follette's approach is quite similar:

And this is Iago. The polished, affable attendant; the boon companion; the supple sophist, the nimble logician; the philosopher, the moralist—the scoffing demon; the goblin whose smile is a stab and whose laugh is an infernal sneer; who has sworn eternal vengeance on virtue everywhere; who would turn cosmos into chaos. This compound of wickedness and reason, this incarnation of intellect, this tartarean basilisk is the logical conclusion in a syllogism whose premises are "Hell and Night." He is a criminal climax; endow him with a single supernatural quality and he stands among the devils of fiction supreme.

One can only speculate why this approach proved so attractive to the judges in both 1877 and 1879. Perhaps the drama, familiarity and simple titillation involved in the contemplation of profound evil provided the winning edge. Certainly, these devil figures provided a wonderful opportunity to use some powerful language of denunciation.[19]

La Follette was also quite clever in choosing for his topic an analysis of a Shakespearean character. It is fair to say that Shakespeare was more universally read and appreciated in the nineteenth century than today. An oration about Iago would naturally interest audiences in 1879. Moreover, the Inter-State Oratorical Contest provided La Follette with an opportunity to perform bits of Shakespeare. He interspersed short Shakespearean quotations among his own words, creating a Shakespearean texture for the whole oration. The quotations in "Iago" would have fallen pleasurably on the ears of La Follette's audiences, and some may have been familiar enough with the text of *Othello* to know when and how La Follette was using Shakespeare.

The many quotations from Shakespeare also furnished a vehicle for La Follette to display his magnificent powers of interpretation. In general, the ornate style of "Iago" served as a self-conscious showcase for La Follette's fine acting talents. When one reads "Iago" out loud, the words roll off the tongue; the rhythm is infectious. La Follette used parallel structure, anaphora, repetition, and alliteration to achieve a dramatic effect. Such combinations as "dangerously difficult," "supple sophist," "greedy glee," "affable attendant," and "ingenious innuendoes" are a delight to declaim. La Follette concentrated particularly on hard "c" sounds, such as "cunning," "cruelty," "crafty," and "cursing." These harsh words were perfect for expressing anger over Iago's foul deeds. One member of the audience, Reverend F.L. Kenyon of Iowa City, was particularly impressed by the interpretive and stylistic aspects of La Follette's address:

He who by the verdict of all took the first prize was the most natural in action and therefore the most effective. His words fitted his thought and his thought filled his words. . . . the truth concerning Iago was so in his mind, that he was able to present to the hearer the truth and the image in such a way as to make them appear living realities.[20]

The ornate style of La Follette's oration occurred in the larger context of real political discourse. James Bryce, in his book *The American Commonwealth*, described oratory of the 1880s as

overloaded with tropes and figures, apt to aim at concealing poverty or triteness in thought by exaggeration of statement, by a profusion of ornament, by appeals to sentiments too lofty for the subject or the occasion. The florid diction of the debating club or the solemn pomp of the funeral oration is frequently invoked when nothing but clearness of exposition or cogency of argument is needed. . . . They have learned how to deck out commonplaces with the gaudier flowers of eloquence; how to appeal to the dominant sentiment of the moment; above all, how to make a strong and flexible voice the means of rousing enthusiasm.[21]

In keeping with the conventions of the day, the major purposes of "Iago" were to arouse enthusiasm and to display La Follette's oratorical skills. "Iago" was peculiarly well-suited for these persuasive tasks and for La Follette's rhetorical aptitudes. The ornate language of "Iago" was meant to be performed, to be delivered with passion, and to engender passion in the audience—but only as a kind of entertainment—a harmless but diverting echo of serious political oratory. Just as people loved to watch a good fight, they enjoyed listening to vehement denunciation. Moreover, La Follette's oration echoed the stimulation of a fire-and-brimstone sermon. Audiences then—as now—took pleasure in being terrified by the description of a living incarnation of evil.

To be judged the best student orator of the entire Midwest was a momentous achievement, and La Follette left Iowa City as a bona fide Wisconsin hero. His train home was delayed for a day in Beloit, Wisconsin, so the local citizens could express their appreciation of his victory. Then, when the train arrived in Madison on May 9, La Follette was greeted by a brass band and most of the student body. The students carried La Follette on their shoulders through the streets of Madison while chanting "The Little Lion of the Northwest." This boisterous parade concluded with a massive bonfire fueled by wooden chairs from the university chapel. Later that evening there was a celebration in the state assembly chamber, where prominent citizens offered speeches of tribute to La Follette. Among others, Colonel E.W. Keyes and Colonel William F. Vilas stressed the honor that La Follette's victory brought to the university and the state of Wisconsin. After these speeches, the crowd clamored for "Iago," and La Follette obliged by presenting his winning oration.[22]

Although "Iago" was not a political oration, it had strong political implications for La Follette. "Iago" generated more public attention and comment in the press than did Rutherford B. Hayes when he traveled to Madison for a political speech about the same time. "Iago" made La Follette's name well-known throughout the state. As David Thelen explains,

La Follette's victory at Iowa City cannot be overestimated. Oratory was probably the basic form of political communication in post-Civil War America, and to be the best orator in six states did indeed entitle him to the admiration of his fellow students [and] to be treated as a state hero. . . . It was an invaluable asset to the young man when he entered politics and was otherwise practically unknown.[23]

Aside from firmly establishing La Follette as the premier student orator in the Midwest, "Iago" had one other important effect. At the end of La Follette's senior year, his scholastic average was disturbingly low because he had devoted himself so unsparingly to extracurricular activities. At that time, the entire university faculty voted on whether or not individual students should receive a degree. When La Follette's turn came, the faculty split evenly on their vote.

David B. Frankenburger argued in favor of La Follette because of his achievements as an orator and publicist, but it took the vote of the university president, John Bascom, to break the tie in La Follette's favor. In the words of Belle La Follette, "Winning the Inter-State Oratorical Contest doubtless helped him get his diploma."[24]

In addition to being the supreme achievement of La Follette's life in 1879, "Iago" is a seminal document for what it foreshadows about his later public speaking. In "Iago" a critic can discern the "rhetorical imprint" of La Follette's discourse, that underlying pattern of distinctive verbal characteristics that marks the entire corpus of his oratory.[25]

In the "Iago" oration, La Follette revealed for the first time his propensity for reducing a complex phenomenon (in this case the play *Othello*) into a simple melodramatic scenario where good and evil are clearly contrasted. La Follette identifies a villain who is deceptive, dishonest, and inhuman and who operates by gradually ensnaring unsuspecting victims. The major thrust of this pattern is to condemn the character of the evil villain. There is no ethical ambiguity in such a scenario because judgment can be reduced to an "equation of right." Its purpose is to encourage outrage over unpunished wickedness. This narrative pattern, which I shall henceforth call the "melodramatic scenario," is expressed again and again in La Follette's rhetoric after 1879.

The question naturally arises, was the melodramatic scenario a habit of mind or a rhetorical formula for successful speechmaking? As one might suspect, it was both. In La Follette's case, the melodramatic scenario was a reflection of a certain world view, the product of a mind that saw things moralistically, in black-and-white terms. Moreover, the melodramatic scenario was an integral part of La Follette's total rhetorical personality—a personality that refused to compromise, that was concerned with loss of innocence and virtue, that was captivated with the concept of the "Evil Principle," and that believed constant vigilance was required against unseen but menacing forces. However, it also seems likely that the melodramatic scenario was, to some extent, a conscious rhetorical strategy. In setting out to win the Inter-State Oratorical Contest in 1879, La Follette drew upon all of the resources and experiences at his command. He gathered ideas for his address from previously successful contestants, most notably O.A. Curtis. He selected the formula of condemning an insidious devil figure, and he spent many days revising and polishing the formula. Thus, La Follette consciously validated the melodramatic scenario as a persuasive strategy.

Throughout his career La Follette used the melodramatic scenario to influence the perceptions of audiences. The scenario functions by illustrating the dangers of a villain in a vivid, easily understood form. It injects drama and suspense, thereby increasing audience interest. It provides an organizational pattern and a sense of structure for ideas. It positions good and evil along a clear story line, hence removing ethical ambiguity and clearing the way for moral outrage. It is ideally suited for reformers because it is a means of cultivating anxiety and a sense of menace. What is more, the logic of the melodramatic scenario is inescapable. Unaware victims must be alerted to their danger immediately, before the dreaded incarnation of evil can close its clever trap. To delay reform for even a moment can be fatal. In the fictive case of "Iago" no reform is possible. The tragedy results because Othello does not become aware of the trap set by Iago until it is too late. But in the legislative world, La Follette could use the melodramatic scenario to urge immediate action. If an audience accepts the image of a sly, malevolent, unseen enemy, then La Follette's call to action takes on added urgency.

The melodramatic scenario exists in nascent—although unmistakable—form in the "Iago" oration. As I shall demonstrate in subsequent chapters, La Follette always had some kind of "Iago" to attack, a villain to excoriate, whether it was the railroads, corrupt politicians, or unfair taxation. After La Follette graduated from the University of Wisconsin in 1879, his rhetoric would move from the world of literary societies and speech contests into legal and legislative arenas. He would apply the lessons learned in constructing "Iago" to the exigencies of political debate, and he would exploit brilliantly his fame as the foremost student orator of his region.

3
Congressman La Follette

On July 4, 1879, two weeks after graduating from the University of Wisconsin, La Follette delivered a speech in Sun Prairie, Wisconsin. Since oratory was the centerpiece of many ceremonial occasions in the nineteenth century, the citizens of Sun Prairie were delighted that they had enticed the winner of the Inter-State Oratorical Contest to address their Fourth of July celebration. Fully aware of the demands of the occasion, La Follette prepared a patriotic, crowd-pleasing address titled "Home and the State." The speech apotheosized the home, showed its primary relation to the state, and proposed a solution for what was then known as the "tramp problem," a phenomenon brought about by the high unemployment of the 1870s. Because of this threatening situation, La Follette proposed that the tramps should be forced to colonize the unsettled areas of the West, where they would regain their self-respect through honest labor such as farming.[1]

La Follette's topic—and his treatment of it—were well received. Several audience members judged "Home and the State" to be the most eloquent Fourth of July oration they had ever heard. For the next year La Follette was busy studying law, but on July 4, 1880, he presented "Home and the State" again, at Reedsburg, Wisconsin. The local and regional press praised the speech for its logic, originality, thoughtfulness, and eloquence.[2]

"Home and the State" added to La Follette's fame as an orator, and on that fame he decided to build a political career. By September 1880, a mere fifteen months after receiving his bachelor's degree, La Follette had opened his own law office and had decided to seek the nomination for district attorney of Dane County. After capturing the nomination, he appealed for votes by stressing his achievements as a speaker. One of his campaign pamphlets, *Opinions of the Press*, was composed entirely of favorable reviews of "Iago." In announcing La Follette's candidacy for district attorney, the editor of the *Wisconsin State Journal* recounted in detail the young orator's victory at Iowa City and the impassioned celebration at home. The editor concluded: "Remembering these things—how much Mr. La Follette honored the University, the State, and the County, on this occasion—the people of his native county will delight to honor the man with their votes in November, for District Attorney."[3]

Because 1880 was a presidential election year, La Follette, while campaigning for himself, also gave several speeches on behalf of Rutherford B. Hayes. They received uniformly enthusiastic responses from Republican audiences and in Republican papers. While the *Madison Democrat* complained that La Follette "talked for all the world like a strolling play actor," it did not deny his effectiveness with Wisconsin voters. That effectiveness was a major factor in his winning the office of district attorney in 1880 and again in 1882. During his tenure as district attorney, La Follette developed his private legal practice and forged a reputation as a zealous public prosecutor.[4]

The most important speech La Follette delivered as district attorney occurred in Madison, on Memorial Day, 1884. The C.C. Washburn Grand Army Post conducted the ceremony, and many influential and politically powerful Civil War veterans were in the audience. La Follette tailored his address masterfully for the old soldiers and their admirers. He condemned the character of the "pernicious" and "wretched" South, and he was even more uncompromising in praising the actions of the northern veterans: "You were right, eternally right."[5]

La Follette's address confirming the values of the Civil War, with the aging veterans present, was probably very moving. His wife, Belle, recalled that "After Bob began, it seemed to me no one moved until he had finished. . . . I see him now in his youth, against the background of trees and sky—at one with his audience, in perfect accord with the spirit of the day." What is more, his 1884 Memorial Day address had long-lasting effects: it confirmed his renown as a brilliant orator and, in the words of Belle, "this address materially helped his nomination and election to Congress in 1884."[6]

Wisconsin Republicans nominated La Follette for Congress on the first ballot. On September 9, 1884, he delivered a short acceptance speech in which he pledged to give himself "unreservedly to the grand work—dedicate to it nights of intense study and days of unremitting toil." His speech developed two main themes: approval of Republican policy on protective tariffs and an attack on the Democrats as the disloyal party of secession. His subsequent campaign speeches continued to exploit these topics.[7]

Once again, La Follette's skill as a public speaker was central to his campaign. Commentators praised him for the lucidity and eloquence of his position on protective tariffs, the major issue of the election. Audiences greeted his speeches with enthusiasm throughout the state. For example, in Monroe, the local paper claimed that La Follette presented "what may be designated in common parlance 'a stinger.' He spoke for nearly two hours eloquently and forcibly mainly on the tariff question, and not only held his audience but his remarks were punctuated with frequent bursts of applause."[8]

Not everyone in Wisconsin appreciated La Follette's rhetoric, however. The Democrats, tired of being labeled as the party of disloyalty and secession, delivered a deliciously sarcastic account of La Follette's attack on southern morals and manners:

he proceeded to wander off down south among the bay of the blood-hounds—clarion cry—grim visage; war—horrid rebellion—black secession—wicked old democrats—bully little republicans, and wound up by a common sample of University rhetorical trill and whang-leather twang.

But even La Follette's opponents admitted that he was effective with audiences. At the same time that the Democratic *Prairie du Chien Courier* ripped La Follette's policies, it conceded that he was "one of the best orators in the state."[9]

La Follette won the election by 491 votes in November 1884, and he became the youngest member of the Forty-ninth Congress when he took his seat in December 1885. According to the custom of the day, freshman legislators were expected to remain silent for a respectable number of months, so it was not until April 22, 1886, that La Follette addressed the House in a political debate. He spoke again on May 6. On both occasions, La Follette captured the attention of the House with a skillful attack against a bill that proposed some new river and harbor improvements but suspended work on fifty-eight old projects. The new improvements were favored by the Democratic majority, while the suspended projects had previously been passed by Republicans. La Follette condemned the proposed legislation because it wasted public funds and did not serve the national interest. Although the Rivers and Harbors bill passed over La Follette's objections, his speech brought him favorable state and national publicity and delighted the Republican leadership in the House. Moreover, La Follette began to establish his reputation as an orator *par excellence* on the national level.[10]

When Congress considered a bill to tax oleomargarine in June of 1886, La Follette spoke in favor of it. He and his constituents viewed imitation butter not only as a threat to Wisconsin's dairy industry but also as a menace to public health. He argued convincingly that the taxing power of Congress could be used to protect the general welfare of Americans. A prohibitive tax on oleo would protect dairy farmers and safeguard the health of citizens by restricting an impure product. In making his case, La Follette praised the contribution genuine dairy products made to "the maintenance not only of the home comforts, the sweetening of home life, but . . . to that which makes the home possible—

the farm itself." The oleomargarine taxation bill passed by a large majority in the House, while La Follette's staunch defense of the dairy industry bolstered his popularity at home.[11]

La Follette opened his second term in the House by defending a bill that later became the Transportation Act of 1887. On January 20, 1887, La Follette argued that the nation needed a regulatory bill because of the "encroachments made by railways on the natural rights of the people." He indicted the "evils" involved in the "vicious abuse" of railroad rates, a practice that "violates not only the simplest and best understood commonlaw obligations, but . . . is against all business principles." The aim of railroad regulation, he claimed, was "perfect service to the public and fair profits upon the great capital actually invested." He believed that the Transportation bill would do much to "arm the individual for an even-handed contest with a corporation."[12]

The most important congressional speech of La Follette's second term was a response to John Carlisle, speaker of the House. After Carlisle delivered a powerful speech in favor of lowering the tariff rates, La Follette felt that he would have to be refuted or Carlisle's speech would serve as an influential campaign document for the Democrats in Wisconsin. Accordingly, La Follette prepared intensively to challenge the speaker. He spent at least two weeks drafting his speech, which involved poring over scores of *Congressional Records* and government reports.[13]

On July 14, 1888, La Follette delivered a technical, point-by-point refutation of Carlisle's speech. He denied the speaker's major proposition that the prosperity of the years 1850-1860 was due to the tariff reductions of 1846. To support his arguments, La Follette presented governmental studies, committee reports, statistical tables, expert testimony, and excerpts from past congressional debates. La Follette's rebuttal of Speaker Carlisle won him Republican Party honors and national recognition. Several newspapers declared that La Follette had decisively defeated Speaker Carlisle in the debate. Perhaps the most significant outcome of La Follette's strong speech was that it contributed to his appointment on the House Ways and Means Committee in the Fifty-first Congress.[14]

In his third term, La Follette participated in the debate over a contested election in South Carolina. The Democratic candidate, William Elliott, who was white, had been certified the winner from a black district. His seat was contested by the black candidate, Robert Smalls, a Republican and a Civil War veteran. On February 13, 1889, La Follette attacked the Democrats of South Carolina for passing an election law that "outrages every principle of honesty and right, tramples under foot the Constitution of the United States, and stifles the voice of the legal Republican voters of that district." But despite La Follette's efforts, Smalls lost his challenge, and Elliott was installed in Congress.[15]

La Follette also played an important role in the debate over the McKinley tariff bill, a measure designed to raise protective tariffs. In his May 10, 1889, speech, La Follette supported higher tariffs to protect domestic metal manufacturing and agricultural raw materials, including hemp, flax, jute, and tobacco. La Follette's speech in favor of the McKinley tariff bill again vaulted him into the national limelight. In particular, he won the praise of his party, state, and region for his thorough and eloquent defense of American agricultural interests.[16]

When Congress debated the "Force" bill in July of 1890, La Follette had another opportunity to voice his concern with protecting representative government. The "Force" bill was a measure designed to prevent the kind of southern election fraud that had occurred in the Elliott-Smalls case of 1889. La Follette's speech of July 2, 1890, objected to southern electoral practices because they prevented free men from determining their own destinies. Congress, La Follette said, was duty-bound to guarantee that "in every part of this country every man shall freely cast his vote and have it honestly counted." After a bitter partisan debate, La Follette and his allies succeeded in passing the "Force" bill in the House by a slim margin.[17]

Several weeks after the debate on the "Force" bill, La Follette gave his last major address as a Representative. The topic was the "Original-Package" bill, and the major issue was whether an article of interstate commerce, such as a cask of liquor, was subject to state laws if it remained in its original package. On July 19, 1890, La Follette spoke in favor of a House measure to guarantee state control of commodities shipped within its borders. During the course of the speech La Follette announced his motives plainly:

there is an opportunity offered here to guard the great dairy and agricultural interests of Wisconsin and the country against a danger plainly threatened by the manufacturers of adulterated dairy, lard, and other food products whose cause is openly and ably championed on this floor.[18]

Much of La Follette's political success can be attributed to his adept oratory delivered on the floor of the House of Representatives. Another important factor was his skill in conducting reelection campaigns. In both 1886 and 1888, he was overwhelmingly renominated by Wisconsin Republicans. As one newspaper editor commented in 1886, La Follette won the Republican nomination because his speeches "struck the popular heart, . . . showed thought and research, and were full of common, practical sense." Republicans chose La Follette again largely because "It was soon discovered that he was clear headed, convincing, eloquent and strong in his utterances, and he at once took rank among the best speakers in the house; and what is very rare in that body, he was listened to with marked attention." Despite his obvious political strength in

Wisconsin, however, La Follette launched vigorous reelection campaigns in his district, and newspaper accounts concurred that he encountered large, enthusiastic audiences wherever he went. For the most part, his extemporaneous campaign speeches reiterated the major arguments and themes that he had developed in Congress, and his constituents responded positively. La Follette won overwhelming victories in both 1886 and 1888.[19]

In 1890, then, it was only natural for La Follette to be confident of the outcome. Because of his position on the House Ways and Means Committee and his sterling performance in protecting the agricultural interests of Wisconsin, La Follette was unopposed for the Republican nomination at the state convention held in August of 1890. His Democratic opponent was Allen R. Bushnell, a popular attorney and veteran of the Civil War. During the early days of the campaign, La Follette remained in Washington, attending to the McKinley tariff until it passed the House on October 1. This left less than a month to campaign against Bushnell, but because of the decisive victories La Follette had rolled up in the past, he was unconcerned. He made a few speeches in Wisconsin, campaigning heavily on his tariff work, then he went into Iowa to speak on behalf of David B. Henderson. As Belle La Follette remembered it, "Wherever he went, there were the same crowds overflowing the halls, the same enthusiasm; and however long he spoke his audience would insist he go on. All the surface manifestations indicated a tremendous Republican victory." But La Follette suffered a stunning defeat. At thirty-five years of age, he was out of political office for the first time in ten years.[20]

La Follette's defeat can be attributed to two factors. The first was passage of the Bennett law, which mandated that all children in Wisconsin be sent to a school where reading, writing, arithmetic, and United States history were taught in the English language. Lutherans and Roman Catholics saw this as an attack on their parochial school systems. La Follette made the critical mistake of acquiescing to this state-wide Republican policy and focusing his attention on national issues, which were less important to Catholic and Lutheran immigrants in Wisconsin. Compounding that error, La Follette did not engage in his usual personal campaigning; he chose to rely instead on his decisive margins of victory from previous contests. On election day, many of his regular supporters stayed home from the polls to express their disapproval of the Bennett law. La Follette's defeat did not go unnoticed in the national press. The *New York Tribune* commented that

The sacrifice of Mr. La Follette to the sectarian disturbances in Wisconsin is one of the most unfortunate results of the election. None of the younger members of the House has won a more enviable reputation than this brilliant and versatile Representative.[21]

Despite the seeming disparity of speech topics and situations during the years 1879-1890, La Follette's rhetoric was unified by themes, values, and tactics originally displayed in his "Iago" speech of 1879. Many of these were embodied by the melodramatic scenario, that narrative form in which La Follette condemned the character of a dishonest, deceptive, and inhuman villain who worked silently and invisibly to entrap innocent victims. Between 1879 and 1890 La Follette isolated and attacked a number of "villains," including tramps, unbridled materialism, the Rivers and Harbors bill, southern Democrats, low tariff rates, and the "Original-Package" bill.[22]

The most garish example of the melodramatic scenario, however, was La Follette's 1886 attack on oleomargarine. La Follette indicted oleo in much the same manner he used to condemn Iago in 1879. Oleomargarine, like Iago, was a "monstrous product of greed and hypocrisy" that "makes its way into the home." Moreover, La Follette declared that oleo was not what it seemed:

Ingenuity, striking hands with cunning trickery, compounds a substance to counterfeit an article of food. It is made to look like something it is not; to taste and smell like something it is not; to sell for something it is not, and so deceive the purchaser. It follows faithfully two rules; "Miss no opportunity to deceive"; "At all times put money in thy purse." It obeys no laws.

According to La Follette, oleo was a "fraudulent and unwholesome article of food" that was "as powerful and irresistible as vicious ingenuity can make it. It is as pitiless as a plague." Just as Othello and Desdemona were unknowingly led to their doom, the innocent dairy industry of Wisconsin was being taken by surprise:

The dairy interest and all that it carries with it is in a distressing condition. It has been driven to the wall and is to-day fighting for a place to stand. It is set upon from all sides by an unseen foe. It is struck from behind. It is taken in ambush. It can make no defense.

Characteristically, La Follette used the logic of the melodramatic scenario to urge immediate action:

All legislation attempted by, or within the reach of the States is impotent to deal with this monster. If there was ever a time in the history of this Government when the essence of the great protection principles should be applied—when this body was solemnly commanded to use its delegated powers for the general good, this is the hour.[23]

While La Follette rarely attacked individuals, he personified activities, products, laws, or proposed policies and condemned their characters as evil. This conspicuous display of moral outrage was central to La Follette's discourse. By condemning the immorality of his nemeses, he could potentially make all of their actions and arguments suspect. Since he characterized his targets as fundamentally deceitful, denials of wickedness did not disprove La Follette's charges. In addition, it was more dramatic and memorable for La Follette to attack the character of his enemies. Such passionate accusations probably lingered in the mind long after the confusing details of debate had vanished. La Follette's expression of moral condemnation not only tended to undermine the character of the subject under attack, but it also elevated his own ethical standing. By objecting to his subject's pernicious character, La Follette enhanced his own morality. In La Follette's view, "The emotions are the native soil of moral life. From the feelings are grown great ethical truths, one by one, forming at last the grand body of the moral law." By strongly linking ethics to emotions, La Follette could act out his own ethicality by displaying emotional outrage.[24]

The rhetorical device of contrast was another aspect of the "Iago" oration that manifested itself in La Follette's congressional oratory. Contrast, in fact, was a natural rhetorical ploy for one who saw the world in such black-and-white terms. Even when La Follette did not use the melodramatic scenario overtly, he tended to sharply contrast his position with his opponents' and to characterize this bifurcation as a moral conflict. In 1879 La Follette contrasted Iago's corruption and immorality with other fictional characters, but in 1890 he contrasted the nobility of Republican tariff policy with the destructiveness of the Democrats' proposal. In attacking the previous Democratic tariff bill, La Follette said, "Comparison and contrast between the Democratic tariff bill of 1888 and the Republican tariff bill of 1890 will be made by this House and by the country." He then differentiated the two bills according to specific items in the tariff schedule. "These measures are most marvelously unlike," La Follette concluded:

It is because one bill favors the protection of American agriculture, manufacturers, and labor, and the other bill opposes this policy; because the Republicans propose to save this market to [sic] this people whenever they can supply it and because the Democrats propose to invite the other countries of the world to take this market from our people whenever it is in their power to do so.

According to this analysis, the Republican bill was good whereas the Democratic bill was evil. La Follette insisted that

these two bills, coming from the same committee, brought forth within the short space of two years, are radically different in parentage, in character, in motive, and in destiny.
They face in opposite directions, they are as wide apart in principle and design as a continent. An ocean could roll between them.[25]

Although his congressional oratory displayed characteristics first revealed in "Iago," La Follette naturally developed some new concepts and techniques. For example, from 1879 to 1890, the Civil War was a central reference point for La Follette. Many of his arguments drew emotional force from the passions engendered by the war between the states. While La Follette was too young to have participated in the Civil War, its memory loomed large in his consciousness, and several of the issues he debated in Congress were interpreted in terms of this conflict. La Follette, like many of his Republican contemporaries, believed that the Civil War was no less than a contest between freedom and slavery, and the North was "eternally right." La Follette's denunciations of southern Democrats were harsh byproducts of his Republican convictions about the Civil War.[26]

In another area, La Follette defended agricultural interests and praised farming as a way of life. In his 1886 attack on oleomargarine, La Follette insisted that the nation's vitality rested with the health of the family farmstead, because

Nearly one-half of all the people in this country are engaged in and directly dependent upon agriculture. The vital forces of every other business, I care not what its character, are drawn from and nourished by it. . . . No other pursuit so universally and profoundly concerns every other citizen of the Republic—no other calling known to civilized man, where so entirely and completely the interests of one is the interest of all.[27]

Conversely, he expressed a distrust of rapid growth, urbanization, and manufacturers. He identified and criticized distressing new changes brought about by industrialization, and he decried the materialism and greed that were replacing cherished agrarian values. In La Follette's Memorial Day Address, for example, he expressed the fear that the nation was turning away from the unity and high moral purpose of the Civil War and embracing in their places the values of greed and materialism. The country, in La Follette's analysis, had undergone disturbing changes since the end of the war:

Twenty years of prosperity and thrift! Farms increased in value and size, the old barns and warehouses [were] not large enough; mills vex the waters of every stream; the thunder of the rushing train echoes in every township; villages spring up and encroach upon the farm; the dwellers in cities trample each other in the hurry of competition; churches turned into stores, stores turned into banks, moneychanging in the house of the Lord and gold piled in vaults where before only cheap merchandise had been kept; faster and faster, on and on we rush, charmed by the siren music of tinkling silver and ringing gold.

The concept that an idyllic age (in this case the holy crusade of the Civil War) was being undermined and replaced by a new, sinister force (in this case materialism) was central to La Follette's so-called "progressive" rhetoric, but its roots can be traced clearly to at least 1884.[28]

In a related matter, La Follette supported railroad regulation in order to control discriminatory corporate practices. He began to articulate the view that individuals and corporations were locked in an unfair conflict. Because of this, La Follette demanded equal treatment under the law for all citizens. La Follette's speech of January 20, 1887, is interesting because of what it presaged about his future rhetorical campaigns. It marked the opening salvo of a continuous battle against the railroad corporations. The issue of railroad regulation was to become a central element of La Follette's political discourse as governor of Wisconsin and as U.S. Senator. What is more, La Follette would refer to this particular speech on several occasions later in his career as proof that he had always stood consistently for railroad reform.[29]

Perhaps more significantly, several of La Follette's speeches from this time objected to forces that undermined representative elections. He opposed electoral determinism and manipulation in whatever form it took, whether it was southern vote fraud or the "cliques and rings" and "political bossism" of the North. He argued that representativeness was the essential element of the American political system, and he regarded the uninhibited electoral process as sacrosanct. Since elections were carried out through balloting, La Follette reasoned that it was essential to protect the integrity of the ballot: "Each citizen's interest," he said, "his property, the taxes he shall pay, the laws he shall obey, his happiness, the future peace and prosperity of his government rest upon the honesty and prosperity of the ballot." No matter what the circumstances, La Follette avowed, elections must be free and fair. Within a few years, his concern with the "sacred rights of every voter" would blossom into a major tenet of his reform ideology. La Follette probably received the full support of his Republican colleagues when he railed against southern and Democratic "crimes against the ballot." But these orthodox Republican arguments were portents of future conflict for La Follette. When fully extended, La Follette's faith in the "sacred rights of every voter" would condemn his own party's system of caucuses and conventions. In 1888, however, the full implications of his convictions were unstated and but dimly perceived.[30]

In 1888 La Follette revealed, for the first time, a tendency to appeal to the judgment of the people, a trait that would later become a trademark of his discourse. Particularly when faced with a hostile setting such as the predominantly Democratic House of 1888, La Follette threatened his opponents with the wrath of outraged voters. Concerning the tobacco tariff bill, he intoned, "You may ignore petitions and refuse to listen to all pleas here, but, gentlemen, there is another court and another day, and from your tyrannical majority both here and in committee we appeal to the people." Throughout his career, La Follette believed he could divine the true will of the people. When necessary, he confidently took his case outside the walls of the legislature to the broader field of public opinion.[31]

One of the most obvious (and wearying) characteristics of La Follette's mature political rhetoric was his technique of using prodigious amounts of evidence to support his arguments. Even as a young congressman, La Follette bolstered his emotional and moral appeals with copious testimony. In La Follette's "Oleomargarine" speech, for instance, he cited masses of expert opinion to support his argument that taxation could be used to regulate commerce as well as to raise revenue. Although other speakers referred to testimony in the debate, La Follette read his at great length, usually verbatim, as if paraphrasing the evidence would interfere with its integrity. In this relatively short speech (about three pages in the *Record*), he cited three Supreme Court decisions, referred to Alexander Hamilton and Thomas Jefferson, and quoted extensively from two scholarly works on the Constitution. Much of his argument was anchored in the authority of John Quincy Adams. La Follette read long passages from a congressional report Adams authored in 1832, and he referred often to an unheralded letter Adams sent to Andrew Stevenson in the same year. La Follette had the letter, which ran three pages, entered into the *Congressional Record*.[32]

La Follette also marshalled stacks of statistics to support his claims. In 1890, while debating southern election fraud, he stated that his statistics were "more powerful and eloquent in their appeal for this great reform than anything or any one will say here or elsewhere." Indeed, La Follette's extensive citation of statistics often overwhelmed his artistic, verbal appeals. Statistics played an especially dominant role in the debate over the McKinley tariff. For example, on May 10, 1899, La Follette predicted that a protective tariff would benefit the tin-plate industry, which in turn would benefit other economic sectors. He extrapolated the following statistical claims from congressional testimony:

What will a protective duty on tin-plate accomplish? It will enable us to make from twenty to twenty-five million dollars' worth of tin-plate in this country annually. What does that mean? It means that to produce the 1,000,000 tons of additional iron ore, the 2,000,000 tons of additional coke and coal, the 450,000 tons of additional pig-iron, the quarrying of 700,000 tons of additional limestone, and the 15,000 tons of Dakota black tin, the 3,000 tons of additional lead, the 6,500 tons of additional tallow and oil, the 20,000 tons of additional sulphuric acid, the 30,000,000 feet of additional box lumber, to turn the pig-iron into sheet-iron, to make the machinery and keep it in repair, and to freight the materials will give constant and remunerative employment to 40,000 men, with their families, making a population of 200,000 directly dependent on this great industry, which will build up quickly in this country under this bill.[33]

Through the extensive use of statistics La Follette attempted to make the benefits of protective tariffs seem tangible, significant, and virtually inevitable. His painstaking research for congressional speeches was a reflection of his desire to reduce uncertainty, to "forever silence further cavil and pettifogging" on a particular dispute. La Follette believed that, with adequate preparation, the absolute truth could be ascertained. It was then the speaker's obligation to systematically impress the truth upon his hearers. When La Follette announced to his opponents in the House, "The cold, hard facts are all against you," it was more than a figure of speech. It was an article of faith.[34]

Not only did La Follette make heavy use of testimony and statistics in his rhetoric, but he revered the public record. In La Follette's mind, the public record was sacred, and those who attempted to distort it were villainous. The most striking example of this attitude occurred during the debate with Speaker Carlisle. In a previous speech, Carlisle had claimed that the representatives from New England were overwhelmingly in favor of uniform tariff reductions in 1857. La Follette challenged this assertion and charged that Carlisle had misrepresented the public record: "With a reckless indifference to plain and established facts," La Follette proclaimed,

this declaration tramples under foot the verified reports of that Congress and plays with the reputation of a distinguished, consistent, life-long protectionist [Senator Justin S. Morrill of Vermont] with a vandal hand. It transforms a devotee of the American system into a heretic and makes him worship the British beast.[35]

Not only can the distinct echo of "Iago" be heard in this passage, but it foreshadows La Follette's enduring concern with the public record. He was always fastidious about basing his own political arguments on what he perceived to be "plain and established facts," and he was careful to have his own views and votes accurately committed to the public record. Conversely, La Follette passionately denounced those who distorted the record or misquoted statements.

His reliance on the public record and the cold, hard facts was somewhat paradoxical in light of his tendency to couple it with passionate oratory that pronounced uncompromising moral judgments upon the opposition. Hence, we have the phenomenon of frequent, lengthy passages of austere evidence, punctuated with the emotionalism of the melodramatic scenario. Nevertheless, this basic pattern would continue to dominate La Follette's discourse for the rest of his career. Indeed, by 1890 he had developed most of the essential elements of his more mature reform rhetoric.

4
The Menacing Machine

On March 4, 1891, La Follette officially became an ex-congressman. He returned to the legal profession and was in the process of reestablishing a thriving practice when, in the fall of 1891, he became involved in an incident that would profoundly affect his status in the state Republican Party. On September 15 La Follette received a letter from Senator Philetus Sawyer asking for a conference at the Plankington Hotel in Milwaukee. La Follette agreed. Sawyer, a wealthy lumber baron, had served in the U.S. Senate since 1881. He was currently involved in a legal dispute concerning the misappropriation of state treasury funds in which, as a bondsman, he was potentially liable for some $300,000. The case was to be tried in the court of La Follette's brother-in-law, Judge Robert G. Siebecker. During the course of the interview, according to La Follette, Sawyer offered him a bribe to influence Siebecker's decision. Sawyer later denied the charge, but because there were no witnesses the facts will never be known. If La Follette had not actually been offered a bribe, however, he was certain that he had been; and that conviction was to play a momentous role in his future political career.[1]

After consulting his friends and advisers, La Follette decided to tell Judge Siebecker about the incident. Siebecker concluded promptly that he could no longer preside over the case; on October 24 he announced his withdrawal but refused to specify precisely why. Siebecker's announcement caused a flurry of public speculation and inspired a number of stories in the press reporting that an attempt had been made to influence the court. Sawyer arranged for an interview with the *Milwaukee Sentinel* in which he denied trying to bribe La Follette. He claimed he did not know Siebecker's relation to La Follette and that he had only offered him a retainer to serve as an attorney "to look up certain records and documents at Madison." Sawyer insisted that La Follette had simply "misunderstood" his intentions. On October 27 Sawyer's version of the incident was published. La Follette answered Sawyer in a statement published in the *Milwaukee Sentinel* on October 29. He provided a detailed account of the meeting, including his precise reaction to the offer of money to make certain that "Siebecker decides the case right." La Follette claimed he replied, "If you struck me in the face you would not insult me as you insult me now."[2]

The response to this public confrontation between the distinguished senator and the ex-congressman was swift and predictable. The Republican Party ostracized La Follette, while the Republican press questioned his honesty and charged that he had ulterior motives. Even those who believed his account were angry with La Follette because they felt he should have kept silent for the sake of party unity.[3]

In an attempt to repair his image, La Follette turned to oratory. Even at the nadir of his political career, he attempted to maintain direct contact with the voters. La Follette was still sought out for his public speaking prowess, and he continued to make local appearances at school picnics, church gatherings, and public meetings. For example, on July 29, 1892, La Follette introduced Governor William McKinley of Ohio to the Monona Lake Assembly in Madison. McKinley's obvious friendliness toward La Follette helped to partially restore his damaged credibility within the national Republican Party.[4]

During the 1892 national election, La Follette campaigned for Benjamin Harrison. He usually spoke twice a day, preaching "the gospel of protection and republicanism" and altering his speeches slightly to accommodate local audiences and circumstances. Despite his rift with Wisconsin's Republican leaders, he was well-received by the highly partisan audiences he addressed. But neither La Follette's eloquence nor the efforts of other Republican spokesmen could defeat the Democrats in 1892. Governor Peck was reelected in Wisconsin, and Grover Cleveland captured the White House.[5]

La Follette realized in 1892 that if he were ever to wield significant political influence in the state again, it would have to come from an anti-Sawyer faction of the Republican Party. Accordingly, he sought to organize a ticket to oppose the "Old Guard" in the 1894 election. Despite the positive public reception La Follette had received in his campaign tour of 1892, he decided that he was not the strongest candidate to challenge the Sawyer faction for control of the statehouse. He feared that if he ran for governor himself, the contest would center exclusively on the controversy surrounding the Sawyer affair. Consequently, he declined to run and cast his support to Congressman Nils P. Haugen. Haugen's candidacy attracted a variety of people who had grievances against the ruling faction. It appealed to ambitious young men eager for an opportunity to participate in politics; it attracted the dairy farmers, led by William D. Hoard, who hated the "Old Guard" for supporting the oleomargarine industry; and it appealed to Scandinavians, who wanted some political recognition from the Republican Party. Haugen proved to be an attractive candidate to all of these groups.[6]

Before the advent of the direct primary, candidates for each political party were nominated through a system of caucuses and conventions. As a result, public speaking and open discussion of issues were not significant parts of the nominating process. To win, it was essential to get voters to attend the local caucuses. This kind of campaign required organization, personal canvassing, and what was known as a "literary bureau"—on which La Follette put particular emphasis. On behalf of Haugen he launched a substantial letter writing campaign that distributed over 1,200 letters. Although the campaign literature made allusions to corrupt bossism and machine politics, it offered no concrete program for changing policy, only the standard promise of better government. Despite La Follette's strenuous efforts, when the delegates convened, they nominated William H. Upham as Republican candidate for governor. Even though Haugen lost the nomination, the 1894 campaign was encouraging for La Follette's organization. The anti-Sawyer faction had carried one-third of the convention delegates on the strength of an unlikely and poorly-financed campaign.[7]

After Haugen's defeat, La Follette returned to his legal practice, but he became ill in the winter of 1896 and had to go south to recover. While away, he was chosen as a delegate to the Republican National Convention. At the convention La Follette delivered a speech seconding the nomination of Henry Clay Evans for vice president. He argued that Evans deserved the nomination because, "when that great blue wave arose in the North, it swept to the sea and crushed the rebellion to earth, [and] he [Evans] went with it on its course from the State of Wisconsin." La Follette's speech was praised widely within the Republican Party. Encouraged by the favorable attention, La Follette decided to run for governor himself.[8]

On July 1, 1896, La Follette announced his candidacy for governor with a simple press release stating that he had received "many letters from prominent Wisconsin Republicans pledging their support if he would but say the word." He conducted an almost identical campaign for himself in 1896 as he had for Haugen in 1894. He sent over 1,000 letters to young, local politicians, urging them to pack the caucuses with La Follette supporters. William D. Hoard asked the dairy interests to support La Follette, and Nils Haugen appealed to his old constituents on La Follette's behalf.[9]

Despite Albert Hall's recommendation that La Follette's campaign be conducted according to an issue-oriented strategy, with specific anti-machine planks, La Follette continued the practice of condemning "bossism" in general while offering no concrete proposals for change. He made only subtle allusions to the corruption of the Sawyer faction and summarized his credentials with the broad statement, "I can at all times be relied on to stand with the people and for the people." His fight for the nomination centered more on issues of party leadership and personalities than on deeper issues of public policy. Partly as a consequence, La Follette failed to obtain the nomination. His organization had estimated that it controlled twelve more votes than needed for victory, but when the delegates convened in Milwaukee on August 5, 1896, they selected Edward Scofield, a candidate from the Sawyer faction. On the night before the convention, twenty delegates told La Follette that they had been offered bribes to switch their votes to Scofield. La Follette's forces were furious; many were participating in politics for the first time, and they found it difficult to accept the inner workings of the nominating process. In a show of party loyalty, however, La Follette's delegates made Scofield's nomination unanimous and pledged their support to the platform.[10]

La Follette campaigned for the Republican ticket in the 1896 presidential election. He gave over twenty-five speeches in Wisconsin dealing with the national issues of the protective tariff and sound money. La Follette delivered his orations with great energy and enthusiasm because of his personal friendship with McKinley and his expertise on the tariff question. By all accounts, audiences relished his rousing partisan appeals. Both McKinley and Scofield carried Wisconsin by decisive margins. As a reward for La Follette's outstanding campaign efforts, McKinley offered him the federal job of comptroller of the currency. But La Follette declined, partly because he feared that the Sawyer faction was trying to remove him from Wisconsin politics. His decision to reject the federal job proved to be a wise one because it appeared to Wisconsin voters that La Follette was motivated by more than a desire for political patronage.[11]

After La Follette's defeat in the 1896 gubernatorial campaign, he began to brood over the causes. He had based his campaign on the unremarkable strategy of condemning bossism and promising honesty in government. Such abstract appeals were not sufficient to distinguish the La Follette faction from its opponent. La Follette decided that an issue-oriented campaign was the best weapon for defeating the Sawyer faction.

As early as September of 1896 La Follette thought that the electoral process needed to be reformed in order to counteract the influence of political machines. He was genuinely convinced that the will of the Republican Party (and not incidentally his own ambitions) had been thwarted by the corruption of the "Old Guard," so he cast about for a means to prevent the Sawyer faction from controlling the nominating process so rigidly. He refined his thoughts over the winter of 1896 until he arrived at the direct primary, an idea that had been debated and experimented with but was not in widespread practice. La Follette consulted closely with Sam Harper, who, in conjunction with Assemblyman William Lewis of Racine, submitted a direct primary bill to the Wisconsin Assembly on February 10, 1897. Although La Follette did not invent the concept of the direct primary, he was to play a vital role in placing it on the public agenda.[12]

From today's perspective the direct primary proposal does not seem very radical, but in 1897 it was an intoxicating concept that, according to Herbert Margulies, "threatened to render obsolete existing political institutions, methods, and customs." From La Follette's view, the direct primary was tantamount to changing the rules of a game he could not previously win. His motives were unquestionably rooted in his personal frustration with the nominating process. Belle La Follette conceded the personal nature of his new campaign:

To meet the specific abuse encountered through direct experience and observation, he worked out a concrete legislative plan: the direct nomination of candidates by the voters. Once the program was clearly formulated, he started in on an educational campaign to win the understanding and support of the people.[13]

La Follette stumbled on the perfect forum for advocating the direct primary when the University of Chicago invited him to present the annual address in honor of Washington's birthday. Since William McKinley and Theodore Roosevelt had been the two previous speakers, it was a great honor for La Follette to be invited. He prepared carefully for the event, cognizant of the distinguished audience that would assemble at Kent Theater. His address analyzed "the political machine, its evolution in our political history, and its menace to representative government." He charged that the modern political machine "has come to be enthroned in American politics." To remedy the abuses of the political machine, La Follette proposed that the caucus and convention system be replaced with a primary election.[14]

In "The Menace of the Political Machine," La Follette advocated publicly a reform program that separated him from the established political faction in Wisconsin. The *Milwaukee Sentinel* reported that the audience, which was described as the "scholarly element of Chicago," responded to La Follette's "masterful presentation" with "frequent and prolonged applause." The influence of the speech, however, extended far beyond the immediate audience. La Follette's address was reported extensively in the press, and the *Milwaukee Sentinel* reproduced the entire text. In addition, La Follette hit upon the idea of contacting small, rural, weekly newspapers throughout the area and offering them an opportunity to distribute a free supplement that contained the text of "The Menace of the Political Machine." He estimated that over 400,000 copies of the speech were circulated through about 300 newspapers. Significantly, "The Menace of the Political Machine" was the opening statement of La Follette's 1898 campaign for governor. As such, it served as the intellectual underpinning and model for a series of speeches that advocated the direct primary.[15]

La Follette followed up "The Menace of the Political Machine" by launching a public speaking blitzkrieg in favor of the direct primary. He spent the summer of 1897 addressing audiences at county fairs all over Wisconsin.

These fairs were sponsored by the county agricultural societies, which were natural allies of La Follette and usually supported him. Some criticized the county fair managers for inviting a controversial speaker like La Follette to an ostensibly nonpolitical affair, but La Follette's power as a "drawing card" tended to overrule the criticisms. After he was greeted by large crowds in his first few appearances, La Follette received many more speaking invitations than he could accept. The county fair addresses generated substantial comment in the press, making La Follette the center of attention, and this free publicity helped him to promulgate his reform program. La Follette himself thought that the county fair speeches were among the most effective of his career.[16]

La Follette used basically the same speech—"The Dangers Threatening Representative Government"—at all of the county fairs. This speech was similar in substance and tone to "The Menace of the Political Machine," but it focused more on the threat of large corporations. In "Representative Government" La Follette claimed that the giant trusts had changed the tenor of American life and were dominating government through the use of political machines. The solution, he said, was to recapture the political process through the direct primary. In addition, he proposed that corporations in Wisconsin be required to pay equitable taxes.[17]

La Follette introduced a preliminary version of "Representative Government" in Mineral Point on July 4, 1897, to a crowd of some 4,000 people from Grant, Iowa, and Lafayette counties, and it won public approval. The fully developed version of "Representative Government" was first delivered at Fern Dell on August 26, where it was "heartily received" by a gathering of Republican clubs. La Follette spoke from manuscript at Fern Dell, and from then on "Representative Government" was virtually the same address at each location. At the Eau Claire county fair in September, La Follette explained his use of the manuscript by saying, "I cannot afford to be misrepresented or misconstrued." A crowd of 3,000 listened to La Follette at Eau Claire, where his speech caused "marked interest and lively discussion." Much the same reaction was recorded at Black River Falls, where La Follette addressed a crowd of 5,000 people on September 9. La Follette's speech helped "attract people to the fair" at Waukesha, where he proved once again his value as a "drawing card." By the time of the Milwaukee State Fair, La Follette's orations had generated intense public controversy, and "Representative Government" was printed fully in both the *Milwaukee Sentinel* and *Milwaukee Journal*. In Milwaukee, when La Follette asked the crowd if his speech was too long, he was greeted by cries of "go on." On September 30 he "attracted a large crowd" at the Hudson's Street Fair, as he did at Cedarburg, where the *Milwaukee Journal* concluded that "the Madisonian has a warm spot in the hearts of Ozaukee County farmers."[18]

"Representative Government" was impressive, concluded B.J. Daly, because it "specifically and in detail told how the will of the people was being defeated by his party bosses and he invited the people of all parties in, to see how the machine worked and to watch the wheels go around, and explained how he proposed to improve things." Daly, a Democrat, also was impressed with La Follette's nonpartisan approach: "here was a man who spoke to me as a citizen, not as a partisan. He did not attack either party as a party; he attacked the bad in both parties, especially in his own. Do you wonder men were impressed?"[19]

La Follette's delivery during the county fair speeches enhanced the impression that he was open, honest, and earnest, though no one ever compared his delivery to that of Webster or Everett. Usually audiences assessed his platform manner as one of strength and energy more than of subtlety. A report in the *Milwaukee Journal* gives the clearest picture available of La Follette's delivery and warrants quoting at length because of its detail:

Whatever purpose he may have had [,] . . . his vigorous oratory cannot have failed to have left an impression on his hearers. . . .

In most speakers such a vast expenditure of energy in the delivery of an oration would become stale and tiresome. But La Follette is infinite in facial expression and gesture. Every inch of his solidly knit frame is brought into play. . . .

And Mr. La Follette is sometimes sarcastic. His words bite like coals of fire; but his face and gestures are unique. Here, as in other phases, they harmonize . . . .

Disgust, hope, honor, avarice, despair, love, anger, all the passions of man, he paints in strong words and still stronger gestures. This may sound like an exaggeration—but into the most commonplace of his word paintings he throws the energy of a man apparently fully impressed with the whole force and truth of his statements. He never wearies and he will not allow his audience to weary. . . .

There is no joke—nothing frivolous. He is in earnest and gives himself up wholly to the work he is doing. It is serious work to him and while he may not possess the finish of some of the noted orators of the day, he certainly does possess their force.

. . . Perhaps this concentration of every power in the man to impress his hearers is a stage trick, but it is well played and beyond detection. It is real and full of life and vitality. . . . You are impressed with the belief that the man is a sort of steam engine. He is iron in the sense that iron conveys the idea of endurance.

La Follette's delivery complemented the substance of his rhetoric and served as a positive contrast to the undesirable attributes of his opponents. Judging from his platform manner, La Follette's way was honest, open, and direct, not deceptive, sly, or insincere. In addition, as the *Milwaukee Journal* suggested, La Follette reinforced the impression of earnestness through the absence of planned humor in the addresses. He could be sarcastic in tone, but never humorous for levity's sake because there was nothing funny about his struggle with the political machine. Indeed, the titles La Follette chose for his speeches suggested the seriousness of present circumstances: the "menace" of the machine; the "dangers" threatening government.[20]

The net effect of La Follette's county fair speeches was to create a widespread public perception that he was the courageous instigator and leader of a farsighted political reform movement. The *Milwaukee Journal* summarized its judgment of La Follette in August 1897:

The movement of which he is the head is formidable, growing, well sustained and best of all, one directed at existing evils and sure to result in better legislation. In what he says about the corporation control of legislature, the present party management can see their doom. He is scathing and unanswerable.

B.J. Daly echoed the sentiments of many when he evaluated the freshness of La Follette's reform program: "He told his plan for a primary election law, then an entirely new idea, and so far as I can learn, original with La Follette." This perception was bolstered by the way county fair managers introduced La Follette, as in this instance from Eau Claire: "He has taken a long step in advance of all of us, and is calling on us to advance to his position."[21]

As might be anticipated, however, not everyone looked on La Follette's growing influence with approval. The *Milwaukee Sentinel* criticized his propensity to claim that the direct primary would be a panacea for all the ills of society: "One might even say that Mr. La Follette's function is to supply average men, who are discontented with corporations, with reasons for their discontent."

Although intended as a complaint, this observation was extraordinarily perceptive and accurate. During the 1890s many people in Wisconsin were drawn together by the commonly perceived threat of large-scale enterprise. Many citizens feared the huge, soulless corporations, and their fears were exacerbated by the sharp economic depression of 1893-1897. Corporations seemed to the public to be escaping their tax responsibilities and to be insufferably arrogant. The average citizen's taxes remained at predepression levels while income declined. On the other hand, wealthy individuals and corporations got tax relief. What is more, farmers and livestock raisers were particularly dissatisfied with Wisconsin's legislation pertaining to railroad regulation and corporate taxation, and the dairy interests believed that the Sawyer faction sacrificed butter production in favor of the big meat-packers who produced oleomargarine. La Follette's county fair speeches drew much of their strength from this upwelling of public indignation, and La Follette gave it a sharp focus and directed it toward a concrete solution.[22]

The county fair speeches were also noteworthy because they broke a political tradition in Wisconsin. In the past, candidates had refrained from running for office until a few months before the party caucuses, but La Follette campaigned for the 1898 election during the "off year." His opponents were unprepared for the aggressive county fair speeches in the summer and fall of 1897. Moreover, the open attack La Follette leveled at his own political party was virtually unprecedented in Wisconsin politics and thrilled the public while it shocked and dismayed the established faction.[23]

After concluding the county fair speeches, La Follette received an invitation to address the "Good Government Club" of the University of Michigan on the topic of primary elections. On March 12, 1898, he delivered an address that was substantially the same as "Menace of the Political Machine." He maintained that a golden age of participatory democracy had been undermined after the Civil War. Industrial development led to concentrations of wealth, which encouraged the growth of political machines. Currently, La Follette maintained, the political machine controlled the electoral process. As before, he offered the direct primary as a panacea for solving the problems caused by the caucus and convention system. The immediate response to La Follette's Michigan speech was unrecorded, but it eventually prompted over 1,000 letters asking for more information about the direct primary plan. In addition, La Follette used the Michigan speech as a political pamphlet for the next three years.[24]

On July 15, 1898, La Follette announced formally that he was running for governor. But whereas in 1896 he had launched his campaign with a terse, formulaic announcement, his 1898 campaign announcement was a persuasive tract that justified his candidacy in specific terms and reiterated the appeals he had developed since "The Menace of the Political Machine." The 1898 document promised to establish the direct primary, ban the use of free railroad passes and franks by public officials, end corrupt practices in political elections, equalize the tax burden, and discourage the formation of trusts.[25]

Even though La Follette conducted an intensive and well-organized campaign, he again lost in the nominating convention. One of the decisive factors in La Follette's defeat was the fact that his opponent, Governor Edward Scofield, had served only one term. Traditionally, the state Republican Party expected successful incumbent governors to serve two terms. La Follette violated precedent by challenging Scofield for the nomination. Another factor in La Follette's defeat was the use of political and financial influence by his enemies. As before, La Follette thought that Scofield's nomination had been bought by the machine, and, in fact, $8,300 was spent to bribe delegates at the convention. In a display of bad feelings, La Follette's delegates refused to make Scofield's nomination unanimous.[26]

Although La Follette lost the nomination, his campaign influenced the party platform. The Republican Party declared against free railroad passes and supported measures to equalize tax burdens, reform state salary practices, and control the influence of private lobbying in legislation. The platform also included a mildly worded election reform plank: "Recognizing that the present caucus and convention law is not free from defects, we favor such legislation as will secure to every citizen the freest expression of his choice in the selection of candidates." The effects of La Follette's 1898 campaign even extended into the Democratic Party, which included planks on equal taxation and the direct primary in its platform.[27]

La Follette did not participate in the fall campaign because he became severely ill and had to cancel his speaking dates. In fact, he spent half of the next year convalescing. As La Follette was recovering, Scofield's administration reluctantly instituted A.R. Hall's anti-pass measure, *ad valorem* taxes on certain railroad equipment, an inheritance tax, and a special tax commission. Nevertheless, La Follette still had a number of reform issues available to justify another campaign in 1900. The Wisconsin legislature had failed to approve a railroad commission, penetrating tax revisions, and, most important, the direct primary.[28]

Instead of conducting an aggressive speaking campaign in 1899, La Follette quietly organized political and financial backing for another try at the governorship. Now the political balance began to shift in La Follette's favor. He received the support of Isaac Stephenson, Emanuel Philipp, and Joseph Babcock—men whose political ambitions had been disappointed by the Sawyer alliance. Stephenson produced the necessary funds to buy the *Milwaukee Free Press*, which became La Follette's metropolitan political organ. When Philetus Sawyer died in March 1898, the inevitability of La Follette's victory became apparent to the "Old Guard."[29]

On May 15, 1900, La Follette formally announced his candidacy for governor. The announcement set the tone for his entire campaign. It was shorter than the 1898 announcement and projected a strong sense of victory. Indeed, the 1900 statement sounded more like a conciliatory acceptance speech than a campaign document. La Follette did not abandon his reform program but stated it without elaborate justification and in delicate language. He claimed that he had

labored to secure the recognition of certain principles as just, equitable and Republican. . . . These principles, and the purposes of those who advance them, will ultimately be accepted as fair and just by those who have opposed them. Each citizen, and the representative of every business interest, must in the end agree that all should share equally in the benefits of government and each should bear a justly proportionate share of its burdens.[30]

La Follette's campaign in 1900 utilized the same intense personal letter-writing program, distribution of literature, and face-to-face canvassing that he had employed before. His political strength was manifested early, as La Follette captured the Waukesha and Oconta caucuses, and his campaign quickly gathered momentum. Faced with this impressive display of political strength, his opposition began to collapse. On July 5, 1900, Senator John Coit Spooner announced that he would retire from office after the expiration of his term in 1903. The public interpreted this as a sign that the Sawyer faction, known as "Stalwarts," were capitulating to La Follette's group. Spooner's announcement left the "Stalwarts" leaderless and without a sense of direction. In contrast, La Follette's organization attracted masses of voters to the caucuses. In particular, La Follette drew upon his traditional base of dairy farmers and Scandinavians, who turned out in record numbers to support him.[31]

When the delegates convened, La Follette was nominated by acclamation. His acceptance speech conformed generally to the model set forth in his May 16 campaign announcement. La Follette promised to work for the primary election law, equal taxation, total prohibition of free passes or discounts to public officials, and elimination of unlawful combinations. He acknowledged the intensity of the battle for the nomination, but he praised his opponents and asked them to put differences aside for the sake of "the triumph of our party in the political battle that is on."[32]

Since in 1900 the Republican nomination for governor was tantamount to a guaranteed victory, La Follette continued his conciliatory strategy. The Republican press widely praised La Follette for his sensitive handling of a delicate situation and for his devotion to party harmony. One of La Follette's political organs, *The State*, played down personal and ideological differences in the party and stressed the prospect of victory with La Follette. Just as in 1896, La Follette campaigned for McKinley and even spent a week outside Wisconsin on his behalf.[33]

La Follette delivered his opening speech of the 1900 campaign at Schlitz Park, Milwaukee, on September 19. He began the address on the leading issue of the day, answering Democratic charges that McKinley and the Republicans were imperialists. He praised McKinley's character, asserted he had no "imperialistic design," and portrayed him as a man "unmoved by the jeers of the jingoes." La Follette claimed that the Spanish-American war had been fought because of a "pure, lofty, disinterested" desire "to end wrongs and outrages, the horrible character and extent of which could no longer be endured." In addition, he repeated familiar Republican arguments about tariff and monetary policy. The final portion of the speech dealt with the direct primary and equitable taxation. La Follette argued that the Republican state platform was the result of a popular movement: "If the proclamations of that platform seem so obviously right to be self-evident today, it is not because the strongest advocates have changed, but because an awakened public sentiment has spoken at last."[34]

The Schlitz Park speech typified La Follette's rhetoric in the campaign of 1900. Since it was a presidential election year, La Follette focused on national issues. Although he did not renounce his reform program, he did not stress it. Such a strategy worked well on two levels. By asking Wisconsin Republicans to close ranks behind the president, La Follette capitalized on McKinley's popularity and avoided a crippling party split. Simultaneously, he demonstrated his own loyalty to the Republican Party—a loyalty that had been nearly broken only a few years before. In 1900 La Follette could afford to be conciliatory to a political faction that clearly had lost its power.

Despite the strong likelihood of victory in 1900, after the Milwaukee speech La Follette launched an ambitious campaign. His literary bureau distributed over 100,000 copies of political tracts throughout Wisconsin. La Follette himself maintained a rigorous speaking schedule that attempted to blanket the state. In a major campaign innovation for Wisconsin, he chartered a special train so he could make more personal appearances. With the train, La Follette could make eight to ten speeches each day. Between September 19 and November 3, he travelled 6,500 miles and made 216 speeches in 61 Wisconsin counties to an audience of nearly 200,000 people. This was unprecedented in Wisconsin political campaigning.[35]

The Democrats opposed La Follette with a weak candidate, Louis G. Bomrich, and their battle cry of "Bryan, Bomrich or Blood!" was no match for the outpouring of public warmth and enthusiasm reserved for La Follette. La Follette was elected governor on November 6 by a record-breaking plurality of 102,745 popular votes. He won 60 percent of all the ballots and carried 64 of 70 counties. In the town of Scandinavia in Waupaca county, he received 240 votes out of the 241 cast.[36]

During the period 1891-1900, the backbone of La Follette's rhetoric continued to be the melodramatic scenario. Nowhere is this narrative device expressed more clearly than in "The Menace of the Political Machine," a speech that proved to be the archetype for virtually all of his subsequent speeches that attacked corporation and machine control of American politics. In "Menace" La Follette's basic task was to convince his audience that the political machine posed a threat to society. He traced the origins of the political machine and explained how it had come to dominate America. In this historical review, La Follette described the past wistfully. Characteristically, he pointed to the Civil War as a noble crusade, a unifying spirit that transcended the petty motives of people:

What sacrifices we were freely making for that kind of government! How ready were we to give our fortunes, mortgage our future, march our brave men to battle, blot out our individual homes and hopes, clothe the dead in glory and the living in mourning—all to preserve a government of the people, by the people, and for the people!

La Follette then made an appeal that was reminiscent of his 1884 Memorial Day Address.[37] He painted a picture of rapid, negative change that was out of control. La Follette maintained that, since the Civil War, industrialization had caused Americans to become preoccupied with materialistic things and to neglect their duties as citizens. He lamented, "Nothing required the good citizen's attention but the material affairs of the nation. The fires never went out in the furnaces, the factories ran day and night." The people devoted their lives to "the hot pursuit of fortune" and did not want "to let business go for politics." Under these circumstances, the political machine had gradually taken over until it had acquired enough power to dictate policies to the people:

When the business man, the scholar, the farmer, the artisan, awoke to the importance of participating in municipal, state and federal politics, they were amazed to find that a new force occupied the field and assumed the right to control.[38]

In addition to attacking the political machine, La Follette also condemned the modern corporation. In his view, the political machine and the corporation existed in a corrupt and symbiotic relationship. The corporation supplied the machine with money, and the machine allowed the corporation to flourish and proliferate. La Follette used the same imagery to characterize the corporation that he used to treat the political machine. "The private corporation," he declared,

is everywhere present to-day. The individual is rapidly disappearing from the business world, and nearly all of the business of the country to-day is transacted by private corporations. . . . nearly everything which ministers to man's comfort or nourishes life, passes under corporate control before it reaches the consumer.

The narrative pattern used in "The Menace of the Political Machine" bears striking resemblance to the one introduced in the 1879 "Iago" oration. La Follette characterized Iago as "artful," "cunning," "sly," and "crafty"; he described the political machine as "artful," "cunning," "sly," "adroit," "unscrupulous" and "debauched." In the "Iago" oration La Follette maintained that "the other characters of the tragedy of *Othello* are but puppets, moving at the will of this master." Similarly, he portrayed the political machine as controlling the destinies of the complacent citizens. In the 1879 speech, the character Iago operated by silently ensnaring his victims, while in the 1897 oration the political machine operated by an "insidious, creeping, progressive encroachment" on the rights of its victims: "The machine—this invisible empire, does its work so quietly. There is no explosion, no clash of arms, no open rebellion, but a sly covert nullification of the highest law of the land." Iago presented the appearance of serving his master while he was actually destroying Othello. So, too, the political machine had "in the beginning the semblance of serving its party but mastered it instead." In short, the political machine was as efficiently evil as the Iago figure, with equally detrimental effects on the moral beings under its control.[39]

Significantly, La Follette characterized the political machine as a kind of engine that threatened to overpower human beings. La Follette was certainly not the first to characterize a political organization as a "machine," but he exploited brilliantly the negative connotations of the metaphor. The machine was dehumanizing and cold; it reflected the vast, impersonal forces of the industrial age. La Follette's recurrent use of the word "machine" as a modifier ("machine men" employed "machine methods") reflected both a horror and a fascination with the trends of modern life. The machine "produced results with mathematical certainty. It was always in operation. It had acquired the trick of perpetual motion." The machine was more powerful and destructive than the men who created it: "The machine is its own master. It owes no obligation and acknowledges no responsibility.... It is independent of the people, and fears no reckoning." It manipulated people mechanically: "The types of its big wheels and little wheels, its pinions and cogs are only too familiar and recognizable.... Every man is placed over the state and every line is laid, every duty assigned."[40]

To underscore further the negative aspects of the political machine, La Follette used one of his favorite techniques: contrast. He contrasted at great length the political machine with the "legitimate political organization." No one in the audience should be confused, said La Follette. The legitimate organization "encourages research," "stimulates discussion," "offers opportunity for the highest public service," "teaches," "reviews," "quickens the sense of obligation and personal responsibility in all the duties of citizenship," while "cliques, rings, machines thrive upon the citizen's indifference to the plain duties of representative government." The legitimate organization "seeks only a fair and honest expression of the people's will," while the machine is "designed to control in defiance of the desires of a majority." Participatory democracy liberates, while the machine "suppresses," "exploits," and "takes tribute." The caucus system results in "wrangling dispute," "disorder," "violence and collision," where men are "badgered" and "bought"; but under the secret ballot system, the polling place is "freed from all annoyances, all espionage, all intimidation," and is so "quiet" that a citizen can "exercise his right." In sum, La Follette said, "there is no likeness or similitude between a political organization that appeals to every voter in the party and a machine that appeals to the most skilled and unscrupulous workers of the party."[41]

La Follette identified several specific harms caused by the machine that needed to be remedied. First, he argued, the machine violated the will of the majority when it arbitrarily selected candidates and rigged elections. He insisted that if voters could not participate freely in the selection of their representatives, then "the first principle of our government fails.... If there be failure here, there is failure throughout." And crucial to representation was the nominating process. According to La Follette, "It is as much the interest and as plainly the duty of the state to as carefully perfect and guard a system of nominating candidates as it perfects and guards the system of electing them."

The machine also harmed society by eliminating the voter's sense of personal responsibility and duty. La Follette argued that "the fundamental principle of a republic is individual responsibility" and that "pure democracy" is the "assertion of the individual as a political factor." La Follette believed in a political system where "the voter can lay his hand directly upon the shoulder of the public servant and point the way he should go." But many citizens had relinquished their personal responsibility during the years of industrialization, and now "cliques, rings, machines" exploited "the citizen's indifference to the plain duties of representative government."

La Follette denied that the problems caused by the political machine could be eliminated by a few minor repairs. He maintained that it was idle to talk of reforming the caucus because the political machine was "inherently bad." In fact, the machine was so clever and devious that it was attempting to change its appearance to trick the voter while maintaining its essential wickedness: "The machine, in some instances, already anticipating the danger of the destruction of this foundation of machine control, under the mask of caucus reform, is seeking to satisfy public interest and save all the elements of the caucus essential to machine manipulation and supremacy." Under the circumstances, compromise was impossible. Indeed, fighting the machine was a great moral crusade akin to the Civil War, and La Follette appealed to his listeners to "emancipate the majority from its enslavement."

During "The Menace of the Political Machine" La Follette built his case for change by cultivating tension and anxiety in the same way evangelistic preachers might illustrate the perils of everlasting damnation to their congregations. Under such circumstances, when the despair of the audience reaches a pinnacle, the speaker offers a simple solution—a panacea. Psychologically, the audience is eager to embrace an easy answer. After creating a sense of urgency in "The Menace of the Political Machine," La Follette asked his audience, "What, then, shall we do to be saved?" His answer was to adopt the direct primary: "Here is our final safety. Here is the ultimate overthrow of the machine." The cure, he said, was to

Go back to the first principles of democracy. Go back to the people. Substitute for both the caucus and the convention a primary election—held under all the sanctions of law which prevail at the general elections—where the citizen may cast his vote directly to nominate the candidate of the party with which he affiliates.[42]

Since La Follette was, in effect, asking Republican voters to overthrow the traditional political order, he needed to address the question of loyalty. Was it dishonorable, irresponsible, or disloyal to change political allegiance? La

Follette addressed this question most fully in "Dangers Threatening Representative Government," where he claimed that those who challenged the political machine were ultimately the most honorable because they responded to a higher sense of loyalty. Moreover, La Follette's supporters were not rejecting cherished Republican principles but rather the corruption of individuals who currently controlled the party:

honestly believing that there are wrongs to be righted, abuses to be corrected, as he [the Party member] desires the success and perpetuity of his party, it is the highest test of party fealty that he shall speak in time a word of earnest warning. . . . [T]hat man is untrue to his state, his party, and himself, who will not raise his voice in condemnation, —not in condemnation of the principles of the political party in which he believes or of the great body of its organization, but of the men who betray it, and the methods by which they control, only to prostitute it to base and selfish ends.[43]

La Follette also claimed that his listeners had a greater responsibility to the past and to the future, and he challenged them to avoid the reputation of being the generation that failed:

Oh, men! think of the heroes who died to make this country free; think of their sons who died to keep it undivided upon the map of the world! Shall we, their children, basely surrender our birthright and say, "Representative government is a failure?" No, never, until Bunker Hill and Little Round Top sink into the very earth.

Characteristically, La Follette insisted that there was no middle ground. Either an honest man was "bound by every obligation of good faith to denounce the betrayal [of the machine], or by his silence he becomes a party to it." On the other hand, those who supported La Follette's direct primary proposal would cover themselves with glory, as he stated in his Acceptance Speech of August 8, 1900: "nothing which has been done by any convention in a quarter of a century will give to every man who has had a share in the work such enduring honor. . . . Into the life of every generation comes some great opportunity for public good. It has come to you to-day." In sum, one of La Follette's major strategies was to define political insurrection as a civic duty of loyal, honorable Americans. Supporters of the machine, on the other hand, were disloyal, irresponsible allies of evil.[44]

Although "The Menace of the Political Machine" and "The Dangers Threatening Representative Government" are similar, there are a few significant differences. For one thing, La Follette used more statistics, examples, and testimony in his "Representative Government" address. The specific content of the evidence in "Representative Government" varied somewhat to suit local circumstances, but in each case he cited a substantial amount of evidence to bolster his arguments. For instance, in Milwaukee, he provided statistics to demonstrate that railroad stocks were overvalued, that 95 percent of the coal industry was owned by the railroad trusts, that the wheat and meat trusts cheated farmers and gouged consumers, that two-thirds of personal property was controlled by corporations, and that trusts evaded paying a fair amount of taxes to the states. In the realm of examples, he provided instances of the negative influences of railway and gas monopolies in Illinois; he cited cases of unfair tax rates among eastern states; he listed four specific reform measures that had been defeated in the Wisconsin legislature, and he provided the Australian ballot as an illustration of a widely accepted election reform that had once been highly controversial. Finally, he cited testimony from official reports that indicted the trusts. Another difference in "Representative Government" is La Follette's attack on "paper" wealth, an attitude that is entirely consistent with his longstanding praise of agriculture as a way of life. Throughout "Representative Government" La Follette tapped the strong hostility his rural audiences felt toward holders of paper wealth such as deeds, bonds, securities, and stocks. He attacked "financial centers of the country" such as New York and Chicago as hotbeds of such "invisible property." He argued that the "officers and directors of great corporations" were escaping taxation at the expense of the farmer and small property holder: "Owning two-thirds of the personal property of the country, evading the payment of taxes wherever possible, the corporations throw almost the whole burden upon land, upon the little homes, and the personal property of farmers." One example La Follette used to prove his point was particularly apropos for his predominately rural listeners:

With horses so cheap that the assessor is the only person that would put a price on them, do you know that the equalized assessed valuation of the horses in Wisconsin, last year, exceeded the assessed valuation of all the notes, bonds, and mortgages by more than five million dollars?

However, La Follette argued, with the direct primary as a political weapon, the farmers and rural dwellers could reverse the burden of taxation by electing people who would tax paper wealth more equitably.[45]

The characterization of political machines and corporations as evil, ruthless, conniving villains posed a rhetorical paradox for La Follette. He needed to portray the enemy as dangerous in order to create public concern for the problem, but he could not go too far or else people might view the enemy as invincible and the problem as intractable. La Follette struck the proper balance in his University of Michigan speech, where he attempted to characterize the political machine as a potent and dangerous enemy; but he never expressed uncertainty about the ultimate outcome of the battle between the people and corruption. Even though the task was arduous, he predicted that the machine was fated to defeat. He claimed to draw strength for his cause from a growing public movement:

The country is awakening, the people are aroused. They will have their own. The machine may obstruct, misdirected reform may temporize, but "be of good cheer, strengthen thine heart," the will of the people shall prevail.

"The fight is on," he exclaimed. "It will continue to victory. . . . There will be no halt and no compromise." Variations of this optimistic assertion that an aroused public would inevitably prevail over evil would become a familiar refrain in La Follette's subsequent rhetoric.[46]

As La Follette had promised, he was ultimately victorious in winning the governorship of Wisconsin. Such an outcome must have seemed unlikely in the aftermath of the Sawyer scandal; but La Follette overcame adversity, and oratory was the keystone in his political resurgence. After a period of relative rhetorical dormancy, his persistent agitation gradually gave him political power and influence while establishing him as a clear alternative to the entrenched faction. Belle La Follette was correct in her belief that the altered political climate in Wisconsin was due "to the cumulative effect of the previous years of work: to speaking campaigns, especially at county fairs, to wide distribution of literature relating to the issues, to newspaper discussion." After three years of intense rhetorical agitation, La Follette had acquired enough support "to mollify the new without antagonizing the old." By the turn of the century, La Follette was a man whose time had come. Through his rhetoric he had captured the governorship and built a broad base of power for later elections.[47]

5
Governor La Follette

Governor La Follette assumed office on January 7, 1901. Three days later he delivered his inaugural address to a joint session of the legislature. Continuing the harmonious tone of the 1900 election, La Follette asked for "comity of relation" to bring about passage of the legislation he proposed. He stressed the "unusual responsibility" of governing the state, and he reminded the legislators that the "demand of the voter to-day is clear and explicit" and "the mandate of the people" must be obeyed. In addition to the direct primary and equal taxation, La Follette urged, among other things, the restriction of political lobbying, economy and efficiency in government, the improvement of public education, and the appointment of women to state boards concerned with educational and charitable matters.[1]

La Follette was confident that Republican legislators would endorse his inaugural address, but conservative Republicans disapproved of it. The *Milwaukee Journal* remarked that La Follette had

used all the tricks of a college orator: he ruffled his eyebrows, held up his index finger, leaned over his little pulpit and nodded his head like a scolding mamma reprimanding her naughty boys. . . . his hearers remained stolid and imperturbed save for an occasional smile on the face of an old-time Stalwart, whose half-hidden axe was well sharpened for the little governor when opportunity presents.

In the words of Albert O. Barton, "A mysterious spirit of battle which appeared to have slept through the campaign . . . suddenly seemed to animate the air."[2]

La Follette introduced his direct primary proposal, called the Stevens bill, to both houses of the legislature on January 28. Proceedings on the bill began on February 12 and continued for several months. The Stevens bill came up for consideration in the Assembly on March 19. Political lobbying for and against the bill was intense. After a tumultuous all-night session, which allegedly included disreputable behavior by opponents of the direct primary, the Assembly approved the Stevens bill, 51-48.[3]

While the Senate continued to debate the direct primary bill, the Assembly considered two bills to equalize railroad taxation. The conflict over tax reform was just as acrimonious as that over the Stevens bill. Finally, on April 23, 1901, the Assembly rejected La Follette's license-fee bill, a proposal that would have required the railroads to pay an additional $600,000 to Wisconsin. The governor was furious. On May 2 he vetoed a recently passed dog-tax bill and used the accompanying message to chastise the Assembly for defeating railroad tax reform. The veto message, read to the Assembly by a clerk, briefly mentioned the small increase on dog license fees but soon proceeded to a scathing condemnation of legislative irresponsibility and unresponsiveness. La Follette concluded that he was

unwilling to present to the people of this state, in lieu of the legislation to equalize taxation which has been promised to them, and which they have a right to expect from representative government, a scheme which, in a general way, may be described as an act to relieve the farmer or city home-owner of a small measure of increased tax upon his realty by imposing a license fee upon his dog.[4]

Later that day the Assembly reacted to La Follette's message by voting to override his veto of the dog-tax bill. Conservatives were outraged by La Follette's "Dog-Tax Veto," but Belle La Follette saw the brilliance of her husband's rhetoric: "It dramatized the abstract principles and made the issue a living force in the everyday thought of the people." Barton believed the "Dog-Tax Veto" pointed out the vivid contrast between the legislature's complete willingness to increase a tax on any citizen while allowing the giant corporations to continue untouched. The "Dog-Tax Veto" "drove home to the common mind . . . the subserviency of the legislature."[5]

In the meantime, the Senate had replaced La Follette's direct primary proposal with the Hagemeister bill, which provided for the nomination of convention delegates through a primary, rather than providing for the direct nomination of candidates by the voters, as La Follette's bill had proposed. The Senate passed the Hagemeister bill on May 3. The *Wisconsin State Journal* predicted that La Follette would veto the Hagemeister bill, and on May 10 he did. In the accompanying veto message La Follette reviled the Senate with a caustic attack on its integrity. The purpose of his May 10 veto message, La Follette said, was to recount the "history of the effort to secure a primary election law in this state, the character of the opposition, and the means employed to defeat it." He then traced his public speaking campaigns since 1897 and his election as governor in 1900. He concluded that the direct primary proposal was a mandate from the people, and he blamed the defeat of the Stevens bill on the insidious, wicked methods of the Stalwarts. Unlike the dog-tax veto message, which was relatively brief, the veto message of May 10 ran to 4300 words and was a major document in La Follette's growing war with the legislature.[6]

As soon as the May 10 veto message had been delivered, the stunned legislature moved to override La Follette. Failing in that attempt by five votes, the State Senate censured La Follette's veto message for transcending "all bounds of official propriety and constitutional right." Published reactions to La Follette's message reflected the deeply divided state of public opinion in Wisconsin. For example, the *Milwaukee Sentinel* stated that the veto message was "unworthy of the chief executive of the state of Wisconsin." Typical of the other side, the *Milwaukee Evening Wisconsin* predicted that "public sentiment will unanimously sustain the veto." [7]

Emanuel Philipp realized that La Follette's message, "printed in the official journal of the Senate as a permanent record, is a stump speech intended for use in political campaigns." Indeed, it might well be said that La Follette's famous veto laid the groundwork for the ensuing reelection campaign. But there were negative effects as well: La Follette developed a solid corps of bitter enemies with extensive resources and political experience. Moreover, after the longest legislative session in the history of Wisconsin, the governor had not passed even one of his major platform proposals.[8]

La Follette developed a life-threatening illness in June 1901 and was forced to drop out of public view for ten months while he convalesced. By March 1902 La Follette was well enough to enter the fray, and he delivered a series of well-received campaign speeches in Oconomowoc, Grand Rapids, and Blue Mounds. In each place, La Follette attacked the state legislature for evading its responsibility to enact tax reform and institute the direct primary system. The *Milwaukee Sentinel* suspected that the governor had "opened his campaign for renomination," and La Follette's political organ, the *Free Press*, cheerfully agreed: "All right, call it the opening of the governor's campaign." [9]

As the 1902 Republican convention approached, La Follette moved the site of the meeting from Milwaukee, where it had been held regularly since 1884, to the University of Wisconsin gymnasium in Madison, away from the corrupting influences of the Milwaukee machine. La Follette won renomination easily on the first ballot. The *Wisconsin State Journal* remarked that "Old things have passed away" and the state had entered a "new era in Wisconsin politics. . . . The youth, the hope, the future, are in town today. They have renominated La Follette." [10]

When La Follette ascended the platform to deliver his acceptance speech, the "convention went wild in its enthusiasm. . . . The mass sent up cheer after cheer." No one expected compromise, and the governor did not disappoint his audience. "The gravest danger menacing republican institutions to-day," he proclaimed, "is the over-balancing control of city, state, and national legislatures by the wealth and power of public-service corporations. . . . It goes directly to the root of government. It threatens to sap the life of American citizenship." La Follette asked if the American people would be servants or masters. He answered, "Surely our great cities, our great states, our great nation, will not helplessly surrender to this most insidious enemy which is everywhere undermining official integrity and American institutions." [11]

Journalists observed that "Every paragraph" of La Follette's acceptance speech "was clean, cutting and direct," and that "every sentence in the speech found a responsive chord in the hearts of the delegates." Moreover, "Almost every sentence was interrupted by applause, and shouts of 'That's right,' 'That's the true doctrine,' 'Good! Good!,' 'Give it to them Bob' and other like expressions." In many respects, the speech was like an "officer's exhortation to his men before the battle," and La Follette's opponents were painfully aware of the warlike aspect of the governor's rhetoric. The *Milwaukee Journal* seemed appalled at the intense political zeal inspired by the speech: "This is not oratory, it is passion. It is fanaticism. It is demagoguery. It is not force; it is frenzy." [12]

La Follette opened the 1902 general election campaign in Milwaukee at the West Side Turn Hall on September 30. A crowd of nearly 2,500 heard him deliver a three-hour speech from a seventy-nine-page manuscript. Notwithstanding the great length of the speech, the "enthusiastic, cheering multitude" was "eager to catch every word that fell from the lips of the governor." The September 30 address consisted of well-rehearsed themes such as attacks on the evil methods of corporation lobbyists, appeals for the direct primary and equal taxation, and a prediction that reform would ultimately triumph. [13]

La Follette's campaign speech generally was praised by the press. Even the *Milwaukee Sentinel* admitted that La Follette had effectively "sounded the keynote" for his 1902 campaign. A prominent member of the audience observed in the *Milwaukee Journal* that the speech "will make a great campaign document," and indeed, La Follette gave substantially the same speech throughout the 1902 contest and circulated it further in pamphlet form. Although he started out delivering this address from a manuscript, he soon came to use the extemporaneous method. La Follette delivered fifty-five speeches between October 7 and November 4. He spoke two to four times each day and reached fifty-three villages and cities. [14]

La Follette won the election with a 47,599 vote advantage over his opponent, David S. Rose of Milwaukee. Although the plurality was less than half of what it had been in 1900, the margin was decisive, considering the Stalwart opposition in his own party. La Follette's faction won a majority of the Assembly seats and added twice as many new senators as did the Stalwarts. But since a number of anti-La Follette senators remained from previous elections, he was still short of a majority in the Senate. The election of 1902 confirmed the suspicion held by many political observers that Wisconsin politics was divided starkly between those who favored La Follette and those who opposed him. Conservative Republicans voted for Rose, and progressive Democrats voted for La Follette. According to David Thelen, "La Follette had succeeded in making his name synonymous with reform in both parties."[15]

Between November 1902 and January 1903 La Follette prepared his "Second Inaugural Address." He was anxious about the speech because he believed that failure to implement his reform program during his second term would cause the public to lose interest. He appeared before a joint session of the Wisconsin legislature to read his message on January 15, 1903, and the three hours it took to deliver the address was a new record for length. In addition to standard arguments for equitable taxation and the direct primary, La Follette advocated a number of other issues, including the prohibition of lobbying, support for a legislative reference library, and better protection for the injured employees of railroad companies.[16]

The most controversial part of La Follette's speech, however, was a proposal to regulate railroad rates through a commission. The issue of railroad regulation was not new in Wisconsin. A.R. Hall had long claimed that rail rates were unfair, but La Follette had wanted to hold this issue in reserve until the proper time. Now the governor argued that the railroads would simply raise their rates in order to make up for the added expense of increased taxes. La Follette maintained that increased railroad taxation "will fail utterly in its object, unless it be supplemented with legislation protecting the public against increased transportation charges." [17]

La Follette attempted to demonstrate through "exhaustive" statistics that Wisconsinites had been cheated out of millions of dollars by the railroads. "Why," he asked,

should Wisconsin have endured this great loss? It is because, and only because, the railroads have continued to exercise such control as to defeat legislation in Wisconsin creating a commission to regulate transportation rates such as the Legislatures of Iowa and Illinois have adopted.

He asked the Wisconsin legislature to establish a state railway commission and to advise the federal government that the Interstate Commerce Commission should be given "authority to regulate rates and prevent discriminations." As a parting shot, La Follette blamed the railroads for making this new issue necessary: "The railroad companies have by their own opposition made legislation for the establishment of a commission to regulate transportation rates a necessary concomitant of tax legislation."[18]

La Follette's 1903 inaugural address was well-received by much of the press. The *Milwaukee Daily News* opined that La Follette's rhetoric exhibited "deep study and a thorough grasp of the problem." The *Wisconsin State*

Journal called his speech a "notable oratorical event" and "a new war cry in Wisconsin politics." The *Milwaukee Sentinel* observed that La Follette's supporters "are loud in their praise" of the address, while his opponents "concede it to be an unusually able and comprehensive document."[19]

Several months after La Follette's message, he told a reporter that if the legislature continued to obstruct his reform program, "the people will take the hide of every Stalwart senator who comes up for re-election." Perhaps the Stalwarts heeded the warning, for La Follette enjoyed some success in the 1903 legislative session. Although the direct primary bill was not enacted, the legislature agreed, after extensive debate and compromise, to put the question to the people in the form of a popular referendum. Since La Follette felt confident of public support, he signed the bill. Moreover, the state legislature approved a bill to tax the railroads on the real worth of property rather than on reported earnings. The *ad valorem* legislation raised the tax bill from $1.9 million to $3.4 million over a two-year period. As La Follette had predicted, the railroads were willing to accept the *ad valorem* legislation because they could make up the extra expenses by increasing rates. But that maneuver would not be possible if the state regulated rate increases. Therefore, when hearings on railroad regulation began on March 17, railroad shippers exerted considerable influence to prevent a rate regulation bill from passing.[20]

To deal with the intense lobbying against the railroad regulation bill, La Follette unveiled a new rhetorical weapon—the "special message." Like the vetoes of 1902, La Follette used these special messages to berate the legislature and make arguments for his position. He sent three special messages to the legislature within a two-week period. The first message, on April 23, repeated earlier arguments that the railroads were charging unfair rates in Wisconsin. In addition, La Follette criticized the railroads' practice of granting rebate payments to favored shippers. He concluded by recommending a "full and thorough examination of the books and accounts of the railroads doing business in the state of Wisconsin." The *Wisconsin State Journal* reported that La Follette's April 23 message caused "consternation in the camps of the railroad lobbyists" and that, "if he had cast a bomb among them it could not have caused greater surprise."[21]

The railroads charged that La Follette had selected atypical examples of rates in his April 23 message, so the governor responded on April 28 with a second message, which offered "a further and more extended consideration of the subject discussed in the first message." The April 28 message was not read by a clerk. Rather, every legislator found on his desk a hefty booklet of 183 pages that listed every station in Wisconsin on two major rail lines and compared the Wisconsin rates with corresponding distances in Iowa and Illinois. On the basis of this analysis, La Follette concluded that "the road is charging exorbitant rates wherever it has unrestrained control of transportation charges."

Moreover, La Follette maintained that certain shippers, in league with the railroads, were granted secret rebates in exchange for political lobbying. This charge caused 156 manufacturers and shippers to sign a resolution of protest stating "We resent the charges and insinuations made in said message" and denying that any "special favors" were received.[22]

La Follette's railroad commission bill was defeated in the Assembly on May 1 and did not even reach the floor in the Senate. The governor responded with yet another special message on May 7, this time requesting that the legislature "enact a law which will prevent any increase in transportation charges by the railroad corporations in Wisconsin." The Assembly passed La Follette's recommendation, but the Senate defeated it.[23]

Although La Follette's special messages failed to gain the enactment of his railroad regulation bill, they were effective in other ways. Belle La Follette reported that the special messages had more than one task to perform: "he hoped to make the fight for it [regulation] so hot that the railroads would let the primary and taxation bills pass in order to stave off a law for rate regulation." In addition, the special messages publicized railroad rates and engendered further public concern. In fact, under the intense public scrutiny that La Follette's messages accelerated, some railroad rates were lowered slightly. A third function of the special message was suggested by Emanuel Philipp, who charged that "Governor La Follette always [has] to have an issue in reserve, and this railway regulation issue would serve his purpose if it were defeated, as it was in the end." La Follette's own remarks tend to confirm the Stalwarts' suspicion. He stated at the end of the 1903 session, "Well, we didn't get all we wanted, but we did pretty well, and we have enough left over for another campaign." La Follette's tactic did not go unnoticed by the press, which cautioned that "Governor La Follette is piling up as much campaign material as possible."[24]

After the 1903 legislative session, La Follette embarked on a lecture tour in the Midwest and the East. In all, he gave fifty-seven Chautauqua speeches between June 23 and September 2. He delivered adaptations of the speech "Representative Government," alternating with a "Hamlet" lecture on Sundays or when he spoke twice in the same community. While La Follette's 1879 speech "Iago" was an attack on an evil villain, his 1903 Hamlet lecture was a defense of an admirable hero. La Follette denied the charges of some Shakespearean scholars that Hamlet was "a mere dreamer" unable to take decisive action. Instead he argued that Hamlet was Shakespeare's "highest conception of man," an individual with refined sensibilities and high moral standards, thrust into a world that was low, coarse, lustful, and brutal. Throughout the analysis, La Follette maintained that Hamlet exercised his will, although he was constrained by conscience.[25]

La Follette's 1903 lecture on Shakespeare reflected several of his lifelong concerns. Most of La Follette's political rhetoric was devoted to the exposure of secrecy and the eradication of wickedness. His analysis of *Hamlet* hinged upon these concepts. La Follette claimed that, by the end of the play, Hamlet realized "there could be no public vindication of the law without *full disclosures* which would *expose the queen*." Moreover, when Hamlet finally acted to kill his wicked uncle, La Follette noted that "the last exaction of the long-violated moral law is about to be satisfied," and the evil king "pays the penalty of his crime in a way to *satisfy public justice*." Although the parallels between La Follette's "Hamlet" lecture and his political rhetoric are relatively tenuous, it is nevertheless tempting to imagine that La Follette identified personally with the Prince of Denmark.[26]

La Follette followed up the Chautauqua tour with extensive off-year campaigning in Wisconsin on the county fair circuit, although as Emanuel Philipp observed, "There have been no 'off years' in this state politically, for a perpetual campaign has been in progress." In the county fair speeches, La Follette resumed his attack on the railroads, using the abundant storehouse of arguments derived from his special legislative messages. The most prominent feature of these speeches, however, was the "reading of the freight rates." The bulk of each speech was devoted to comparing freight rates in Wisconsin to rates in other states. The invariable conclusion was that Wisconsin consumers were being cheated by the greedy rail lines.[27]

Audiences knew in advance that La Follette would read the freight rates, but he continued to draw large, supportive crowds wherever he went. According to Barton, "ordinarily, statistics and figures are repellent to an audience, but in these instances the interest of the hearers was held in spite of them." The *Milwaukee Journal* described a typical county fair audience as "made up chiefly of the residents of surrounding towns and cities. On the track were farmers and working people. It was largely an out-of-town audience in which the Scandinavian element was conspicuous and the German element lacking." The *Journal* concluded that such an audience supported La Follette "heart and soul." In all, La Follette spoke at twenty locations in Wisconsin, at such places as Plymouth, Appleton, Eau Claire, Madison, Evansville, Antigo, Rhinelander, La Crosse, and Chippewa Falls.[28]

After the 1903 Chautauqua and county fair campaigns, speculation began that La Follette intended to seek a third term as governor. While a third term was not unprecedented, there was a strong tradition of serving only twice. Throughout the fall of 1903 La Follette refused to reveal his intentions, preferring to keep his opponents guessing. He had enjoyed only sporadic success as governor—the primary bill had passed, but it could still possibly be defeated at the polls; the rate commission and maximum rate bills had been killed; and the *ad valorem* taxation had been approved, but there was no way to prevent increased railroad prices. If La Follette chose to pursue these issues in 1904, it would be his fifth bid for the gubernatorial nomination.[29]

Sensing the worst, La Follette's opponents organized resistance. One estimate claimed that nine out of ten newspapers opposed the possibility of La Follette serving a third term. The *Wisconsin State Journal* opined, "The only way to dislodge him is to take him by the rhetorical seat of the pants and throw him down hard." The *Milwaukee Sentinel* followed this prescription by attacking La Follette as an insincere political demagogue interested only in reelection. In addition, La Follette's Stalwart opponents challenged his railroad statistics in a 240-page book called *The Truth About Wisconsin Freight Rates*. Referred to as the "Red Book" because of the color of its covers, this document contained 400 statistical tables designed to show that railroad regulation was failing in other states.[30]

By December of 1903 La Follette's opponents had developed two potentially damaging arguments against railroad regulation. First, the railroad companies had voluntarily reduced their rates slightly and now claimed that further reductions were impossible. Thus, a railroad commission would be pointless. Second, the Stalwarts argued that railroad regulation had been tried in Wisconsin once before and had failed. Critics of La Follette's proposal pointed to the Granger-inspired Potter laws of the 1870s as proof that railroad regulation was not feasible. La Follette attacked these two arguments on January 29, 1904, when he spoke to the Rock County Grange at Milton Junction. His speech, titled "Granger Legislation and State Control of Railway Rates," was the opening shot of the 1904 campaign.[31]

La Follette responded to the railroad rate reductions by taking credit for forcing the railroads to behave more responsibly. Furthermore, he argued that lowering the railroad rates proved that they had been excessive and amounted to an admission of guilt: "What a confession this whole proceeding makes! How completely are they unmasked." The rate reduction "completely overturns all their denials; it destroys the value of all their testimony, and gives away their entire case." At the same time, La Follette argued that even though the railroads had cleverly reduced their prices slightly, the rates were still higher than in other states that employed rate regulation. Thus, a railway commission with the power to control rates was still needed in Wisconsin.

La Follette also attacked his opponents' assertion that the old Granger railroad laws had been a complete failure. He admitted that the Granger statutes "were far from perfect with respect to the provisions for their enforcement. But they were essentially correct in principle and reasonable in their terms." He characterized the Granger movement in Wisconsin as "the first great struggle in this country between the railroads and the public, to determine which should be master."[32]

Although the Milton Junction speech was a strong campaign document, La Follette did not yet reveal his intention to seek another term. Since the Stalwarts claimed that no one had requested La Follette to run again, in

February the *Mt. Horeb Times* published a "Call to Governor La Follette," which asked him "to again accept the position whose trust you have discharged with such fidelity to the people and such honor to the state." The *Wood County Reporter* of April 19 argued that "The State of Wisconsin cannot afford to put in his place at this time any other man." In April and May of 1904 La Follette responded to these "calls" by campaigning actively in Milwaukee, La Crosse, Ripon, and Racine.[33]

By the time of the state nominating convention on May 18, the conflict between Stalwarts and "Half-breeds" (half Republican and half Populist) had become so bitter that the anti-La Follette forces bolted and formed a "rump convention" at another site. Since La Follette's faction had complete control of the regular convention, the party platform was a mirror image of the governor's political agenda. This situation was the culmination of La Follette's efforts to control the Republican Party, and he declared triumphantly in his May 19 Acceptance Speech:

NO CANDIDATE [F]OR MEMBER OF THE LEGISLATURE OR FOR ANY STATE OFFICE SHALL RECEIVE THE SUPPORT OF THE PARTY ORGANIZATION, UNLESS HE NOT ONLY DECLARES FOR THE PARTY PRINCIPLES, BUT UNLESS HIS CHARACTER HAS BEEN SUCH AS TO GIVE VERITY TO HIS DECLARATIONS. . . . In the next legislature no man will find a place there with a right to be called a Republican member of that legislature, who is not proven as worthy to be accepted as a faithful and trusted representative.[34]

La Follette toured the Chautauqua circuit in the summer of 1904 to raise funds for the general election campaign. Afterwards, he began campaigning in Wisconsin. He realized that control of the legislature in 1904 was essential or his reform program would certainly falter. In 1900 La Follette had disregarded the election of the legislature. In 1902 he had endorsed certain candidates. But in 1904 he campaigned heavily in the districts of his political opponents. In addition, for the first time La Follette openly endorsed Democrats who were running against Stalwart candidates. La Follette urged voters to support men who stood for reform, and he pleaded for citizens to disregard party affiliation.[35]

La Follette needed a powerful rhetorical weapon in 1904 to influence the election of the legislature. In April and May of 1904 he had experimented with a new tactic, which he called "reading the roll" to the people of Wisconsin. After considering a specific issue, such as the railroad commission bill, he then would read the official vote of the legislature, usually including only the "wrong" votes of Stalwarts. By the fall of 1904 "reading the roll" had become a central feature of La Follette's campaign speeches. His address of November 4 provides a good example of this tactic:

I want to read you the names . . . of the distinguished senators of the stalwart organization who stopped legislation in the interests of the railroads in the senate of the state of Wisconsin. (Great Applause.) Now there is nothing personal about this, you understand. You see a man's record who goes there as a representative is a record that all the people of the state are interested in, not only his own constituents, but all the rest of the state, because his vote affects everybody and all the business of the state as you know, and a man surely ought always to make a record there that he takes great pride in. I am quite sure that these distinguished gentlemen will feel under great obligations to me for communicating to the people of the state the distinguished services which they have been rendering to them. (Cheers) When the stalwarts, who voted to kill that bill which simply aimed to put the bars up so that the railroads could not raise the rates any more than 20 to 69 percent higher than Illinois or Iowa, the distinguished gentlemen who did that service for the people of the state by killing that bill in the senate are: Senators Beach, Bird, Eaton (hisses), Gaveny, Green (hisses), Hagemeister, Johnson, McDonough, Morse, Mosher, O'Neill, Riordan, Roehr (hisses) Rogers (hisses). (A voice—"Cash"). The Speaker, I didn't say that. Rogers, Willey, Whitehead. Every name I have given you is the name of an eminent stalwart. (Applause)[36]

Notwithstanding the sarcastic, ironic tone, reading the roll call was psychologically similar to reciting the objective, immutable facts of history, which could be rationalized as "education" of the voters. The impartial appearance of reading from the public record camouflaged this highly partisan method of attacking his adversaries. But in reality, as the above passage indicates, La Follette used "reading the roll" as a means of embarrassing and ridiculing his political opponents. Aside from "reading the roll," La Follette's 1904 general election campaign speeches repeated the same themes that had dominated his rhetoric for the past two years.[37]

In the 1904 gubernatorial campaign La Follette spoke for forty-eight days in succession and averaged over eight hours a day on the platform. He won the 1904 election by a plurality of 50,952, and the direct primary measure was approved by about the same margin. Only three Stalwart opponents survived La Follette's "roll call" campaign. For the first time, La Follette had control of the entire legislature, making the 1904 victory a "momentous climax . . . to his whole ten-year crusade."[38]

Since the direct primary controversy had been settled in the recent referendum, La Follette was now free to concentrate on other issues, including civil service reform. In his 1905 inaugural address, he maintained that state jobs should depend on "merit and fitness" rather than on political connections. It was probably not a coincidence that such a recommendation countered the damaging accusations that La Follette was interested only in building up a political machine. Other recommendations included support for a graduated income tax, legislation to curb political lobbying, and a plan to establish a state department of forestry.[39]

But the most important issue facing Wisconsin, La Follette maintained, was railroad regulation. "The railroad is a natural monopoly," he argued:

Its line, once established in a given territory, naturally excludes other capital from investing in the field which it covers. Of all monopolies, the railroad is the most extensive and far-reaching in its control of industrial forces.

Thus, railroad regulation was "the most important work in the government of this republic for this generation of men."[40]

The first item taken up by the legislature after La Follette's 1905 inaugural address was electing a U.S. senator to replace Joseph V. Quarles, an avowed Stalwart. La Follette had been coy about whether he would be available for the position. However, when the "Half-Breed" controlled legislature chose La Follette for the office, he accepted the offer in a brief speech delivered on January 25, 1905.[41]

La Follette called the past decade in Wisconsin "epoch-making"—a time in which the state obtained "the enactment of broad and comprehensive statutes which bulwark and fortify the foundations of representative government." He stated,

I cannot but feel, I was elected governor of this state because the people believed I stood for certain things in government, and that I would not relax my efforts until I had done all in my power legitimately as governor to accomplish certain results.

Therefore, he warned, "if there should appear any conflict in the obligation I entered into when I took the oath of office as governor," he would reject the senatorship and remain in Wisconsin. Most important, La Follette saw the office of U.S. senator as an opportunity "to carry a message, out of our service here, into the wider field of national legislation."[42]

Once La Follette had been selected for the Senate and his legislative program started to be enacted, he moderated his aggressive rhetoric in 1905. Since the Stalwart opposition had been effectively eliminated, there was no longer any need for a combative approach. The *Milwaukee Daily News* noticed that La Follette "subordinated as best he could the strong, vicious, and revengeful side of his nature," and although he sent six special messages to the legislature in the regular session, they were to a great extent more technical than polemical. La Follette's major triumph of the session occurred on May 18, when the railroad regulation bill was approved. The *Milwaukee Journal* marked the occasion by exclaiming, "How he has done it we do not know. But he comes out of the long struggle an unquestioned victor."[43]

During the summer and fall of 1905, La Follette went on the Chautauqua circuit, delivering "Representative Government" in twenty-five different states. Robert Stuart MacArthur, upon hearing one of the addresses, admitted that La

Follette "had remarkable success in drawing, holding and arousing great Chautauqua audiences," but he added, "the ardency of his zeal leads him occasionally, in the opinion of many hearers, to unfairness and even to fanaticism." One of La Follette's booking managers, Charles L. Wagner, noted that "he was not a big return card. He told more than his share at his first appearance. . . . He was certainly a ranter, but a pleasing one." Another booking agent aptly summed up the overall impression La Follette left with Chautauqua audiences: he exhibited "genuine intellectual integrity; a real interest in human welfare; [and an] earnest, vigorous presentation of his message."[44]

La Follette promulgated his reform ideology nationally on the Chautauqua circuit, but he gave Wisconsin no word on precisely when he would resign the governorship and assume his duties as senator. On November 21, La Follette called for an extra session of the legislature to meet the next month. On December 5, 1905, he appeared in person to deliver his final legislative message, in which he called for the construction of a new state capitol building, a "second-choice" amendment for the direct primary law, and investigation of insurance companies and public service corporations. In a separate communication, he announced that he would resign the governorship but remain active in Wisconsin politics: "No office and no honors could tempt me to forego the right to work aggressively in this field, where the best of my life has been spent, and where I shall ever feel that my first and last obligation rests." When the legislature adjourned on December 19, however, it had not passed any of the governor's recommendations for reform. La Follette's opponents interpreted this outcome as a sign that his political influence was waning. In any event, it was a rather disappointing anticlimax to his earlier legislative triumphs.[45]

Since La Follette delivered "Representative Government" scores of times while he was governor, the melodramatic scenario continued to be his dominant rhetorical technique. He did not confine the melodramatic scenario to "Representative Government," however. Indeed, one of the most vibrant examples of this device occurred in his May 10, 1901, veto message. La Follette used the melodramatic narrative form typical of earlier speeches to attack the character of his opponents. He maintained that the political machine used insidious, unethical methods to defeat his direct primary bill:

An array of federal office-holders, joining with certain corporation agents and the representatives of the machine in the regular legislative lobby, moved upon the capital, took possession of its corridors, intruded into the legislative halls, followed members to their hotels, tempted many with alluring forms of vice, and in some instances brought them to the capitol in a state of intoxication to vote against the bill.

In addition, he accused the lobbyists of "a systematic campaign of misrepresentation" and "persistent falsification and malicious assault." Such an aggressive onslaught served two purposes. First, it functioned as a call for La Follette's supporters to rally against a dangerous, powerful, and evil enemy. Second, it distracted public attention from criticism of the governor.[46]

By 1902, La Follette had amended the melodramatic scenario slightly. In light of the fact that his reform initiatives had been frustrated, he began to define obstructionism as another wicked characteristic of his villainous opponents. At Blue Mounds, in 1902, he averred that

> The nation, the state, like the individual, has every day its duty to perform. As with the individual, evasion of duty destroys character, stimulates vice, breeds trouble. He who preaches the doctrine of delay, who is the apostle of procrastination, who would stay advance, is the enemy of good government, and the instrument—almost always the willing instrument—of evil.[47]

Another manifestation of the melodramatic scenario was La Follette's use of a special kind of evidence to bolster his claims about the grave danger threatening America—testimony from respected historical figures, whom he surrounded with a mystical aura. In his Acceptance Speech of July 16, 1902, La Follette recounted in almost poetic language the famous "prophecy" of Chief Justice Ryan, a revered Wisconsin judge of the 1870s:

> I see him now as then—his bowed figure, his transparent face, his luminous eyes, through which, undimmed with age, shone the genius of one of the great intellects of the last century. Again I hear his vibrant voice across almost a generation of time:
> "There is looming up a new and dark power. I cannot dwell upon the signs and shocking omens of its advent. . . . For the first time really in our politics, money is taking the field as an organized power. It is unscrupulous, arrogant, and overbearing. . . . money as a political influence is essentially corrupt; it is one of the most dangerous to free institutions."

La Follette used a similar technique in his speech of April 22, 1904, when he summoned the prophets of the past as witnesses for his cause. He cited James A. Garfield on the "modern barons," Matt Carpenter on monopolies, John Sherman on combinations, and the usual passage from Chief Justice Ryan. La Follette invited the audience to compare his present proposals with past concepts articulated by distinguished predecessors: "I have been denounced as radical and extreme in my utterances upon these subjects. I ask you to turn to the record and find anything anywhere I have uttered that will compare with what I now give you from the lips of John Sherman."[48]

Citing prophets of the past such as Ryan and Sherman aided La Follette's case in several ways. By associating a prophet's name with La Follette's cause, the governor attempted to fend off charges of political heresy. If the need for reform was seen clearly in the 1870s by a venerated "prophet" of the past, La Follette reasoned, then his legislative program was far from radical. Furthermore, the quotation from Ryan fit seamlessly into the well-established narrative pattern of the melodramatic scenario. After 1902, the technique of citing prophets from the past became a mainstay of La Follette's rhetoric.

Aside from the melodramatic scenario, La Follette continued to use other techniques he had developed in earlier periods. One such technique was the extensive citation of statistics. During his years as governor, statistics about railroad rates were centrally important. The key to La Follette's use of statistics was that he always adapted them to the specific circumstances of the audiences he addressed. For example, on September 2, 1903, he addressed a county fair at Plymouth, Wisconsin. He analyzed a number of commodities that were shipped via rail to or from Plymouth, such as cheese, butter, livestock, and grain. In the case of lumber, he literally read a statistical table to the audience. The table compared the rates for lumber that people in Plymouth had to pay with the rates in Iowa for an equal distance of shipping. He concluded, "You must pay that much more than your neighbor in Iowa who lives at the same distance in that state from the shipping point that you do from Milwaukee."[49]

La Follette's county fair speeches were effective because he provided tangible evidence from everyday experience that Wisconsinites were being charged inequitable railroad rates. Many of his hearers probably suspected that railroad rates were unfair, but La Follette told his county fair audiences exactly how much money the railroads were stealing from their pockets. The "reading of the freight rates" was also effective because the sheer volume of the statistics lent substance and credibility to La Follette's arguments. Moreover, La Follette had the advantage of using statistics on the attack. The initial presentation of statistics in a controversy is especially persuasive since the audience has nothing with which to compare. On the other hand, the defender, or refuter, has to refer to the attacker's statistics, make them understandable, and show that they are inaccurate or that the attacker's conclusion is mistaken. Thus the task of the refuter is twice as complicated, and the thrust of the refutation risks becoming lost in a morass of details. Finally, La Follette coupled his statistics with strong moral statements about the injustice of the rail rates. Listeners would be likely to grasp immediately the strong moral statements and assume that the statistics supported them.

Prior to 1904, La Follette's reform initiatives had been defeated repeatedly in the legislature. Because of this, La Follette faced the rhetorical problem of inspiring his supporters to fight on in the face of adversity. The techniques he selected to address this problem had been well-rehearsed in earlier campaigns.

First, he appealed to the duty and responsibility of the voters to enact needed reforms. As he told his audience at Oconomowoc, the direct primary was the "one way for you to meet and master the political situation as it exists today. . . . Your interests are at stake. You are in the majority. Upon you rests the responsibility." In his 1902 Acceptance Speech, La Follette predicted that Wisconsin "will do its plain duty now, as it did in that greatest epoch of the country's history. It will meet the issues with rectitude and unfaltering devotion."[50]

Second, La Follette insisted that the alternative to fighting the machine was political and economic slavery. In 1904, at Milton Junction, La Follette posed a simple choice for his listeners: "the people of this state must either tamely submit, . . . or provide against" the abuses of the railroads. "The only security that the people of Wisconsin have in this great contest lies in pressing forward without halt or stop." The greatest danger, he proclaimed, was compromising with the enemy: "No siren song, sung in double chorus for 'harmony' and 'compromise' will result otherwise than in sacrificing all of the ground gained during the protracted struggle."[51]

But, La Follette warned his audiences, those who fought for freedom had to pay a price. They could expect to be ridiculed and abused by the enemy. In 1904 he instructed his followers to

expect to face the violent misrepresentation and personal abuse of every conceivable character. That comes as a part of the sacrifice which must be made to the cause. But those who have borne the heat and burden of the battle in Wisconsin for eight years are veterans now. They do not shirk from the combat. They do not hesitate to face the fire. They will not retreat or lie down.

La Follette concluded with a stirring battle cry: "this fight begins today. . . . from this hour until the close of the polls on election day, there shall be no halt and no stop."[52]

Despite hard struggle and setbacks, however, La Follette assured his followers of ultimate triumph. In Grand Rapids he declared: "We may stumble; we may be delayed. We shall never be driven back; we shall never surrender. We shall ultimately triumph." In Blue Mounds La Follette drew upon a concept he articulated in the "Iago" oration: "The principles of right are eternal. They have all the time there is in which to vindicate themselves, no matter how falsely misrepresented, how maliciously assailed." In sum, La Follette chose the path of minimizing expectations of immediate success, while stressing the prospects of ultimate victory. The task of reform was so difficult, he said, that minor defeats were inevitable, but he praised reform Republicans as tough fighters who were not afraid of an uphill battle. He was certain that loyal citizens would do their duty by voting against the corporations and the political machines.[53]

Not all of La Follette's rhetoric from 1901 to 1905 was a continuation of previous themes. For example, in 1901 La Follette defined his campaign promises as a "binding contract" that could not be broken. In vetoing the Hagemeister bill, La Follette stressed "the binding character of my official obligation" to the people. He portrayed the promises of the 1900 Republican platform as a legal contract. It was, he said, a "contract pure and simple," and "to violate the promises of that platform is to cheat and betray the voter." By characterizing the 1900 Republican platform as a binding contract, La Follette justified his own actions and cast doubt on the trustworthiness of Republicans who opposed the direct primary.[54]

La Follette introduced another technique of redefinition in his "Second Inaugural Address." To strengthen his appeal for regulation of railroad rates, La Follette defined railroad prices as a tax on the people of Wisconsin. Apologists for the railroads claimed that any business had a right to charge a fair price for its services. But La Follette, in defining railroad rates as a tax, was able to tap into the public's historic resentment of unfair taxation. He claimed that

Railroad transportation is a tax upon the commerce of the country. It is a tax from which no one can escape. Every producer, every consumer, every man who buys, every man who sells, must pay railroad transportation. It pervades every phase of our existence; it is a part of every hour of our daily life. . . . How essential it is that this tax imposed by the railroads should be fairly and justly levied.

In the same address, La Follette also assured his listeners that railroad regulation could not possibly harm its object. This argument fit into the overall pattern that La Follette was not a radical and that his policies would not lead to economic collapse or anarchy. The linchpin of his case was that the courts would ensure that the railroads would not "be deprived of a reasonable profit." La Follette insisted that his proposal required nothing more than fairness from the railroads. It was simply designed to end "reprehensible and inexcusable forms of favoritism." If the railroads objected to a regulatory commission, he concluded, it was only because they had something to hide.[55]

By 1904 La Follette was forced to answer certain charges leveled by his opponents. In response to the accusation that, as governor, he was using the railroad issue solely for the purpose of gaining political power, La Follette argued that his position on railroad regulation had never changed. On April 22 he reminded his audience that he had advocated creating "a commission to control transportation rates" in 1887. Thus, La Follette had not seized upon a convenient issue to further his political ambitions. On November 4, however, La Follette admitted that he was ambitious, but he defined this trait as an ultimate virtue:

Now, they say that I'm awfully ambitious, and I am. . . . I'll tell you frankly here tonight I'll be very glad indeed, I am very anxious indeed, to connect my name, with others, in getting upon the statute books some legislation here in Wisconsin that will be just and fair to the railroads and just and fair to the people.

He maintained that the record of a good railroad law "will stand there on the statute books long after I'm dead—will be a better monument, a better legacy to leave my children than anything else I could leave them."[56]

Concerning the subject of his reputation, La Follette claimed on April 22, 1904, that his opponents had subjected him to "personal abuse and vituperation." Without repeating the specific charges, he attempted to make his opponents look cruel for assailing his character. In a strong emotional appeal, he remarked, "My two little boys will be men some time, and now and then it comes to me, what will they think when they read those newspapers." By condemning patently unfair attacks, La Follette attempted to cast doubt upon all criticisms of him, whether legitimate or not. Moreover, an enemy who hurled lies must be sly, dishonorable, and nasty, fulfilling the stereotypes La Follette had long developed of the corporation lobbyists. The whole issue of personal attack, however, was ironic because La Follette brought the abuse upon himself. He attacked the character of his opponents, then he condemned them for making his personality a legitimate issue.

His speech of April 22 was infused with a sense of personal suffering or martyrdom. La Follette revealed that the fight for reform had damaged his health, but he vowed, "as long as there is left in me the breath of life there will be no man in the state of Wisconsin who will cry out against the corruption of the people by the corporations more vehemently than I will." In addition to his physical suffering, La Follette claimed that he had suffered financially because of his reform crusade. Indeed, he asserted, he could have tripled his income if he had worked for the railroads as a lawyer instead of choosing public service. The theme of personal suffering helped neutralize charges that La Follette was an insincere demagogue interested only in his political career. Physical and economic suffering indicated selfless devotion to the cause and reinforced the sense of ethical zeal so integral to a successful crusade. La Follette offered his "suffering" as tangible proof that he was committed to the struggle.[57]

The scorecard for La Follette's tenure as governor was most impressive. During his years in office he had obtained a primary election law, a railroad commission, taxation of railroads and public utilities on the basis of actual physical worth, a civil service law, regulation of telephone and telegraph companies, conservation laws, banking regulations, anti-lobbying rules, and labor legislation. As before, La Follette's oratory played a central role in his political achievements. After an initial period of compromise and conciliation, La Follette returned to his role as an agitator and popularizer.[58]

La Follette used public speaking to educate the voters, to advocate his reforms, and ultimately to remove his opponents from the legislature. He devoted himself almost exclusively to three issues—the direct primary, equal taxation, and railroad regulation—and he timed the introduction of each issue to match the public's mood and the political situation. He agitated relentlessly on these topics through a variety of sources, including campaign speeches, pamphlets, and official messages. In addition, he introduced new campaign techniques such as reading "the freight rates" and "the roll call" to increase public awareness and cultivate discontent with the railroads and the legislature. In short, his methods were combative. Rather than working quietly to adapt his agenda to the legislature, he insisted that his ideas be enacted unchanged, and he battled to make the Assembly and Senate conform to his proposals.

La Follette achieved unrivaled success with this rhetorical formula. Since his reform program had national implications, Wisconsin sent him into the "wider field" of the U.S. Senate. As La Follette departed for Washington, he had a firm political agenda in mind and a tested method of persuasion with which to enact it. But, as he would discover, neither the agenda nor the method were necessarily appropriate for the "wider field" in 1906. The problems of an entire nation were too complex for simplistic solutions, and national leaders were a different kind of audience than Wisconsin state legislators and dairy farmers.

6
Senator La Follette

After joining the Senate, La Follette's first major speaking opportunity came during the debate over the Hepburn bill, which was designed to amend the Interstate Commerce Act of 1887. The Hepburn bill called for a system of uniform bookkeeping and auditing of railroad accounts, but not the power to fix rates unilaterally. La Follette was not satisfied with the Hepburn bill because it did not go far enough. Instead, he decided to argue for amendments to strengthen federal regulatory powers. La Follette spent several weeks preparing for the debate, and, when he entered the Senate chamber on April 19, 1906, he had a speech manuscript of 148 printed pages, which he delivered to crowded galleries over a period of several days.[1]

When La Follette started speaking on April 19, senators began to walk off the floor, leaving La Follette virtually by himself to address the crowded galleries. As La Follette saw his colleagues leaving the chamber, he believed he was being punished for breaking the tradition that freshman senators should remain silent, so he proclaimed defiantly:

Mr. President, I pause in my remarks to say this: I can not be wholly indifferent to the fact that Senators by their absence at this time indicate their want of interest in what I may have to say upon this subject. The public is interested. Unless this important question is rightly settled seats now temporarily vacant may be permanently vacated by those who have the right to occupy them at this time. . . . I do not ask to have Senators called back here who feel no interest in what I have to say. I know that the country will take interest in the discussion that I shall make of the defects of this proposed legislation.

La Follette's blatant threat of the wrath of the people, a familiar theme in his discourse, brought a cheer from the gallery and reportedly caused many legislators to listen more attentively to him thereafter.[2]

Throughout the debate, La Follette drew heavily from his storehouse of railroad statistics and arguments used in his Wisconsin campaigns. He

74 Robert M. La Follette, Sr.

contended that railroad competition was being undermined by rebates, discrimination, and combinations and that this resulted in unreasonably high rates. Moreover, he argued that exorbitant rail rates damaged the American home and family: "Transportation and transportation charges affect the daily life of every man who must support a family in this country." The proposed Hepburn bill, he argued, would not correct these abuses. Clearly, stronger legislation was needed. Because of extensive public subsidization of the railroad industry, La Follette claimed, the rail lines owed the public a special debt, and the interests of the general public should be foremost in drafting new laws. Characteristically, La Follette claimed that an intelligent, calm public would never support laws that would harm the railroads; thus, there was nothing to fear from the advocates of reform. La Follette called for legislation that would be just and equitable to shippers and the public alike. Despite an impressive personal performance in the Hepburn bill debate, La Follette's amendments were all rejected, and he received little support from fellow Republicans.[3]

La Follette's next major speaking opportunity occurred in March 1908. The Panic of 1907 brought about a call for emergency currency. In response, Senator Nelson Aldrich proposed that 500 million dollars be raised as emergency currency and that this sum be backed by bonds from state, city, and railroad sources. La Follette was utterly opposed to the concept of supporting public currency with private railroad bonds, and he saw the Aldrich bill as proof that government was being controlled by private interests. Instead, La Follette proposed a penetrating revision of banking and currency laws. He also used the Aldrich bill debate as an opportunity to pursue the issue of railroad valuation. He was determined to reject railroad bonds as security unless their value was based on the actual worth of the physical assets.[4]

Once again, La Follette prepared meticulously for the debate over a period of several weeks. On the day of the speech, Senator Aldrich had all provisions regarding railroad bonds struck from the bill. But La Follette delivered the speech as prepared, and he predicted that the railroad provisions would be reinserted later. La Follette began his attacks on the proposed bill on March 17 and continued on March 19 and 24. The purpose of the Aldrich bill, he claimed, was to restore confidence in worthless railroad bonds by using them as backing for emergency currency. Moreover, he argued that the extra currency created by the Aldrich bill would be used simply for further dangerous speculation.[5]

In his speeches on the Aldrich bill, La Follette used the melodramatic scenario to indict the evils of concentrated wealth. Over a period of time, he recounted, the banking industry had gradually fallen under the influence of a few powerful and wealthy businessmen. As a result of their combined scheming, La Follette charged, masses of capital have been brought under one management, to be employed not as the servant of commerce, but as its master; not to supply legitimate business and to facilitate exchange, but to subordinate the commercial demands of the country.

Now, he claimed,

Trained men, who a dozen years ago stood first among the bankers of the world as heads of the greatest banks of New York City, are, in the main, either displaced or do the bidding of men who are not bankers, but masters of organization.

As part of the melodramatic scenario, La Follette used a theatrical metaphor to convey the idea that things were not as they seemed. He complained that

The press set [the Panic of 1907] all forth as it appeared on the surface. It portrayed the great financiers hurrying to and fro, setting a prop here, a prop there, holding midnight meetings in Morgan's library, seeking some way to avert the calamity that threatened prosperity and a nation's honor. It was a thrilling picture, but it was false. . . . How perfect the stage setting! How real it all seemed! But back of the scenes Morgan and Stillman were in conference.

The Aldrich bill of 1908 was "plausible in appearance," said La Follette, but "hollow at heart." Railroad bonds appeared in the "guise of reenforcement to failing credit," but "Let no Senator be deceived," there was a secret motive. The financial system of America was in reality controlled by a handful of men who issued orders to "the dummy directors, the fillers-in, the figureheads," who only appeared to have any authority.

As with most conspiracy theories, La Follette's relied on circumstantial evidence for support. On March 19, for instance, he admitted that "It is not always possible . . . to produce record evidence showing step by step the operations of these great powers." But, he claimed, the pattern of circumstantial evidence pointed clearly to the conclusion that an elite group dictated the business of America. "It all fitted together like a piece of mosaic," he explained:

any man with ordinary intelligence, who sees the same names repeated over and over again on the various directorates . . . will understand how the important business interests are in fact welded and fused together into one mass under one control.

The logic of the melodramatic scenario demanded that the Senate put a halt to the menace of concentrated wealth: "Let no man think he is not concerned; that his State or his constituency is not interested. There is no remote corner of this country where the power of Special Interests is not encroaching on public rights." Every day, La Follette warned, this evil force became "a greater menace to the industrial and commercial liberty of the American people." But, La Follette said,

> I do not direct my attack against a Rockefeller, a Morgan, a Harriman. They are but types. They but embody an evil. Back of these men is the THING which we must destroy if we would preserve our free institutions. Men are as nothing; the System which we have built up by privileges, which we have allowed to take possession of Government and control legislation, is the real object of my unceasing warfare.

If the Senate did not act to destroy this dangerous system, he warned, it would have to face the wrath of the people.[6]

La Follette was unable to block passage of the Aldrich bill, which was approved in the Senate on March 27. Differences between Senate and House versions of emergency currency legislation were worked out in conference and approved in the House on May 27. The conference report came up for approval in the Senate on May 29, one day before the Senate was scheduled to adjourn. Just as La Follette had predicted, the railroad bond provisions had been reinserted. La Follette was so outraged by the conference report that he planned to join with Senate Democrats in a filibuster.[7]

La Follette began his part in the filibuster on May 29, 1908, one day before adjournment, and he held the floor for a record-breaking eighteen hours and forty-three minutes. In a rambling discourse, he repeated the arguments he had made on March 17, 19, and 24. During his speech La Follette was feverishly ill, and the temperature in the Senate chamber was stiflingly hot. As the hour of final adjournment neared, anger built on the floor. At one point La Follette was convinced that he had been poisoned by a glass of milk and eggs that had been brought to him while speaking. La Follette yielded the floor to a colleague at 7:05 A.M. the next morning, but due to a tactical mistake his allies lost the floor and the Aldrich-Vreeland bill passed.[8]

Despite the disappointing finale, La Follette's address of March 17, dubbed the "Money Power" speech, sparked much positive comment in the press, and his office was overwhelmed with requests for copies of the address. What was more, he received support from some unusual quarters. The New York Board of Trade was sufficiently impressed by La Follette's speech to request twenty-five copies. Usually, about 85 percent of requests for reprints came from the Midwest, La Follette's natural constituency, but in this instance almost half of the requests came from large Eastern cities. A number of smaller business people and manufacturers saw La Follette's analysis of the Money Trust as precisely correct.[9]

In March 1909, the tariff issue again became the center of debate in Congress. Conservatives opposed reducing tariff rates because they wanted to protect domestic industry, while progressives wanted to discipline powerful corporations by revising tariffs downward. La Follette and a group of progressives including Jonathan Dolliver, Joseph Bristow, Albert Beveridge, Moses Clapp, and Albert Cummins opposed the conservative Aldrich tariff bill in the Senate. La Follette's group divided up the labor and research in order to provide comprehensive opposition to the complex bill.[10]

La Follette challenged the cotton and woolen schedules on June 9 and 11. Characteristically, he cited statistics to demonstrate inequities in the tariff rates. Large manufacturers, he concluded, were benefiting at the expense of ordinary people. Moreover, he stressed the impact high tariffs had on the American home, a theme he had developed earlier in relation to railroad rates. A high protective tariff, he maintained, "reaches everything that goes upon [the citizen's] table, everything that goes to clothe and warm his family and provide for their comfort."[11]

La Follette's most important role in the tariff debate, however, was not as a speaker but as a strategist and coordinator for the progressive faction. Throughout the debate, La Follette and his allies sought to expose the selfish motives behind the Aldrich tariff bill by interrupting the proceedings with tough questions and roll call votes. Although, in the judgment of many, the progressives were impressive in debate, Aldrich controlled the majority, and the tariff bill passed the Senate on July 8. La Follette was one of only ten Republicans who voted against it.[12]

In August 1909 a revised version of the Aldrich tariff bill was resubmitted to the Senate as a conference report. La Follette planned to speak against the Payne-Aldrich bill, but the speakers' list was manipulated to prevent him from addressing the Senate. Prior to the vote, on August 5, La Follette obtained the floor long enough to threaten his opponents:

I make this explanation that it may go into the *Record*. As I shall have occasion many times to state my views with respect to this tariff legislation between now and the convening of Congress in December next, I forego the opportunity to have spoken here with less disappointment.

The Payne-Aldrich bill was approved in the Senate by a comfortable margin. This time, La Follette was one of only seven Republicans to vote against it. Despite the fact that he failed to prevent passage of the tariff bill, La Follette was satisfied about one aspect of the outcome—he was now a prominent leader of a small but determined coalition. In June 1909 he remarked, "When I came here I stood alone in this chamber. Now there are nearly a dozen men who stand with me."[13]

As La Follette suggested on August 5, he did not limit his speaking to the Senate. Indeed, he went on major speaking tours in 1906, 1907, and 1908 in between legislative sessions. Whenever his reform agenda was frustrated in the Senate, as it often was, he made a point of forcing roll call votes so he could obtain a public record of those legislators who were obstructing reform. He wanted to take the "record" to the broader public of concerned citizens. This tactic, which he perfected during his campaigns in Wisconsin, was intended to bring public pressure to bear on his political opponents, to promulgate his political reform, to aid the reelection of fellow progressives, and to raise money. In addition to "reading the roll" on his speaking tours, he delivered variations of "Representative Government."[14]

Although La Follette had used "reading the roll" extensively in Wisconsin, it was perceived as a novel and effective political weapon on the national scene. Moreover, reading roll call votes was a means for La Follette to confront his enemies in a way that would not be perceived as a personal attack. La Follette defined this technique as "educating" the voters. As he explained in his *Autobiography*,

It was plain to me that the people needed to be educated on men as well as measures. I therefore formulated my plan so to conduct the discussion with respect to men that it would be impersonal in its character and would go directly to the record of the representative and deal with concrete facts. La Follette said to his wife in 1907, "I read the roll call in an unbiased way, following an impartial judicial presentation of the measure voted upon. I never mention anyone's name save as it comes in the course of the roll call."[15]

In conjunction with La Follette's national speaking tours, he launched a journal devoted to progressive reform. He planned the publication in December 1908, and the first issue appeared on January 9, 1909. *La Follette's Weekly Magazine* contained articles from progressive authors, editorials by La Follette, and featured "roll call" votes on important issues. La Follette's editorials were usually drawn from speech manuscripts, so there was little that was strikingly new in the publication, but it provided him with another medium to spread his political doctrine and to "educate" the public.[16]

By 1910 La Follette's influence in the Wisconsin state legislature had eroded, and many progressives feared he would not be returned to the Senate. Ironically, La Follette was unable to speak in his own reelection campaign to the Senate. He was ill with a serious gallbladder disorder, and he had no campaign funds. Fortunately for La Follette, fellow progressives came to his rescue and spoke on his behalf. Political surrogates made 108 speeches in eleven Wisconsin counties in the primary election, and prominent national progressives provided financial support. In addition, La Follette's political organization was efficient in organizing and turning out the vote. La Follette candidates swept the primary election and triumphed in the general election. When the Wisconsin legislature reconvened, La Follette was easily returned to the Senate.[17]

After his victory in the 1910 election, La Follette believed that traditional party lines had broken down, and he thought that progressives had become a national force. He planned to make the national Republican Party a vehicle for progressive reform in the same way he had captured the state Republican Party in Wisconsin. When he returned to Washington on December 3, 1910, he helped to found the National Progressive Republican League (NPRL). La Follette drafted the declaration of principles for the organization and coined the phrase, "The will of the people shall be the law of the land." The NPRL was launched officially from La Follette's Washington home on January 21, 1911. The organization stood for direct election of U.S. senators, "a thoroughgoing Corrupt Practices Act," adoption of referendum, initiative, and recall, and direct primary nominations for all elective officials. The platform was to be used as a charter for forming state organizations.[18]

La Follette was convinced that effective national reform could only come with a progressive in the executive branch. In 1908 he had sought the Republican nomination for president. But his platform, which was based on his senatorial positions, failed to excite much interest, and he received only the support of Wisconsin's delegation at the national convention. By May of 1911, however, he had accumulated a significant amount of support for a presidential bid. When Theodore Roosevelt initially stayed out of the race, La Follette declared his own candidacy. At first, progressive Republicans saw La Follette as their best chance to block Taft's renomination. By October La Follette's candidacy had gained momentum, but always lurking in the background was the figure of Roosevelt. When the former president refused to rule himself out of the race, a number of progressives began to abandon La Follette. In the face of political defection, La Follette forged ahead with his candidacy.[19]

While this political maneuvering transpired, La Follette wrote a series of magazine articles that told the story of his career. The campaign autobiography, assisted by Ray Stannard Baker, was serialized in *American Magazine*. Installments began in October 1911 and continued through July 1912. In telling his life story, La Follette featured his struggles with the machine in Wisconsin and drew heavily on his political triumphs in his home state. The last two installments criticized the records of Roosevelt and Taft for obstructing progressive reform.[20]

After finishing the magazine articles, La Follette started a major speaking tour. Between December 27, 1911, and January 5, 1912, he delivered a series of extemporaneous speeches in Ohio, Michigan, Illinois, and Indiana. Then, on January 22, he addressed Carnegie Hall in New York City. In these speeches, he repeated his standard positions on railroad valuation, railroad rate regulation, and tariff revision. He also criticized Roosevelt and Taft for failing to support progressive positions. La Follette was delighted with the large, enthusiastic crowds that turned out for the speeches. Despite this positive reception, however, La Follette's campaign was being swamped by the rising tide of enthusiasm for Theodore Roosevelt. When he entered the race officially, even La Follette's staunchest allies urged him to support Roosevelt.[21]

By the end of January 1912, La Follette was exhausted from months of strenuous campaigning and discouraged by the desertion of former supporters. He was further burdened by the news that his daughter Mary faced a serious operation on February 3, the day after he was scheduled to give a major address in Philadelphia. La Follette considered cancelling the engagement, but he feared the public might believe he had withdrawn from the race. So he decided to go ahead with his address to the Periodical Publishers' Association in Philadephia on February 2, 1912.[22]

La Follette arrived at the banquet hall at 11:00 P.M., after Woodrow Wilson had just completed a brief, charming address. The audience was tired, satiated, and listless. La Follette had not been able to eat during the day, and he had taken a small shot of whiskey to steady his nerves before the speech. He was initially well-received, but La Follette soon alienated his audience. His major theme that large corporations controlled newspapers and that only periodicals were free from corruption offended the newspaper people in the audience. La Follette soon became belligerent with the bored, hostile listeners. He tried to extemporize but only became rambling and incoherent. La Follette stumbled on in humiliation for nearly two hours. The worst fault was that he had misjudged his audience: the purpose of the banquet was to reconcile newspapers and magazines. The Philadelphia speech was like a caricature of La Follette's rhetoric: it intensified his worst tendencies yet left nothing of his congeniality and ability to win over an audience. When the speech was over, La Follette returned to his room, physically nauseated. He left that night to join his wife and daughter in Wisconsin.[23]

The press blasted La Follette the next day, claiming he had suffered a "mental breakdown" or a "collapse" and announcing that he had withdrawn from the presidential race. Rumors circulated that La Follette was drunk or insane, when in fact he was suffering from the results of unrelenting stress and toil. His physician diagnosed the trouble as lack of sleep and ordered him to rest. When La Follette cancelled his speaking dates, reports of his withdrawal intensified.[24]

After resting, La Follette vowed to win the presidential primaries in North Dakota and Wisconsin. He began his tour of North Dakota on March 12, 1912, and made numerous speeches at railroad stations and auditoriums across the state. La Follette realized his health was a major issue in the campaign, so in response to Gifford Pinchot's charge that La Follette was a "disabled steam engine," he proclaimed, "my firebox is intact, . . . my drive wheels are strong and . . . my sandbox isn't empty." The metaphor was ironic, considering La Follette's campaigns against the railroads.[25]

La Follette's speech at Valley City Normal School typified his rhetoric during the 1912 primary campaign. One of the major tasks of the speech was to explain why he had changed his position over the years on protective tariffs. He argued that when he had supported protective tariffs in 1890, "we had a competitive system between those who were engaged in the manufacturing business in this country." But since 1890 combinations and trusts had formed, and, sheltered by the "high tariff wall," they had destroyed competition and caused prices to rise. In addition, La Follette attacked Roosevelt for failing to recognize this condition and take decisive action: "just when the trust organizations of this country assumed proportions that were beginning to be alarming," Roosevelt abrogated his responsibilities. After the 1908 election, many Republicans expected high tariffs to be reduced, but Taft and the "Stand-pat" Republicans refused to enact more equitable rates.

La Follette defined the guiding principle of progressive Republicanism as acting in the public interest. Typically, he presented a black-and-white view of his position contrasted with his opponents':

Every issue that has divided the Progressive Republicans from the Stand-pat Republicans . . . has been along a line of cleavage as clearly defined as anything can be, and in every case the Progressives stand for the interests of the public as against the interests of privilege. That is all there is to the Progressive Movement. It can be summed up in a single word,—SERVICE. Service to the public, that is it.

In reviewing his own record of service, La Follette reminded his audience that he had consistently advocated railroad regulation. He argued that railroad rates should be "based upon the amount of money actually invested in the railroads, rather than on fictitious capitalization." Furthermore, he claimed that the problem of high prices would never be solved "unless you apply the same principle to these trusts and combinations that we have applied to the railroads in the State of Wisconsin; . . . get the real, true value of their property," and regulate them on that basis.[26]

The Washington correspondent of the *Minneapolis Sunday Tribune* presented a vivid visual image of "Fighting Bob" during his speeches in North Dakota:

Supposedly coming from a sick bed, the Wisconsin senator looks anything but a sick man. He is tense, vigorous and full of fighting ire. Picture this "little giant" with the bushy head of hair, tramping up and down the platform, face, hands and figure in nervous action as he drives home his points. Picture him leading carefully up to his arraignment of the popular idol of the day [Roosevelt] and as one prominent North Dakotan described it, "getting away with it," and you have a picture of "Bob" La Follette on the stump. . . . There is no shrinking in his manner. He is already laying his plans for 1916 and means to carry on the fight. There is an indomitable something in this little fighting man that evokes admiration whether willing or unwilling.

Many voters must have shared this impression of La Follette, for he won big in North Dakota, beating Roosevelt 58 to 39 percent, with Taft receiving just 3 percent. In Wisconsin, La Follette beat Taft by a three-to-one margin, with

Roosevelt receiving a tiny fraction of the vote. However, in April of 1912 La Follette went on another speaking tour in areas that had shown strong support for Roosevelt. He began speaking in Nebraska on April 5 and proceeded through Oregon, California, South Dakota, Ohio, and New Jersey before returning to Washington. Predictably, with the Republican establishment opposed to him, he lost all of the remaining primary elections.[27]

When the Republican convention met in Chicago in June 1912, both Taft and Roosevelt needed La Follette's delegates. La Follette decided to use his forty-one delegates to help prevent Roosevelt's nomination. Although the convention rejected La Follette's platform, he took satisfaction in the fact that Roosevelt was defeated. Many, such as Woodrow Wilson, attributed Taft's nomination to La Follette's determined speaking campaign against Roosevelt during the primaries. Paradoxically, La Follette was furious with Roosevelt for bolting the Republican Party because he feared the Bull Moose Party would endanger the chances for a progressive Congress. La Follette did not publicly endorse any presidential candidate in the fall campaign, although many perceived that he tacitly supported Wilson.[28]

In October 1912 La Follette published the first of five serialized articles in *La Follette's Magazine* that presented his view of the presidential campaign. These articles comprised the concluding chapters of *La Follette's Autobiography* when it was later published as a book. In the first three articles La Follette recounted how he was not a quitter in the 1912 election. He also discussed directly the rhetorical debacle at Philadelphia, denying that he had suffered a breakdown or lost his health. The last two articles were a scathing attack on Roosevelt. La Follette even went so far as to accuse Roosevelt of conspiring with the big trusts in order to capture the White House. In sum, the *Autobiography* is a bitter monument to La Follette's hatred and distrust of Roosevelt.[29]

After La Follette's harangue against Roosevelt in the 1912 campaign, he was probably satisfied that he helped—however little—to put Woodrow Wilson in the White House. At first La Follette was cautiously optimistic that Wilson would be a political ally, but he soon discovered that the president was fiercely partisan and exercised a tight, exclusionary congressional leadership. In 1913 La Follette delivered a series of speeches in the Senate, but they were predictable and received relatively little attention. Nonetheless, during this time La Follette advocated open hearings on proposed tariff legislation, introduced a bill to supplement the Sherman Anti-Trust law, defended women's suffrage, and gained passage of the La Follette Seamen's Act, which protected the rights of maritime workers. Ironically, in the words of Fred Greenbaum, this "almost forgotten law was his pride and joy," and it was "the only statute to bear La Follette's name [alone]."[30]

Although La Follette did not yet know it, the debates of 1913 marked the end of an era in his rhetoric. During the previous seven years La Follette had advocated reform in such areas as protective tariffs, railroad rates, and the banking industry. The most remarkable thing about La Follette's rhetoric during this time was its inflexibility. Although he introduced a few new concepts as a senator, for the most part he continued to sound the same themes and use the same rhetorical techniques that had been so successful in Wisconsin. But while La Follette represented well the interests of his region and constituency, he lacked the finesse and the willingness to compromise required for national leadership. On the other hand, he proved to be a significant voice in the Senate and a leader of progressive Republicans. His public speeches did not usually obtain their immediate goals, but they did provide an important part of the atmosphere in which progressive legislation was eventually forged. As war stalked Europe, however, La Follette's rhetoric would turn from domestic affairs to international issues, and he would be challenged to adapt to a new set of problems and demands.

7
"Willful Men"

Prior to 1914, La Follette had not paid much attention to foreign affairs. As governor of Wisconsin and then U.S. senator, La Follette had been preoccupied with domestic matters. His first important policy address that concerned international affairs occurred on February 12, 1915, when he advocated the La Follette Peace Resolution, which called for neutral nations to organize in order to seek peace in Europe, to make rules for limiting arms and regulating export of war supplies, and to establish an international tribunal to settle disputes. La Follette's resolution resembled a rudimentary League of Nations, which was ironic because Woodrow Wilson opposed La Follette's ideas in 1915, and La Follette helped block adoption of Wilson's League in 1919.[1]

La Follette's resolution was a source of friction between him and Wilson in 1915, and the tensions continued to increase as La Follette delivered a series of speeches in the Senate that attempted to undermine the president's foreign policy. On January 27, 1916, La Follette spoke against Wilson's request for a strengthened military, and on March 10 he supported the Gore Resolution, which warned Americans not to travel on armed, belligerent ships. On July 19-20 La Follette delivered a seven-hour speech in the Senate that opposed a naval appropriations bill. In each case, Wilson's position prevailed.[2]

Because Wisconsin progressives did poorly in the 1914 elections, La Follette campaigned heavily in his home state before the 1916 senatorial contest. Moreover, with the advent of the Seventeenth Amendment in 1913, La Follette now faced primary and general election races instead of being appointed by the Wisconsin state legislature. He began his speaking campaign for the 1916 primary on August 14 at Sun Prairie and continued for two weeks, making seven or eight speeches per day. He discovered at the outset that his constituents were most concerned by the war in Europe. Thus, he stressed his approval of American neutrality and his opposition to military build-up. In addition, La Follette received campaigning help from fellow progressives, including senators

Clapp, Gronna, Kenyon, and Norris. After defeating his primary opponent by a convincing margin, La Follette faced a strong Democratic challenger, who attacked him for his stand on preparedness, his failure to support Wilson, and his "pro-Germanism." La Follette concentrated his speeches on the dominant issue of the 1916 election—the conduct of American foreign policy. He refused to endorse the Republican national platform or its candidate, Charles Evans Hughes. This was widely perceived as approval for Wilson, which helped swing some Democratic voters to La Follette. The *Wisconsin State Journal* endorsed Wilson for president and La Follette for senator.[3]

The result of this intensive campaign was an impressive victory for La Follette in the general election. He won sixty-nine of seventy-one counties and almost doubled his opponent's tally in the popular vote. Surprisingly, he was at the height of his popularity in Wisconsin in November of 1916. Farmers supported his agricultural measures, and laborers were satisfied with his efforts in the areas of railroads, working conditions, and the rights of organized labor. Nearly every Wisconsinite backed his fight against special privilege in a democracy. The transcendent issue of the campaign, however, was foreign affairs, and La Follette's rhetoric accurately reflected the opinions of his constituents, especially of German-Americans. La Follette and others interpreted the election results as a mandate from the people for peace.[4]

In February 1917 Wilson asked Congress for authority to arm American merchant ships to defend themselves against German submarine attacks. La Follette helped organize a filibuster against Wilson's request. The Senate met on March 3 for a continuous, twenty-six-hour session that ended in adjournment. La Follette had agreed to be the final speaker—the one who would feel the most pressure—but at the last moment the speakers' list was manipulated to prevent La Follette from obtaining the floor. When the chair refused to recognize La Follette, he stood in the center aisle screaming that he would not be silenced. A group of hostile senators rushed at him, and Senator Harry Lane defended La Follette with a sharpened rattail file. Eventually, the Senate compelled La Follette to sit down; but, along with his allies, he managed to block the bill through parliamentary procedure, and the Senate adjourned without approving Wilson's request.[5]

Woodrow Wilson reacted angrily by publicly stating, "A little group of willful men, representing no opinion but their own, have rendered the great Government of the United States helpless and contemptible." The *New York Times* of March 5, 1917, published a survey of thirty-three editorials on the filibuster, and fully three-fourths supported Wilson's condemnation of La Follette. Dozens of newspapers questioned La Follette's loyalty and patriotism. The *Cincinnati Post* even referred to the Wisconsin senator as "von La Follette."[6]

When the Senate reconvened, it proposed a cloture rule to limit debate. On March 8, 1917, La Follette opposed the cloture rule, but he lost. By April 1917 a Declaration of War on the part of Wilson was a foregone conclusion. Indeed, on April 2, Wilson asked for war. Two days later La Follette refused to allow the war to be declared by unanimous consent. He delivered a three-hour speech to a crowded floor and galleries in which he argued that a declaration of war was unnecessary.[7]

La Follette systematically attempted to refute Wilson's Declaration of War, including the president's assertions that the German government was especially evil or barbaric. La Follette contrasted Germany with England and concluded that England was at least as lawless as Germany. At the end of the speech, La Follette assigned blame. He claimed that Woodrow Wilson was solely responsible for bringing America to war. On the other hand, La Follette's proposals, which he had advocated since 1915, would have averted conflict. La Follette stated that his primary motive for delivering a speech on this occasion was because he wanted the record to show the true facts of how and why the United States went to war. His April 4 speech prompted another round of denunciations in the press, and he was even hanged in effigy and ridiculed in his home state of Wisconsin.[8]

After America entered the conflict, La Follette opposed a number of Wilson's initiatives, but he voted for necessary supplies to conduct the war, and he did not block its efficient execution. He did, however, vote against measures that restricted individual freedoms or penalized ordinary citizens. La Follette condemned the conscription bill on April 27 and argued that a draft was irrational and unfair. In May he voted against the espionage bill, which restricted freedom of speech and curtailed individual rights. He attacked the war revenue bill in August 1917 because it placed an unfair burden on common people. Instead, he proposed that the rich—the beneficiaries of the war—should finance it. In the same month, he introduced a War Aims Resolution that argued for the right of Congress to control national wartime goals, not the president. The resolution also required the United States to disavow any motives of conquest or territorial acquisition. La Follette's proposal was opposed by the Wilson administration, and it triggered more criticism from the press. The *New York World* called La Follette "pro-German," and Senator Atlee Pomerene said that La Follette was "trifling with the integrity of America." There was even some talk of expelling him from the Senate.[9]

There were several rhetorical motifs that underpinned La Follette's foreign policy discourse from 1915 to 1917. One of the most dominant motifs was the melodramatic scenario, that persistent narrative form that extended through all of his political communication. During these years, La Follette attacked two targets with the melodramatic scenario: international trusts, particularly munitions manufacturers, and Woodrow Wilson.

La Follette argued that international trusts wanted to start a world war because it would be good for business. The trusts, through bribery and corruption, controlled political leaders and hence could influence policies worldwide. Moreover, similar to Iago, the villainous trusts and munitions manufacturers engaged in a systematic campaign of deception and misrepresentation. In the United States, the corporation-controlled press distorted the news in order to mislead the public into war, and the major cause of this conspiracy was greed. On July 20, 1916, La Follette claimed that privilege demanded more profits: "Intervention means war. War means blood and killing and bereaved families and unmentionable horrors. And all for what? Profits! Privilege profits!" War would generate huge earnings for the wealthy at the expense of the poor. In La Follette's opinion, allowing greed to dictate national policy was morally indefensible.[10]

Typically, the melodramatic scenario had a consistent kind of logic. One concession to the enemy, one compromise, and the nation would start sliding down the slippery slope of destruction. For example, on July 20, 1916, La Follette claimed that if the military was given an increased appropriation, it would lead to ever greater appropriations, until "forever and forever, unless there be revolt, you have changed the destiny of this country."[11]

The second target of the melodramatic scenario was Wilson. La Follette attacked the president for his dictatorial tendencies, and he characterized Wilson as a ruthless master. On March 10, 1916, La Follette claimed that Wilson wanted "unlimited and exclusive prerogative of the Executive in dealing with foreign affairs" and "absolute power to make war at will." Moreover, Wilson conducted his affairs in secret and did not consult Congress in formulating legislative proposals. La Follette fostered the image of Wilson sitting in the White House manipulating Congress and dictating national policy through his powerful organization. Wilson, through intermediaries, violated individual freedoms and the sanctity of the home. For instance, in condemning the draft on April 27, 1917, La Follette created the following menacing scene:

The main purpose of this bill is to clothe one man with power, acting through agents appointed by him, to enter at will every home in our country, at any hour of the day or night, using all the force necessary to effect the entry, and violently lay hold of 1,000,000 of our finest and healthiest and strongest boys, ranging in age from 19 to 25 years, and against their will, and against the will and wishes of their parents or family, deport them across the seas to a foreign land. . . . Some underling . . . raps at the door with the butt of his musket and tells the parents that he has come to take their boy.[12]

Another familiar motif in La Follette's rhetoric was an intense concern with the public record. Since La Follette was almost always in the minority during this period, he was preoccupied with registering his opinions and establishing his right to be heard. For example, on the matter of cloture, he said: "This matter may not interest the Senate, but I shall read it into the RECORD in order that it may go elsewhere, to be read and considered." La Follette wanted to record his objections for those outside the Senate, and, ultimately, for the judgment of history. Since he often saw little hope of influencing the Senate, he would wait for future vindication. In retrospect, it is clear that La Follette's April 4, 1917, speech was delivered mainly for the record, since war was a foregone conclusion, and the structure of the speech painstakingly reconstructed events and assigned blame. On April 4 La Follette did not seriously try to influence senators or establish viable counterproposals. In a related matter, La Follette routinely had roll-call votes read into the *Congressional Record* because he wanted a complete accounting of who had voted for what. On September 10 he remarked that the published roll-call votes would make "wholesome and interesting reading for the people of this country."[13]

La Follette also continued his habit of using extensive evidence to support his arguments. From 1915 to 1917, he quantified the war dead and casualties and provided statistics on the monetary costs of conflict. In addition, he cited massive amounts of historical precedent and testimony to support his arguments. In several different speeches to the Senate he cited historical authority such as Hamilton, Clay, Webster, and Lincoln to prove that Wilson's actions were unconstitutional and that the best statesmen disapproved of rules that limited the free exchange of ideas. In other speeches La Follette provided expert opinion to support the claims that volunteers fight more effectively than conscripts and that coastal defenses for the United States were adequate.[14]

One type of evidence that was quite important from 1915 to 1917 was testimony from the common people, especially those from the agricultural heartland. La Follette stated that the common people had wiser judgment than many of their political leaders. He contrasted the calm deliberation and wisdom of midwestern farmers with the hysteria and distortion of the eastern, corporation-controlled press. Consistently, La Follette claimed that Wilson's policies violated the true will of the people. As proof, he often cited letters and telegrams from ordinary people, and he sometimes had masses of correspondence entered into the *Congressional Record*. A major policy consequence of this tenet was that La Follette continuously advocated national referenda to insure the public's input into foreign policy, including the question of a war declaration. La Follette claimed that the people should decide a question as vital as war, particularly since the common person did the dying.[15]

La Follette argued that ordinary people were opposed to war and would react against it. He admitted, however, that public opinion was often strangely quiet. He asserted that the public's outrage was largely being denied expression because of government repression of basic freedoms. On April 4 he stated that expression of public opinion may be temporarily dormant, but "there will come an awakening; they will have their day and they will be heard. It will be as certain and as inevitable as the return of the tides, and as resistless, too." In the end, the will of the people would be victorious. When the Senate voted against his proposals, he threatened them with the wrath of the people and the harsh judgment of the voters.[16]

La Follette supplemented the pleas of common citizens with poignant emotional appeals about the human costs of war. On several occasions he vividly depicted the horrors of death, separation, starvation, human degradation, and cruelty. For example, on April 27, 1917, he decried "the anguish of those at home, of families broken up, hopes blasted, bodies crippled, insanity and disease, debt and poverty, and want and famine, which are only a few of the results of every great war." Another type of emotional appeal concerned the financial hardships suffered by common citizens supporting the costs of the war. La Follette used the metaphor of a crushing weight to illustrate this. He argued that many would be ruined by "the measure of the load which goes upon the bended backs of the American people, . . . when the tax burden comes, when the weight begins to press down, . . . [and] these men . . . are grunting and sweating under the burden of the doubled cost of living." La Follette's main objection to Wilson's schemes for financing the war was that they benefited the few at the expense of the many. On August 21 La Follette argued that the rich lived in "luxury and security," while the masses paid for war "with their lives and the greatest sacrifice of all—with the blood and life of their loved one." In La Follette's mind, this inequality was revolting to the moral senses.[17]

Without doubt, La Follette's rhetoric from 1915 to 1917 provoked a steady stream of negative reactions and criticisms from the press and public officials. In September of 1917, however, an event transpired that eclipsed the earlier controversies. La Follette accepted an invitation to address the Nonpartisan League convention in St. Paul, Minnesota, on September 20. Most of the St. Paul speech contained a tribute to the Nonpartisan League and the Granger Movement and a discussion of war taxation. However, in response to a question from the audience, La Follette digressed on the causes of the war. He claimed that America had "suffered grievances . . . at the hands of Germany," but not sufficient provocation for war: "I say this, that the COMPARATIVELY small privilege, for the right of an American citizen to ride on *A MUNITION LOADED SHIP FLYING A FOREIGN FLAG*, is too small to involve this government in *THE LOSS OF MILLIONS AND MILLIONS OF LIVES!!*" He insisted that Wilson knew the *Lusitania* carried munitions but did nothing to prevent Americans from boarding the ship. The audience cheered these remarks. Then, La Follette briefly defended the right of free speech during wartime. At the close of the speech, the audience gave him a standing ovation, and La Follette counted the evening as a great success.[18]

The next day La Follette was shocked to discover that the St. Paul speech had created a storm of controversy. The Associated Press story from St. Paul claimed that he had said "We had *no* grievance against Germany" [italics added]. In addition, the AP claimed the tenor of the meeting was disloyal and that La Follette argued that the sinking of the *Lusitania* was justified. These errors occurred despite the existence of three stenographic reports of the address. Throughout the United States, speakers and editors characterized La Follette's speech as treasonous. According to David Thelen, after the St. Paul speech La Follette "became the main focus of official and vigilante campaigns to suppress antiwar spokesmen." A number of organizations sent resolutions to Congress calling for La Follette's expulsion. The most influential of these was the Minnesota Public Safety Commission, which formally presented its expulsion petition to the Senate on September 29, 1917.[19]

The Senate scheduled La Follette to make a major address on October 6, 1917. Most observers believed that he would defend himself against charges of disloyalty that arose primarily because of the St. Paul speech. As the day approached, several of La Follette's opponents prepared to attack him, and they manipulated the schedule so that La Follette would have no opportunity to refute them. The public, sensing the likelihood of an impassioned personal defense, packed the galleries on the morning of October 6. In addition, most of the senators were present. La Follette "appeared composed" as he entered the Senate and took his place. He obtained the floor, as had been prearranged, through a question of personal privilege. He stood nearly motionless at his desk and read the speech from manuscript in an unemotional, even detached, way. When he finished the speech, there was from the galleries a spontaneous outburst of applause that had to be silenced.[20]

After La Follette concluded, three senators replied: Frank Kellogg of Minnesota, Joseph Robinson of Arkansas, and Albert Fall of New Mexico. Robinson's speech was the most thorough and memorable of the three. Although it was probably unintentional, Robinson's speech also synthesized the scattered attacks on La Follette that had been filtering in for seven months. Robinson started his speech standing at his desk near the front of the floor, across the aisle from where La Follette sat. He began calmly, but as the speech progressed, he became more agitated and abusive. The virulence of Robinson's attack shocked the floor and galleries into complete silence. A United Press correspondent described Robinson's speech as "the most unrestrained language that ever has been heard in the Senate." In marked contrast, La Follette sat quietly at his desk, making notes for a possible rebuttal. Finally, La Follette turned in his chair so that he could face Robinson directly. Robinson moved toward him, shaking his fist, while La Follette regarded him with disdain. At the climax of the speech, Robinson violated the Senate custom of never addressing a colleague directly. He jabbed a finger at La Follette and shouted: "I want to know where you stand."[21]

La Follette was unable to obtain the floor before adjournment to refute his attackers. However, Senator Fall did permit him to make a brief statement. La Follette announced that he had come prepared to substantiate all of the claims he made in the St. Paul speech, and he desired to answer the charges just made against him. He stated that he would "have to avail myself of some other means of communicating the facts to the public." La Follette probably never suspected that the October 6 address would be his last public speech to answer charges of disloyalty.[22]

In La Follette's speech, there are three interrelated persuasive purposes. In a sense, there are three separate speeches, superimposed in layers. Each layer needs to be peeled off to unlock the persuasive secrets of the work as a whole. The three layers are: (1) policy advocacy; (2) counterattack; and (3) apology.

The top layer proposed a legislative agenda for the Senate. From a structural perspective, this function was the most obvious one. Ironically, La Follette's ostensible purpose for delivering the speech was the one that violated audience expectations most directly. The audience expected a personal defense from La Follette, but on the surface, at least, he did not offer an apology.

La Follette argued that there were two connected problems in society. First, he claimed that there was an organized campaign on the part of business and government to persecute citizens who criticized the war. Second, he maintained that Wilson's administration tried to intimidate Congress into mindlessly supporting the president's war program, which led to unacceptable human and monetary costs. He proposed two policies for the government: citizens should be free to discuss the war in all of its aspects; and Congress should declare the purposes and objects of the war. La Follette supported these policies with copious testimony, historical authority, and legal commentary and precedent, particularly as it applied to the Constitution. At the end of the speech, he refuted possible objections to his proposals and suggested benefits that would accrue from them.

The second layer of La Follette's speech was a counterattack on the characters and actions of his accusers. Early in the speech, La Follette characterized the charges made against opponents of the war, including himself, as "malicious falsehood" and "libel and character assassination." In general, he did not dignify the charges by repeating them; he merely portrayed them as unfair, untrue, and reckless. In addition, he argued that the "war party" and "the war-mad press and war extremists" had impure motives. The expulsion petitions and charges of treason were an attempt to punish him for a lifetime of political opposition to concentrated wealth, special privilege, and corporate control of society. The real issue, therefore, had nothing to do with La Follette's loyalty to his country. Moreover, said La Follette, his chief opponents in the war controversy were those who would profit politically or economically from an expanded, protracted war. He also attacked Wilson directly: "The President's leadership" was responsible for the "awful death toll" and the "fearful tax burden." In short, Wilson's actions meant the United States must *bear the brunt* of the war."

The third, deepest layer of the speech was La Follette's defense of past actions. Early on, he established the fact that this speech would go beyond the St. Paul controversy; it would concern the condemnation of all those who opposed the war. Here La Follette used a defensive strategy that B.L. Ware and Wil Linkugel have called "transcendence."[23] "If I alone had been made the victim of these attacks," he insisted, "I should not take one moment of the Senate's time for their consideration." But that was emphatically not the case, so he intended to defend the rights of all citizens to speak freely during wartime. Throughout the remainder of the speech, La Follette stated his own opinions and complaints on behalf of citizens in general. Such a strategy removed the focus of the debate from the specifics of the St. Paul debacle to the larger issue of constitutional rights. Not only did this tactic raise La Follette to a more defensible vantage, but it enhanced his character by demonstrating concern for others. It also placed him in the familiar posture of a crusader for the people—morally superior and on the attack.

At the same time La Follette executed the strategy of transcendence, he argued implicitly that his activity could not be reasonably defined as disloyal. On the contrary, La Follette defined his actions as responsible, positive, and loyal in the truest sense. This tactic of redefinition had been used before in Wisconsin, where La Follette had argued that challenging the political machine was the highest form of party loyalty. During the October 6 speech, he contended that "it was the right—the constitutional right—and the patriotic duty of American citizens . . . to discuss the issues of the war." Thus, La Follette defined critical free speech as not treasonous but actually a duty of conscientious citizens. By implication, those who did not think and speak critically about the war were irresponsible and disloyal to the principles of democracy.[24]

In terms of Congress's right to establish war aims, La Follette maintained it was "an evasion of a solemn duty on the part of the Congress not to exercise that power at this critical time in the Nation's affairs." Congressional control of the war was essential to the functioning of democracy: "on this momentous question there can be no evasion, no shirking of duty of the Congress, without subverting our form of government." Again, La Follette defined his own activity in a positive light and his critics in a negative light.

The remarkable thing about La Follette's speech is that its three persuasive functions existed so harmoniously together and that each layer stood so well on its own as an organized, rational message. The deliberative layer created the impression that La Follette would not be deterred from his legislative agenda by his critics. It drew attention away from the St. Paul incident by forcing his attackers to refute policy arguments. As part of the policy advocacy, he argued that there were significant problems in society that needed to be solved. This indicted Woodrow Wilson's administration and other members of the "war party" and the "war-mad press." So, the deliberative layer did some of the work of the counterattack layer by discrediting his opponents.

The second layer of the speech attacked the actions and characters of La Follette's tormentors. Primarily, it attempted to destroy the credibility of the charges made against him. Further, the second layer forced his opponents to spend time answering the attacks; and, potentially, it put them on the defensive. The counterattacks also served a warning that he would not be verbally assaulted with impunity; he was capable of inflicting pain on his opponents, as well.

In the deepest layer, the actual apology, La Follette created definitions that exonerated his past actions. But each of these definitions, when applied to the actions of his opponents, functioned implicitly as attacks. His opponents were *not* behaving patriotically, according to La Follette's definitions. Therefore, La Follette skillfully combined policy advocacy, counterattack, and apology in the same, seamless address.

The immediate effects of the debate of October 6, 1917, were predictable. Senator Robinson's admirers received his speech well. The *St. Louis Republic* reported "The intense earnestness of the Arkansas statesman and his masterful oratory held the crowded galleries spellbound, while Democrats and Republicans alike on the floor nodded approval of his sentiments." Similarly, La Follette's sympathizers loved his address. It was particularly celebrated by Eugene Debs, who called the speech a "classic." In the nation's heartland, many agreed with La Follette—perhaps a majority. But because of the paranoid social climate, few voiced their support publicly.[25]

As a result of the outcry over the St. Paul speech, and particularly because of the flood of expulsion petitions, the Senate opened an investigation into La Follette's loyalty. From the beginning, most of the committee members wanted to bury the issue, and they delayed active consideration for fourteen months. The majority was uneasy about the La Follette case because of the disturbing precedent it would set to expel a senator for "expressing unorthodox sentiments." By the time the Senate voted on the expulsion resolution, the war had ended, which cooled the patriotic fervor that had burned during the conflict and lessened the animosity toward La Follette. In addition, on May 24, 1918, the Associated Press retracted its original story concerning the St. Paul speech and issued an apology. This event was widely publicized, and major newspapers wrote sympathetic editorials. Finally, the 1918 election put La Follette in a pivotal political position, which motivated Republicans to keep him in his seat. In January of 1919, the Senate defeated the expulsion resolution 50-21. In 1923 the Senate acknowledged the frivolous nature of the disloyalty charges when it voted to reimburse La Follette five thousand dollars to cover his legal expenses.

Even though La Follette was vindicated technically in the Senate after the war was over, in many respects his political opponents achieved their objectives. The furor over the St. Paul speech and the ensuing loyalty investigation occupied La Follette's attention almost exclusively for over a year; and, as a consequence, his effectiveness as an antiwar spokesman was severely curtailed. Moreover, La Follette found it to be nearly impossible to obtain an effective, national forum for his defense. He received no invitations to speak outside the Senate, and his congressional addresses had to be moderated during the loyalty investigations. He had only the Senate floor, his own limited-circulation magazine, and a few, local, sympathetic newspapers to make his case to the nation. These minor sources were drowned out by a deluge of critical commentary across the country. Thus, La Follette had to fight a pervasive, negative climate of opinion more than an easily defined opponent who could be engaged directly.

La Follette's October 6 speech and his other rhetorical efforts were not immediately effective in restoring his reputation. But, over a longer period, he was exonerated. The single misquotation "We had no grievance against Germany" apparently triggered most of the denunciations. When the Associated Press apologized, it seemingly discredited all of the charges against him. La Follette's vindication, however, must also be attributed to the rhetorical choices he made on October 6. Since La Follette identified himself so strongly with freedom of speech, it was difficult to damage him without also undermining the Constitution. La Follette successfully forced his accusers into an extreme position with which few were comfortable. During the fever of the war, people were driven to extreme positions, but in the guilty aftermath, the majority realized the wisdom of La Follette's arguments. Indeed, it was the way in which the public record of La Follette's position interacted with subsequent political and social events that won him exculpation. The public's eventual revulsion toward the war, symbolized by its rejection of Wilson's League of Nations appeals in 1919, placed La Follette's actions in a new light. In addition, many admired La Follette's courage, conviction, and consistency; few doubted his sincerity save his most bitter detractors.

To a large extent, La Follette addressed a future audience in his October 6 speech. Where persuasion was not immediately feasible, he opted for placing his arguments in the public record. He was content to submit his case to the judgment of the future. On the freedom of speech issue, history judged him kindly. Particularly in the post-Vietnam era, historical commentators have admired La Follette's opposition to World War I and his steadfast support of basic constitutional rights.[26]

A final reason for La Follette's acquittal was the behavior of his opponents. Critics such as Robinson indicted themselves through their speeches and actions. Robinson violated Senate decorum and shocked many with abusive rhetoric. His discourse flaunted the values of decency and fair play, and his inflamed, irrational rhetoric stood in sharp contrast to La Follette's calm demeanor and measured discourse. Moreover, Robinson discredited himself through the use of highly exaggerated or patently false statements. He said, for example, "I can not find language within the rules of the Senate to appropriately characterize the sentiments uttered" by La Follette on October 6. To a fair observer, however, there was nothing extreme or disloyal about La Follette's speech. When Robinson called his adversary's October 6 speech treasonous, it was difficult to take Robinson's other charges seriously. In sum, Robinson's speech is remembered chiefly today for being one of the most intemperate in the history of the Senate, while La Follette's address is regarded as a classic argument for free speech and representative government.[27]

In May 1919, with questions about his loyalty laid to rest, La Follette considered the peace treaty negotiations conducted by Woodrow Wilson in Europe. As news of the treaty reached Washington, La Follette became disturbed by the concessions Wilson made in order to reach a settlement. La Follette believed that Wilson disregarded the principles of his "Fourteen Points" speech, delivered in January 1918. La Follette had approved of Wilson's address at the time, and he thought America was now honor-bound to make the peace treaty conform exactly to the fourteen points. The Treaty of Versailles was signed on June 28, after which Wilson returned to the United States. On July 10 Wilson presented the treaty to the Senate for ratification. After studying the treaty, La Follette argued in his magazine that it "violates the pledged word of the President of the United States . . . and besmears the fair name of this nation."[28]

During the debate over the treaty, La Follette spoke a number of times. On October 16 he opposed the treaty provision that assigned the Shantung Province of China to Japan, arguing that America did not have the right to transfer a part of China to another country: "The question simply is . . . whether or not we shall become a party to a gigantic theft of territory and valuable rights from China, a sister Republic, an ally in the late war, for the benefit of the most despotic Government on earth."[29]

La Follette attacked the section of the treaty that established an international labor authority on October 29. He opposed it because labor law would be enacted in secret conference and the new organization would do nothing to protect the rights of American laborers. Moreover, La Follette condemned the authority of a foreign governmental body that did not express the will of the American people:

> My point is that, regardless of the particular law involved, this article of the treaty not only takes from the American people the right to determine what laws they shall have upon their statute books, but by giving to an extranational authority the right to enforce laws within our territory it strikes at the heart of our sovereignty as a Nation.[30]

On November 5 and 6 La Follette attacked President Wilson for exceeding his authority in negotiating unilaterally the Treaty of Versailles. Much of this speech was an examination of historical precedent concerning the constitutional obligations of the president to consult the Senate on treaty matters. In Wilson's case La Follette concluded that in the history of the country "there never has been such an exhibition of autocratic power as that to which this body has submitted at the hands of the present Executive."[31]

On November 13 La Follette attacked Article X of the League Covenant, which promised to preserve the territorial integrity of all nations. He claimed that the territory seized from the Austro-Hungarian Empire was divided up in violation of

> every principle of ethnology and racial alignment. . . . We, sir, if we become a member of this league of nations, assume the obligation of standing guard over this territory, with all its rivalries and hatreds and its petty and artificial governments brought into existence by the mere word of the two or three men who controlled the Paris conference.

Such untenable boundaries would have to be defended with the lives of American soldiers, "by the boys raised in South Dakota, in Wisconsin, in Pennsylvania, in New Jersey, and elsewhere."[32]

La Follette presented his final speech in the treaty debate on November 18. He characterized the treaty as the culmination of an international conspiracy. In particular, he claimed that the British had plotted to control the world, and the treaty was "plainly the consummation of the long-considered and well-planned program of the imperialists who dominate the British foreign office." Joining the League, La Follette said, "would make us the object of endless jealousies and hatreds, involve us in perpetual war, and lead to the extinction of our domestic liberty."[33]

On November 18 La Follette introduced six reservations to the treaty and asked for a roll-call vote on each. All six reservations were soundly rejected by the Senate. The next day the Treaty of Versailles was defeated both with the Lodge reservations and without. La Follette played a significant—though not central—role in undermining the League of Nations. Although some Democrats credited La Follette with blocking the treaty, he believed the most important figures in the opposition were William Borah, Hiram Johnson, and James Reed.[34]

La Follette opposed the Treaty of Versailles for different reasons than did many senators. He was not opposed to joining an international body *per se*, but he viewed the treaty as a bad ending to a bad war. He objected to provisions that furthered international imperialistic interests and violated principles of self-government for other nations. Above all, La Follette perceived his opposition to the treaty as entirely consistent with his opposition to entering the war. He would have supported a just international organization, but not one he believed was exploitative, undemocratic, and would have resulted in further world conflict.[35]

The years from 1914 to 1919 offered many opportunities for La Follette to make brave stands on issues of war and peace, but, with few exceptions, his rhetorical methods and themes remained surprisingly constant. Although he addressed such issues as American entry into World War I, conscription, war financing, sedition, and the Treaty of Versailles, his discourse was controlled by long-standing premises and concerns. La Follette continued to condemn the selfishness and greed of the giant trusts and corporations, especially arms manufacturers. He claimed the purpose of war was to promote profits and oppress people, and he decried the inequalities between the few and the many. Corporations grew fat in war, he argued, while common people paid the price in sacrifices, taxes, and blood. On the topics of conscription, the Armed Ship bill, and treaty negotiations, La Follette transferred opprobrium from the corporations to the White House. He characterized Wilson as a ruthless master who dictated policy unilaterally and reached decisions in secret conclave, able to defy the law of the land at will.

In opposing the proposed League of Nations, La Follette objected to secret negotiations and international conspiracies that attempted to control the destinies of subject peoples. Furthermore, he feared the loss of self-determination that membership in an international league could bring. La Follette believed the goals of many foreign powers conflicted with American values of representation and individual freedom. He affirmed the free will of nations as well as of individuals and opposed outside control at all levels of the human community.

La Follette expressed faith in the power of symbolic persuasion to influence world opinion. He believed mighty adversaries could be defeated on the strength of a concerted moral crusade.[36] He extended the concept of popular will to international affairs and maintained that the will of the people should be expressed through petitions, referenda, and elections. La Follette claimed the wisdom of America resided in the common people, particularly the agricultural population of the Midwest. He praised the calm judgment of the people and was confident that their good sense would ultimately prevail. Moreover, he threatened the Senate with public wrath for shirking its responsibility and ignoring the true will of the people.

La Follette continued to be preoccupied with establishing a clear public record. He aimed to explain his position and make his voice heard above the clamor of war. His strategy was designed for long-term rather than immediate effects. La Follette recorded his objections to the war confident he would be exonerated in the future. Even when his loyalty was questioned, La Follette never wavered from his convictions, and in the end he was vindicated. As La Follette returned to domestic reform in 1919, he was to encounter a changed mood in America. He would struggle to adapt his old rhetorical formulas to a different world than the one he had encountered before the war.

8
"Forward, Progressives!"

After the Treaty of Versailles had been defeated in November 1919, La Follette and the rest of the Senate began to consider domestic matters, the most pressing of which was railroad legislation. La Follette favored continuing the government control of railroads established during the war, but on December 1, 1919, conservative senators introduced the Cummins bill, which was designed to return the rail lines to their private owners and guarantee a good return on the owners' investments. The Cummins bill based its financial provisions on the face values of railroad securities rather than on the actual physical assets of the companies. Moreover, it would furnish a federal subsidy to compensate for the period of government control during the war. In short, the Cummins bill would undo much of what La Follette had labored to establish. To counteract this threat, La Follette worked closely with the railroad brotherhoods and with farm groups such as the Farmers' National Council, the Farmers' Union, and the Grange. Farmers opposed the Cummins bill because they thought it would result in higher freight rates; labor opposed it because they desired greater government control over the workplace.[1]

Supporters of the Cummins bill argued that government control of the railroads during the war had caused heavy financial losses. La Follette challenged this view in five separate speeches, totaling thirteen hours, which he delivered on successive days, starting on December 9, 1919. In his opening speech he argued that the financial failures of the railroads were not due to government operation. On the contrary, he said, statistics indicated that the railroads had already been failing when the government assumed control, and under government stewardship the lines had begun to show a profit. La Follette concluded that the country needed more time for "a complete demonstration of the success or failure of the system." In three other addresses, La Follette attacked the rate provisions of the Cummins bill. He argued that the bill would tax people unfairly, that financial returns would be based on fictitious "book value" of the property, and that the bill undermined the Adamson-La Follette physical valuation law of 1913. In his final speech, La Follette attacked the anti-strike provision, which "denied labor the right to quit in a collective body."[2]

Throughout the debate, La Follette indicted the character of the private railroad industry, calling it "sordid" and claiming that it "schemed," "plundered," and "looted." He accused the railroads of dishonesty and deception in record keeping. He blamed the twin crises of high prices and labor unrest facing the nation in 1919 on the domination of America by the giant corporations, and he threatened the Senate with the wrath of the people if they failed to curtail the corporate menace by defeating the Cummins bill. La Follette was the only senator who vehemently opposed the Cummins bill throughout the debate. On December 20 the Senate approved it, 46-30.[3]

Throughout the Cummins bill debate La Follette had been suffering from poor health. In January 1920 he was incapacitated by a case of influenza coupled with a recurring gallbladder disorder. He was absent from the Senate for several months, but he returned on March 19 to vote for the final rejection of the Treaty of Versailles. While La Follette was away, he plotted political strategy for his home state. The progressives in Wisconsin had been badly divided by the war, and Stalwart Republicans controlled the statehouse. In the face of this, La Follette attempted to reforge a progressive coalition among several influential groups in Wisconsin. Farmers were disenchanted with profiteering on agricultural produce, higher costs of manufactured goods, and a sense of helplessness and isolation. What was more, the usually conservative German Democrats felt alienated by the social climate created by the war. Both of these groups found a spokesman in La Follette, and although the conservative Republicans maintained nominal control, "Fighting Bob's" political base was coalescing once again. The Social Democrats, the Nonpartisan League, the railroad unions, and the Wisconsin branch of the Committee of Forty-eight also lent support to La Follette's cause.[4]

As a spearhead for his coalition, La Follette wrote a platform for the "La Follette Republicanism" ticket in the April 6 national delegate contest. His platform called for the repeal of the Espionage and Sedition Acts, restoration of civil liberties, abolition of the draft, and government ownership of railroads, natural resources, and agricultural processing facilities. In addition, he favored government encouragement of collective bargaining organizations. The contest for convention delegates was the first test of strength in Wisconsin between La Follette and the Stalwarts since the end of the war. The "La Follette Republicanism" slate carried the state by 50,000 votes and received 24 of 26 delegates. Important as the victory was in Wisconsin, La Follette's delegates were isolated at the national convention. La Follette's nomination and the minority platform were heartily booed, while cries of "Bolshevik!" echoed through the hall.[5]

Faced with this unequivocal rejection by the GOP, La Follette began to search for a new political vehicle for his ideas. The nomination of Warren

Harding for president by the Republicans left a number of progressive factions disaffected, including the Committee of Forty-eight, which was composed of those who had supported Theodore Roosevelt in past campaigns. The Committee of Forty-eight and the Labor Party discussed the possibility of La Follette heading up a coalition party. He consented to be an independent presidential candidate if the progressive factions could agree to a program substantially similar to his 1920 platform, but they could not. Leaders of the Labor Party distrusted white-collar professionals from the Committee of Forty-eight, while middle-class progressives were horrified by the Labor Party's revolutionary ideology and rejection of capitalism. Without a unified coalition of progressive groups, La Follette refused to mount a campaign.[6]

Since La Follette was not up for reelection in 1920, he did not need to campaign actively. Moreover, he was under doctor's orders to avoid strenuous activity. Nonetheless, he did appear in Milwaukee on October 21 before an audience of 7,000 people. This address focused on the Esch-Cummins Act and was La Follette's first outside the Senate since the St. Paul speech of 1917. As was La Follette's custom by now, he read from a manuscript to avoid being misquoted.[7]

La Follette repeated many of the arguments against the Esch-Cummins Act that he had made in the Senate. He called the act a "mass of cleverly concocted camouflage" and stated that the real intent of the bill was "buried in a mass of verbiage." In reality, he said, the act laid "the foundation for the economic exploitation of all producers and all consumers for the benefit of a monopoly." Moreover, he attacked the Esch-Cummins Act because it would "destroy the right of collective bargaining." In La Follette's analysis, "The only hope of the people of this country for relief lies with the small group of independent Senators and Congressmen who . . . have the constructive vision and the courage to fight for legislation in the interests of the people." The *Milwaukee Journal* noted that, in the October 21 address, La Follette "spoke with much of his old-time vigor. The oratorical power which has been so potent a power in Wisconsin politics for 20 years is still in evidence."[8]

When La Follette returned to Congress after the 1920 elections, he spoke against the Winslow-Townsend amendment, a measure designed to strengthen the Esch-Cummins Act. He presented a statistics-laden speech on February 21 and 22 to prove that the amendment was even worse than the original bill. He claimed that the Senate was attempting to "fasten new burdens" upon the American people. He objected to the fact that the proposed amendment removed all government restrictions on profit for the railroads, and he offered a counter-amendment that placed a ceiling on profit guarantees. La Follette's measure was defeated, and the Winslow-Townsend bill passed; but he garnered some favorable publicity from his speeches. The *New York Times* duplicated some of La Follette's statistical tables and commented that the speech was "not marked by a conspicuous oratorical effort, but consisted principally of quotations from reports, statistics and tables."[9]

La Follette returned to Wisconsin in March to make several speeches, the most important of which was an address to the People's Reconstruction League. He delivered the address on March 25, 1921, in the Assembly chamber of the state capital. This was La Follette's first speech in Madison since 1916. His political advisers warned him to avoid the sensitive war issue, but La Follette insisted on confronting this ghost head-on. During the speech he raised a clenched fist and shouted, "I would not trade my war record with any living man." The audience sat in stunned silence for a moment, then exploded into tumultuous applause. An old political foe of La Follette's, witnessing the display, declared, "I hate the son of a bitch; but, by God, what guts he's got." La Follette, however, knew more than his political advisers. World War I had not been popular, especially in Wisconsin, and La Follette exploited this fact brilliantly.[10]

La Follette returned to the Senate in April, and although he was busily engaged in committee assignments and report-writing, he made few significant speeches during the remainder of 1921. When La Follette did take the floor, he echoed familiar themes and continued old rhetorical habits. On May 16 he began a series of remarks against the Naval Expansion bill, which called for resumption of the ship-building program originated in 1916. He accused the munitions and armor manufacturers of "stealing from the Government and from the public. . . . [T]hey ought to be in the penitentiary, wearing stripes." In September La Follette attacked a revenue bill because, he argued, never "in the history of this country has such a burden of taxation been laid upon the people as that which they are required to bear to-day, and must continue to bear during this and succeeding generations."[11]

In January 1922 La Follette condemned the election of Senator Truman Newberry of Michigan because he had used campaign funds illegally. The issue, La Follette declared, was "whether it is possible to buy a seat in the United States Senate." He warned his colleagues "against this insidious foe revealed to-day . . . in its full ugliness and strength." Nonetheless, the Senate voted to seat Newberry over La Follette's objections. On March 22 La Follette spoke against the Four Power Pact, which was a proposed treaty between Great Britain, France, Japan, and the United States. La Follette rejected the Four Power Pact for the same reasons he had opposed the Treaty of Versailles: it was imperialistic, exploitative, undemocratic, and it served the "great interests which control the Governments" of the participants.[12]

The Four Power Pact was ratified by the Senate despite La Follette's strenuous dissent. In fact, virtually all of La Follette's positions were spurned by the Senate in 1921 and 1922. He was frustrated by the political climate in Washington and admitted in private that he was discouraged by the lack of progressive reform.[13]

One of La Follette's conspicuous successes during this time was his role in uncovering the Teapot Dome scandal. La Follette became suspicious in May of 1921 when control of the naval oil reserves was transferred from the Secretary of the Navy to the Secretary of the Interior. By March 1922 La Follette had read reports that Secretary of the Interior Albert Fall had leased the naval oil reserves in California to a private driller. Soon after, rumors circulated that Fall had also leased the Teapot Dome reserve in Wyoming. After investigating the charges on his own, La Follette introduced a resolution in the Senate on April 21, 1922, calling for Fall to furnish detailed information concerning the leasing of the oil reserves.[14]

On April 28 La Follette accused the Interior Department of corruption and called for an official inquiry into the "subject of leases upon the naval oil reserves." He indicted the oil companies as "hungry exploiters," "burglars," and "pillaging interests" who "exploit this rich field" and make use of a "ruthless system of pillage." After La Follette completed his charges, not a single senator rose to refute him. In fact, his resolution passed unanimously, a satisfying victory for him in a period marked by disappointment.[15]

In June 1922 La Follette became concerned about two recent Supreme Court decisions—one ruling that child labor laws were unconstitutional, the other holding that labor unions were subject to anti-trust laws. When the American Federation of Labor (AFL) invited La Follette to address their convention on June 14, he decided to use the occasion to criticize the Supreme Court. In his address of June 14 La Follette asked the AFL to support a constitutional amendment that would allow Congress to override a Supreme Court decision. He attacked the Supreme Court for initiating "a process of gradual encroachments" on the power of Congress, and he proposed that no inferior court be permitted to rule on the constitutionality of an act of Congress.[16]

La Follette objected to the high court because it exercised "supreme power over the happiness, the rights, and the very lives of the 110,000,000 people of the United States." In addition, La Follette reasoned, the federal judiciary was not elected by the people. This fact violated "the immortal principle that the will of the people shall be the law of the land." Hence, there was no accountability to the voters, and "this absence of direct responsibility to the people has led the Federal judiciary, and particularly the Supreme Court, to assume and exercise an arbitrary power wholly inconsistent with popular government." La Follette argued that the "choice is simple but fateful. Shall the people rule through their elected representatives or shall they be ruled by a judicial oligarchy?"[17]

La Follette's arguments appealed to AFL members, who "stood on chairs, pounded tables and shouted at the top of their voices." The labor convention endorsed La Follette's ideas, but his speech drew sharp criticism when it was reported in the press. Dr. Nicholas Murray Butler, in an address before the

New Jersey State Bar, called La Follette's proposals revolutionary and destructive, and Butler's remarks were read into the *Congressional Record*. Senator Frank Kellogg of Minnesota claimed that La Follette's speech subverted representative government. On June 21 La Follette responded to this criticism by claiming that few had seen or heard his Cincinnati speech. Consequently, he read the entire address into the *Congressional Record*.[18]

Because the tide of reform sentiment had ebbed in Wisconsin, La Follette was concerned about his reelection chances in 1922. The Republican National Committee actively opposed him, and the Stalwart faction in Wisconsin waged an intensive anti-La Follette campaign. The conservatives attacked La Follette for his war record and for his proposals concerning the Supreme Court. In addition, they labeled La Follette the "Socialist candidate" because the Socialist Party of Wisconsin commended him for his stand against imperialism.[19]

In response to the opposition, La Follette went on an intensive public speaking campaign in Wisconsin. He made his first major campaign address in Milwaukee on July 17 to an audience of over 5,000. Once again, he was advised not to mention his war record during the speech, but in response to a question from the audience, he proclaimed proudly that he would not trade war records with anyone. The audience applauded enthusiastically. Henceforth, in every speech he deliberately discussed his stand on the war, and the response was uniformly favorable.[20]

Realizing their tactical error, the Stalwarts soon dropped the attack on La Follette's war stand and charged instead that he was a lonely and ineffectual voice of protest in the Senate and that he did not represent the views of Wisconsinites. La Follette's campaign met this challenge by presenting testimonials from respected national leaders attesting to his value as a statesman. La Follette received support from individuals such as Senator George Norris, William Allen White, and Roscoe Pound, Dean of the Harvard Law School.[21]

La Follette spoke for six weeks in the northern part of the state, and his son Phil represented him in the south. Traveling by automobile, La Follette was able to make two or three speeches per day. Such a campaign had not been waged by La Follette since the last Senate race in 1916, and Bob Jr. thought his father had never been more effective. This judgment was supported by the electoral results; La Follette carried all but one county in the state and was renominated by a landslide.[22]

La Follette opened his general election campaign in La Crosse on October 19, where he spent an hour defending his war record. He also claimed that "we have lost democracy in this government in the last 60 years. . . . It will require a terrible sacrifice on the part of coming generations to bring back the government to the people." Over the next ten days La Follette took his message to Green Bay, Kaukauna, Appleton, Oconto, Marinette, Merrill, and Antigo. After concluding his Wisconsin itinerary, La Follette felt secure enough in the outcome to speak on behalf of political allies in other states. La Follette carried every county in Wisconsin in the general election, winning by a large majority. The press interpreted his electoral triumph as a sign that he was the national leader of progressives in America. The *New York Times* commented that "Today La Follette is stronger than at any other time in his career," and he would be "the most powerful legislative factor in the next Congress." Moreover, the *Raleigh News and Observer* noted that La Follette's "success under all the circumstances is the most remarkable exhibition of personal power in American politics in the present decade."[23]

In March 1923 La Follette's doctors insisted that he withdraw from public life for a time in order to conserve his health. His doctors consented to a tour of Europe provided that he avoided public speaking and other strenuous activities. He left the United States in August 1923 and returned in November. Throughout his tour he followed his doctors' orders and avoided public speaking, but he did record his travel impressions, which were later printed in the *Washington Herald* and *La Follette's Magazine*.[24]

Although La Follette gained valuable insights about Europe, the tour did not improve his health. Nevertheless, he returned to the Senate after the Christmas recess. On February 11, 1924, he spoke in favor of a resolution calling for Secretary of the Navy Edwin Denby to resign. La Follette called the Denby-Fall case "a putrid eruption on the body politic and important largely because it indicates a generally diseased condition." The Senate adopted the resolution, and Denby resigned one week later.[25]

Shortly after delivering the Denby speech La Follette became ill with a respiratory infection that developed into bronchial pneumonia. La Follette's failing health and old age were reflected in the lessened intensity of his rhetoric. A reporter who witnessed La Follette's performance during the Denby speech wrote:

His face had lost some of its old color. His voice had not quite the angry power it used to have, but still it was a strong voice; perhaps a little pleasanter to listen to because somewhat mellowed. He read his speech . . . but I noticed that his hand was steady as he held the manuscript. . . . He was more moderate than of old. Success and power, for he is now the most powerful single factor in the Senate, and perhaps, too, advancing in years, have mellowed him.

By 1922 La Follette was known in Wisconsin simply as the "Old Man," and as his health and age increasingly concerned him, he became friendly on a social basis for the first time with conservatives. La Follette also devoted less time to researching his own speeches, relying on the services of the People's Legislative Service to provide material for his arguments. Moreover, he devoted correspondingly less time to polishing his speeches to perfection.[26]

La Follette's discourse from 1919 to 1924 continued to exhibit well-established rhetorical habits. His attacks on the railroad and oil monopolies were bolstered heavily with statistics and testimony. Moreover, La Follette could still be heard threatening the Senate with the wrath of the people if it failed to curtail the corporate menace. Finally, the unrepentant senator refused to apologize for or moderate his positions regarding World War I. The most dominant rhetorical motif, however, remained the melodramatic scenario. For example, on October 21, 1920, La Follette characterized the big trusts as sordid schemers, "sinister interests plotting for their own enrichment." By April 28, 1922, La Follette claimed the oil monopolies had "corrupted Government servants, ruthlessly seized and exploited the natural resources which Nature gave to man, and systematically robbed the people through extortionate prices."[27]

La Follette's single innovation during this period was the addition of a new evil villain: the Supreme Court of the United States. However, he continued to use the melodramatic scenario to indict this sinister menace. On June 14, 1922, he maintained:

By a process of gradual encroachments, uncertain and timid at first, but now confident and aggressive, sovereignty has been wrested from the people and usurped by the courts.

To-day the actual ruler of the American public is the Supreme Court of the United States.

Typically, La Follette cast the melodramatic scenario in the form of historical narrative:

Until recent years the Supreme Court ventured to assert this great power to override the acts of Congress, only upon rare occasions, and at widely separated intervals of time. . . .

For several years before the outbreak of the Great War, however, the people had become aroused to this dangerous situation and a continuous campaign was being conducted to check or correct it. . . . But the judiciary was not checked. On the contrary, it availed itself of this period, when the attention of the people was diverted by the problems of war and of reconstruction, to extend its powers and to nullify the acts of Congress with greater boldness than it ever before displayed. . . . We have created—or, at least, have suffered—to grow up within our land a Frankenstein which must be destroyed or else it will destroy us.

La Follette also portrayed the Supreme Court as a disease, and in a revealing mixed metaphor he advocated that "The time has come when we must put the ax to the root of this monstrous growth upon the body of our Government."[28]

By 1924 the political structure of American life was convincingly conservative in both major parties. The fragmented progressives looked to La

Follette to lead the fight against conservative doctrine. As the scandals of the Republican administration continued to unfold, La Follette's supporters began to think in terms of a third-party ticket. The Conference for Progressive Political Action became the focal point for a possible third party, and La Follette was the only progressive figure of presidential stature to lead them. La Follette collaborated with the Conference on a political platform to submit to Wisconsin voters in the April 1, 1924, primary. The citizens of Wisconsin approved the platform, and twenty-eight progressive delegates were elected to the Republican National Convention. La Follette decided to offer his platform as a minority report at the national Republican convention, but not to place his name in nomination. If the Republicans adopted his platform and fielded a progressive candidate, then La Follette would not run as an independent.

The platform reflected La Follette's political agenda for the past decade. It demanded that "the Federal government be used to crush private monopoly, not to foster it," and he advocated measures to protect natural resources, control the railroads, reform taxation, discipline the federal judiciary, aid American agriculture, protect the rights of industrial workers, and make the electoral process more representative. In international affairs, he favored "firm treaty agreements" to reduce armaments, abolish conscription, and outlaw war. Not surprisingly, his platform was rejected, and Calvin Coolidge was nominated for President. Three weeks later, however, the Conference for Progressive Political Action (CPPA) asked La Follette to be its presidential candidate. La Follette announced that he would run for president, but as an independent candidate—not on the CPPA ticket. Nevertheless, he sent his platform to be read to the CPPA convention, which endorsed it by acclamation the next day.[29]

The statement accompanying La Follette's platform contained the essence of his 1924 campaign. In most respects, La Follette could have written this document twenty years earlier. "The rank and file of the membership of both old parties is Progressive," La Follette claimed.

But through a vicious and undemocratic convention system and under the evil influences which have been permitted to thrive at Washington, both party organizations have fallen under the domination and control of corrupt wealth, devoting the powers of government exclusively to selfish special interests.

La Follette argued there was only "one paramount issue" in the 1924 campaign: "To break the combined power of the private monopoly system over the political and economic life of the American people":

If the Progressives will but unite with a single purpose to meet this issue fearlessly and squarely they may rely with entire confidence upon the support of the plain people who are the victims of the present system and who have the right and the power, through the ballot, to control their own government.

La Follette's platform statement focused especially on the needs of American farmers. The present agricultural crisis, he claimed, was caused by the "consistent policy of administrations of both parties in leaving monopoly a free hand to set the price on everything the farmer buys and everything he consumes, including farm machinery and implements, fertilizer, and household necessities." To benefit all of society, La Follette advocated the

> organization and development of a national cooperative marketing system, under the control of the farmers themselves, free from interference by the government or its agencies. The government must recognize that agriculture is entitled to be placed upon an equal footing with other industries of the nation.

If this were done, he concluded, it would "benefit the consumer through eliminating the unjust toll of middlemen and speculators in food products."

La Follette emphasized that he was "unalterably opposed to any class government, whether it be the existing dictatorship of plutocracy or the dictatorship of the proletariat. Both are essentially undemocratic and un-American. Both are destructive of private initiative and individual liberty." In La Follette's analysis, the entire political debate could be reduced to one conflict:

> With the changing phases of a thirty-year contest, I have been more and more impressed with the deep underlying singleness of the issue.
> The supreme issue is not railroad control. It is not the tariff, banking or taxation. These and other questions are but manifestations of one great struggle.
> The supreme issue, involving all others, is the encroachment of the powerful few upon the rights of the many. This great power has come between the people and their government. We must, with statesmanship and constructive legislation, meet these problems, or we shall pass them on, with all the possibilities of violent conflict and chaos, to our children.

Given the simplicity of La Follette's analysis, he presented Americans with a simple choice: "We must choose, on the one hand, between representative government, with its guarantee of peace, liberty and economic freedom and prosperity for all the people, and, on the other, war, tyranny, and the impoverishment of the many for the enrichment of the favored few." The choice for representative government, he said, would be no easy task. It would involve

> sacrifice, courage, and unsparing activity from every man and woman engaged on the people's side. But so long as the Progressives keep faith with the people and remain steadfastly true to the principles which are at stake, we can face the vast financial resources and the specious arguments of our opponents with full confidence of success.

La Follette claimed he was fighting for the old principles of society advocated by Jefferson, Jackson, and Lincoln. As an independent, La Follette said, "My appeal will be addressed to every class of the people and to every section of the country." To prove that his policies would not lead to chaos or anarchy, La Follette pointed to his record in the Senate and in his home state of Wisconsin. "Happily," La Follette said,

we can point to great progressive commonwealths like Wisconsin, where prosperity has been enjoyed by business, agriculture and labor alike, where honest taxation and efficient government has been substituted for graft and corruption.[30]

After announcing his candidacy, La Follette asked Louis D. Brandeis to be his running mate, but Brandeis refused. La Follette then settled on Senator Burton K. Wheeler of Montana, a disaffected Democrat. A variety of organizations endorsed La Follette, including the Socialist Party, the railroad brotherhoods, civic reform groups, women's groups, and individuals such as Professor John Dewey and Helen Keller. The American Federation of Labor endorsed him by default, since the major parties virtually ignored organized labor. E.W. Scripps directed his chain of twenty-five newspapers to endorse La Follette, but that constituted the extent of his support in the national press. The Republican Party perceived La Follette's candidacy as a serious threat and labeled him a party "infidel." Some of Roosevelt's old supporters denounced La Follette's programs as radical, and Charles Dawes, Republican candidate for vice-president, charged La Follette with "leading the army of extreme radicalism."[31]

La Follette's campaign had organizational problems from the start, not the least of which was getting his name on the ballot. He was forced to rely on Socialist help in many instances, and in California he appeared on the Socialist ticket, which lent credence to charges that La Follette sought to undermine capitalism. Moreover, the coalition of diverse political elements in his organization began to disintegrate almost from the outset. Lower-class laborers and middle-class, traditional progressives distrusted each other, and agriculturalists were uneasy about the assertiveness of the labor unions. In addition, financing was a constant worry. The labor unions promised much but delivered little in the way of cash. The major source of funding came from an accumulation of small, individual donations. By late August Belle La Follette confided that the campaign was chronically underfinanced and understaffed. Despite these difficulties, the La Follette-Wheeler ticket was able to appear on the ballot in nearly every state in under two months' time.[32]

La Follette, ever alert to new media, appeared with Calvin Coolidge and John Davis in September 1924 in a "talking" film in which the candidates stated their platforms. The films, made by Dr. Lee DeForest's phonofilm, were historic in that it was the first time that the voices and visual images of presidential candidates were shown together. La Follette also saw radio as a promising medium for promulgating his reform ideology. Radio, in La Follette's view, had the advantage of educating the voters on issues firsthand, thereby eliminating misrepresentation by the press. Although a radio hook-up cost $3,500, La Follette felt it was worth the cost, and he planned to open his campaign with a radio address. Live speeches at political meetings had been broadcast before, but no one had ever made a political address solely to a microphone. The *New York Evening Journal* called La Follette's radio address a "unique experiment in American politics."[33]

La Follette spoke on Labor Day for thirty-five minutes, a short address by his standards, but well suited for the electronic medium. His audience was estimated at several million listeners, with radio speakers set up at auditoriums and other public gathering places. La Follette had rehearsed this address carefully, and his son gave him hand signals during the speech to indicate how his voice carried over the loudspeakers. The Labor Day speech was modeled on La Follette's platform statement of July 4, as were all of his subsequent speeches in the campaign.[34]

La Follette commented after the address that he was unaccustomed to speaking without a visible audience:

I will admit that I missed some of the folks who have sat down close in front at some of my meetings, but I visualized my audience. I thought of friends in Wisconsin who I knew would be listening, and farmers out in the Northwest and laboring men attending their picnics and Labor Day meetings.

He humorously assessed one advantage of radio: "Of course I do not flatter myself that the whole country paused while I delivered that speech; but I will say that I never had a more respectful hearing or fewer interruptions." La Follette did experience some minor difficulties with the new medium later on in the campaign, however. When an audience member in Kansas City asked him to speak louder, he replied,

I have been advised . . . that if I bellow too loudly the radio doesn't get it. . . . I have got to shoot right at this thing. What I like when I am speaking to an audience is freedom; I like the freedom of the stage; I like the freedom that comes from not being tied down to a miserable manuscript.

On another occasion, after straying too far from the microphone, La Follette remarked, "I wish I had some straps to put my feet in."[35]

La Follette began his in-person speaking campaign at Madison Square Garden in New York City on September 18 and ended it in Cleveland on November 1. In between, he delivered at least nineteen major addresses in fourteen states in the East and Midwest. Throughout the campaign, La Follette faced large, enthusiastic crowds. Audiences were enchanted by La Follette's charisma and energy. Many commentators noted the poignant drama of watching the sixty-nine-year-old orator attack the special interests with the same fervor and militancy of his youth.[36]

When La Follette returned to Wisconsin on November 2, over 3,000 friends and supporters escorted him from the Madison train station to the capitol, after which he made a few brief remarks. He remembered that 45 years earlier he had been escorted from the station to the capital in a similar manner when he had won the Inter-State Oratorical Contest. He then declared, "Providence willing, I believe I shall last long enough to see the nation freed from its economic slavery and the government returned to the people." Although La Follette did not know it, this brief extemporaneous speech in Madison would bring his career as an orator to a close. He would write a few more editorials, but he would never deliver another public speech.[37]

Although La Follette claimed to appeal to "every class of the people and to every section of the country," his rhetoric during the 1924 campaign was best suited to audiences in the agricultural heartland of America. Indeed, his speeches were particularly vibrant when discussing the plight of farmers. In Kansas City, for instance, he was almost lyrical in recounting the settling of the West. "It is inspiring to me," he said, "as it should be to any man, to stand on the threshold of this great prairie empire stretching to a thousand miles in three directions. Here a new America had its beginnings." He told about the homesteaders:

the home builders who faced sickness and death, drought and flood. . . . They reared families, suffered from hunger and disease in their determination to build this western empire. . . . By 1890, this rich territory was peopled by prosperous, educated, home-owning farmers. They were not tenants. They were owners. They feared no man. I love to think of this heroic achievement. It is one of the most heroic achievements in American history.

But then, he continued, about 1898, a change began:

Something ominous happened. Men saw it but dimly, but they felt an unseen power that was striking at the security they had attained. Something was happening to the farmers, not in this section alone, but all over the country. Something was destroying their independence. Somebody, some thing, was taking from them the wealth they produced.

The evil villain, La Follette argued, was organized monopoly.[38]

La Follette claimed in Kansas City that the well being of the American farmer was paramount. "There are few political crimes," he said, "that arouse me as does the direct participation of this government of ours in the destruction of the farmer." Throughout the campaign, he advocated the proposals to aid agriculture spelled out in his platform. As he promised his audience in Des Moines, "we will initiate and carry through measures for the immediate relief of the farmer. . . . The farmer cannot wait. The country cannot wait."[39]

During the campaign La Follette attempted to tap the hostilities of farmers by attacking the great financial centers of the East, particularly Wall Street. "The railroads of the country are interlocked with the packers, with the millers, with the commission men, with the grain pits," he claimed in Kansas City. "Together they form an economic system, ruled from Wall Street." In Syracuse he maintained that the

independent bankers, particularly in the West, have learned that they have little in common with the financiers of Wall Street. . . . they have seen the great banks of cities reaching out with their branches like a greedy octopus to absorb their little business.[40]

By contrast, La Follette's appeals to organized labor and industrial workers were ambivalent. He wanted to separate himself from radical elements in the labor movement, and he avoided any appeals to class consciousness. He insisted that his campaign was "not a class movement. It draws its strength from the common people in every walk of life," including "farmers and workingmen, storekeepers and factory owners." His definition of labor was the broadest one possible, as he expressed in his "Labor Day Address":

As we are the outspoken champions of all who labor, it is fitting that we should inaugurate our campaign on Labor Day. But we recognize no narrow definition for the laboring millions of this country. The farmers, the business men who give honest service in return for righteous profits, the women who toil in the homes, the offices and the schools of the land,—all these we regard as laborers for the common good as truly as the wage-earners in the shops and mills and mines, and on the railroads.[41]

La Follette failed to establish that he was a particular friend of unions or that he could be counted on to create special policies for industrial workers (as he had for farmers). La Follette's frame of reference was agricultural, and he stressed his record as former governor of a farming state. In addition, La Follette was an outspoken critic of violent strikes as a tool for unions. He told Pittsburgh workers,

Any man who resorts in an industrial dispute to violence is a criminal, and should be dealt with as such, whether he be a paid gunman of a corporation or a traitor to organized labor and the principles for which it stands. But I insist that it is the first function of the Department of Justice to enforce the law in the public interest, without favoritism either to capital or labor.[42]

Whether consciously or not, La Follette created the impression that labor was simply another weapon in his fight against the big trusts and that he was inherently more interested in disciplining monopolies than in the organized power of workers. Labor leaders such as Samuel Gompers, however, were not particularly opposed to monopoly *per se*, because they often found it easier to negotiate contracts with large corporations. Such a paradox probably played a role in the weak support labor afforded La Follette in campaign contributions and votes. The entire labor movement donated only $50,000 to La Follette's campaign, half of which came from the AFL. Donations to La Follette from other sources totaled $460,000. The exact number of votes workers cast for La Follette is unclear, but several samples from New York City revealed he got between 25 and 33 percent of working-class Italian votes but only about 15 percent of the votes cast by Irish laborers.[43]

La Follette's 1924 campaign seemed to gain momentum through the early fall, but by the end of October his popularity began to plummet. Large audiences and enthusiastic receptions did not always translate into votes. Newspaper accounts consistently stressed the great drama of La Follette's political meetings and his status as a celebrity, facts that proved irresistible to spectators, whatever their political convictions. Overall, however, political fervor for La Follette was most intense in the Midwest. Elsewhere, voters feared that a radical La Follette would mean an end to prosperity. Given the choice between "Coolidge or Chaos," the answer was clear for most. Coolidge won the election in a landslide with 54 percent of the vote, compared to 16.5 percent for La Follette and 28.8 percent for Davis. La Follette's showing was the largest popular vote ever garnered by an independent candidate up to that time. He carried only the state of Wisconsin, but he placed second in eleven states in the Midwest and West.[44]

La Follette and his staff blamed two causes for the loss—the attempt to unite diverse and sometimes hostile factions and the appeal of prosperity, job security, and stability offered by the Republican Party. After the election La Follette observed that the Conference for Progressive Political Action collapsed and disintegrated quickly because it had been composed of self-serving political and economic factions that were not primarily interested in progressive reform, *per se*. Although La Follette was disappointed, he expressed sympathy for workers who were afraid to risk their livelihoods by revolting against the political establishment. However, La Follette's family and close supporters were especially bitter about the failure of labor unions to support his candidacy.[45]

Another major cause for the loss was the skill of La Follette's political opponents. Republicans cultivated fears about La Follette's radicalism. His staff considered the claim that La Follette would bring about a depression the most crippling attack of the campaign. Moreover, his opponents maintained a steady barrage of charges that La Follette was a demagogue, another "Marat," or a tool of the communists. Other damaging perceptions were that he was pro-German, that he wanted to undermine the Supreme Court, or that a vote for La Follette might deadlock the election. By contrast, Coolidge did not deliver many speeches, choosing instead to act presidential and to use state occasions as a vehicle for his campaign. Such a strategy gave Coolidge dignity and respectability and underlined the desperation of La Follette's crusade. In the meantime, Coolidge's underlings could savage La Follette's credibility.[46]

Although La Follette was disappointed by the outcome of the 1924 campaign, he was far from crushed. In the aftermath of defeat, he wrote in *La Follette's Magazine*, "Under the lash of these masters of America the wonder is not that so many millions were intimidated and voted for Coolidge, but that so many millions stood by their convictions and voted the Independent ticket." Before the month was out, La Follette began to lay the foundation for the next congressional election. "The Progressives will close ranks for the next battle," he predicted:

We are enlisted for life in the struggle to bring government back. We will not quit and we will not compromise. . . . Without money and with little organization we have shaken the mighty in their seats. . . . Our task is great, but our cause is greater.
   Forward, Progressives, for the campaign of 1926![47]

But La Follette never lived to participate in the campaign of 1926. The presidential contest had taken a heavy toll on his fragile health. In December La Follette became ill, and in May 1925 he suffered a heart attack. He died on June 18. La Follette wrote his own epitaph shortly before his final illness: "I would be remembered as one who in the world's darkest hour kept a clean conscience and stood to the end for the ideals of American democracy."[48]

9
Conclusion

When looking back over La Follette's entire rhetorical career, one can see some differences over time, but the overriding impression created is that of consistency. Although the topics of La Follette's discourse differed in each chronological period, the essential values, techniques, and stylistic devices were remarkably unchanged. His early speeches—even one delivered in a college speech contest—strongly foreshadowed his mature political discourse. From La Follette's student days until the end of his life, he always had some kind of "Iago" to attack, whether it was tramps, oleomargarine, corrupt political machines, money trusts, railroads, Theodore Roosevelt, munitions manufacturers, Woodrow Wilson, or the Supreme Court. La Follette may have changed his incarnations of the "Evil Principle" in the decades after his 1879 presentation of "Iago," but many of the basic themes, assumptions, and psychological tendencies remained the same.

The central unifying element in La Follette's rhetoric is the melodramatic scenario. La Follette began each instance of his simple, moralistic narratives by alluding to a golden age of the past that insidiously came under attack from a villain. The evil adversary unfairly ambushed and, ultimately, enslaved the innocent, unaware victims. La Follette concluded the plot of his melodramatic scenario by pleading for immediate action in order to avoid total submission to the wicked master. In addition, the villain always exhibited three general traits: deceptiveness, dishonesty, and inhumanity.

As a means of reinforcing the unseen yet deadly method of the villain, La Follette used figures of speech that might loosely be called "consumption" metaphors. In the "Iago" oration, the villain's scheme was like delicately-administered poison—too low a dose for the victim to become alarmed, yet enough to ensure a steady wasting away. Seven years later, La Follette characterized oleo as a "plague," a term that also expresses the slow-acting but lethal method of the villain. In addition, La Follette accused oleo of "eating the heart out of an industry [dairy farming] which is to this Government what blood is to the body." The diseased heart metaphor again suggests a gradual death, undetectable at first, but inevitably fatal if not contravened. In a 1907 attack on the U.S. financial industry, La Follette used yet another variation on the consumption theme: "legitimate commercial banking is being eaten up" by financial speculators. As a final example, in 1922 La Follette called the Supreme Court a "monstrous growth upon the body of our Government," which conveys the idea of a malignant tumor that slowly robs vitality from the body politic. All of these manifestations of the consumption metaphor express the concept of an initially hidden, but almost inevitably fatal, entrapment.[1]

An important part of the melodramatic scenario is the concept that the villain springs his clever trap while the unaware victims are distracted by special circumstances. In the "Iago" oration, Othello and Desdemona were so distracted by their love for each other that they did not notice Iago's evil machinations. In La Follette's 1886 attack on the oleomargarine industry and his 1897 assault on the political machine, the innocent victims had been blinded by economic prosperity and spiritual smugness. In vetoing an unacceptable election reform bill in 1901, La Follette explained that the citizens of Wisconsin had been lured into a false sense of security with his election as governor. In condemning a national bill to raise emergency currency, he claimed that the country had been confused by the Panic of 1907. In both his 1916 assault against the munitions industry and his 1922 criticism of the U.S. Supreme Court, he insisted that the population had been diverted by World War I. In each of these cases, a current crisis resulted because people failed to be vigilant about a danger from within. While the victims were always innocent, they made the mistake of being unaware; thus, the people must be forever on guard against the "Evil Principle," in whatever form it may take.[2]

Throughout his career, La Follette characterized the villain as powerful, manipulative, and nearly invincible. In 1879 Iago controlled the fates of all the characters in *Othello*; in 1886 oleo made its way into every home and threatened the foundation of American life; in 1897 the political machine dictated public policy at will and controlled every political position; in 1901 machine lobbyists invaded the hotel rooms of legislators and the very corridors of the Statehouse. In 1908 La Follette identified a "System" that controlled all of industry and banking. The scope of the evil master's influence was ultimately not limited to control of the United States, however. During the controversy surrounding World War I, La Follette claimed that the "great financial masters" had "world-wide power." Thus, by 1916, La Follette had expanded the scope of the villain's domain from the United States to the entire globe. In fact, the scope of the villain's malevolent influence had been increasing steadily in La Follette's rhetoric—from a Shakespearean play, to the oleomargarine industry, to state-wide political corruption, to the dangerous consolidation of national wealth and power, to world-wide domination by financial masters.[3]

As La Follette demonstrated throughout his career, the melodramatic scenario had the potential to persuade people to enlist in his reform crusade. Under ideal conditions, it created a sense of menace or anxiety, the belief that something was wrong. Such a feeling, of course, was necessary for a social reformer like La Follette. He had to demonstrate that there was a need for change. If the audience accepted his description of reality, then action had to be taken immediately because further delay would be fatal. Thus, the melodramatic scenario served well the purpose of a reformer because it tended to spur action.

The melodramatic scenario also was appropriate for a wide range of audiences and circumstances because it provided a vivid, compelling story in an unambiguous, easily-understood form. It had elements of color, suspense, and drama. All of these factors increased audience attention and interest. Consequently, La Follette was able to obtain a hearing, which was again essential for a social reformer. In addition, by virtue of its nature, the melodramatic scenario forced audiences to make a clear choice between good and evil. This necessitated a vote for reform because the alternative was unthinkable. Finally, since melodrama deals inherently in the currency of strong emotions and outraged sensibilities—the unfairness and wickedness of the villain's deeds—the melodramatic scenario encouraged the moral outrage necessary to fuel a reform crusade.

Not only did the melodramatic scenario help to motivate La Follette's political converts, but it provided a way of making sense out of the world, both for himself and his followers. On a basic level, it provided an organizational structure for the substance of his discourse. All of his speeches unfolded in a similar way, which allowed La Follette to produce them quickly and efficiently. But more importantly, the melodramatic scenario provided a clear explanation for events in society. If one of La Follette's proposals was blocked, it was not because his proposal lacked merit but because the enemy subverted it unfairly. If major newspaper editors supported military preparedness, for example, it was only because an unseen master dictated that position. On the other hand, La Follette's version of events was difficult for disbelievers to refute because the villain was, by nature, sly, insidious, secretive, and invisible. Obviously, an unseen opponent is impossible to disprove with absolute certainty.[4]

The melodramatic scenario provided two major reasons to support La Follette's policies: the negative consequences of the villain's actions and the bad character of the enemy. In each speech, he specified the negative consequences of the villain's actions. The enemy caused clear harms to society, such as intruding into homes with impure products, dictating who will hold political office, impeding necessary legislation, stealing wealth from society, or encouraging war. These serious problems could only be solved by embracing a specific panacea such as the direct primary proposal or blocking dangerous legislation such as the emergency currency bill.

Another major reason to support La Follette was the bad moral character of the villain. Throughout his career, La Follette made the moral characters of his opponents and their proposals a major issue. The conspicuous display of moral outrage was central to his discourse. By condemning the immorality of his adversaries, he could make all of their actions and arguments suspect. Denials of wickedness in such an atmosphere only tended to reinforce the validity of his charge. If the villain was cold, immoral, devious, dishonest, secretive, etc., that was sufficient reason to oppose any action the enemy might take. According to this reasoning, bad character led to bad deeds. Even if a villain's policy did not seem to be harmful on the surface, it still should be opposed because it was, no doubt, part of a sly scheme. In addition, it was more dramatic and memorable for La Follette to attack the character of his enemies. Such potent personal attacks tend to linger in the mind long after the confusing details of debate have vanished. Finally, La Follette's vehement expression of moral outrage not only undermined the character of his opponents but also elevated his own ethical standing. As La Follette stated in "Iago," "The emotions are the native soil of moral life. From the feelings are grown great ethical truths, one by one, forming at last the grand body of the moral law." By linking ethics to emotions, La Follette could act out his ethicality by displaying emotional outrage and, not incidentally, provide a contrast with the cold, unfeeling villain.[5]

In the specific case of La Follette, the melodramatic scenario was also a manifestation of his perceptions and mental customs. It was produced by a person who saw the world in stark, black-and-white terms; his rhetoric reveals an unyielding, moralistic personality. La Follette consistently reduced complex social and economic problems into simple scenarios where a villain attempted gradually to ensnare an unsuspecting victim. These scenarios occurred in a world of sharp contrasts; the action was based on the direct comparison of opposites, the derivatives of good and evil. This clear delineation made the construction of melodrama possible; it enabled the villain's actions to be perceived unambiguously. There was no middle ground to complicate the simple plot or to obscure the sense of moral outrage.

In La Follette's melodramatic narratives, the "equation of right" was always stated boldly. La Follette typically talked in terms of moral principles rather than changing circumstances; and, once convinced that he was correct, his verdict became as absolute as the immutable laws of the universe. Because he was fighting against a ruthless, resourceful enemy, he allowed no compromises. He believed that constant vigilance was required against an insidious villain who sought to undermine society. Significantly, over the course of his career, La Follette had many different names for the same monolithic enemy. The oleo industry, the political machine, organized monopoly, the money trusts, concentrated wealth, special privilege, and the System were all manifestations of the "THING" that had to be destroyed in order to restore representative government to the people.

While the melodramatic scenario influenced the perceptions of audiences, it had an equally powerful impact on La Follette himself; in other words, it had a strong self-persuasive quality for the speaker. In a sense, he became captive to an *idée fixe*, and the process by which this happened is analogous to the acquisition of a powerful habit. The first expression of the melodramatic scenario in "Iago" was a natural manifestation of La Follette's world-view and rhetorical personality. "Iago" was praised so lavishly that, consciously or unconsciously, the melodramatic scenario was likely to emerge again. As it was successively repeated and reinforced, the mental habit became more deeply ingrained. Eventually, the melodramatic scenario began to determine rhetorical behavior.

Once La Follette's discourse became subsumed by the melodramatic scenario, it was limited in the paths that it could follow rationally. Compromise with the enemy, for example, was impossible, and only certain types of solutions were adequate to cope with the problems he had outlined. Moderate remedies were patently insufficient to cope with the monstrous "THING." Moreover, the belief in an all-consuming, insidious plot tended to be self-confirming. La Follette could fit every observation or piece of evidence into a sinister mosaic. Such a pattern of thought limited his capacity for new perceptions and creative solutions. Because he thought in terms of the melodramatic scenario, he became incapable of addressing the problems of America in any other way. In short, the melodramatic scenario constrained the perceptions of the speaker as well as the audience.

La Follette's rhetorical imprint projected a compelling view of reality for many audiences because he was elected governor of Wisconsin three times and served for two decades in the U.S. Senate. The dairy farmers and rural-dwellers of Wisconsin, who formed the backbone of La Follette's support, feared the social changes of industrialization, urbanization, and the rise of large, complex organizations. They believed that the wholesome, good, old values of rural America were under attack by insidious villains—political machines, big corporations, railroads, and money trusts. They feared having their lives controlled from afar by the masters of Wall Street. Of course, not everyone in Wisconsin or the Midwest saw the world this way, but La Follette's most loyal supporters probably did.[6]

La Follette was able to articulate these amorphous nightmares, to give them shape and form through the melodramatic scenario, and to provide solutions for stopping the menacing villains. The panaceas he offered, such as the direct primary, were amulets against disturbing social changes (which were in actuality beyond anyone's control). Nevertheless, La Follette captured the anxiety and discontent of his followers and focused it into a powerful reform movement that reached its zenith in Wisconsin around the turn of the century. As the twentieth century progressed, these attitudes became less potent as a political force, although by no means did they disappear.

While the precise character and plot elements in the melodramatic scenario are probably unique to La Follette, it can be categorized as a species of what Richard Hofstadter called the "paranoid style" in American politics. According to Hofstadter, the paranoid style is "a way of seeing the world and of expressing oneself" that recurs in history. While it tends to be exhibited by members of the political right, it can come from any part of the ideological spectrum; however, "In America it has been the preferred style only of *minority* movements." In addition,

the fact that movements employing the paranoid style are not constant but come in successive episodic waves suggests that the paranoid disposition is mobilized into action chiefly by social conflicts that involve ultimate schemes of values and that bring fundamental fears and hatreds, rather than negotiable interests, into political action.

Several examples of the paranoid style provided by Hofstadter relate closely to La Follette's rhetoric: discourse produced by the Populist movement and those who sought to expose a munitions makers' conspiracy during World War I. While La Follette was technically a Republican for almost all of his political career, his rhetoric expressed many of the concerns of these two groups and existed concurrently with them.[7]

Despite the many years he held public office, La Follette is perhaps best understood as an agitator. Most of his rhetoric was devoted to introducing reform ideas and to popularizing them. He did not seem comfortable as an incumbent. As David Thelen has observed, La Follette "preferred exposure, publicity, and election campaigns to the boring daily routine of administering laws and appointing officeholders." La Follette's rhetoric was ideally suited for the long fight, where he had an entrenched enemy to assault. Once in office he continued to seek confrontation with powerful adversaries and to generate issues for extended campaigns.[8]

La Follette brought confrontational tactics into the capitol in Wisconsin and the halls of Congress in Washington. As governor he used surprise legislative messages and vetoes to take his enemies off guard. In the Senate he was a frequent participant in the filibuster, a form of political protest that enabled a small but potent faction to thwart or at least forestall legislative decisions. La Follette used the filibuster as a means of obtaining publicity for his views, of capturing the attention of a large audience, and of wearing down his opponents. In the filibuster La Follette found a natural vehicle for his rhetorical style—very long and redundant speeches that exposed evil and used enormous amounts of evidence.

The scene of La Follette standing virtually alone on the floor of the Senate, speaking to the galleries, is an apt symbol for much of his rhetorical career. Both as governor and senator, La Follette used political office as a platform for addressing the public. Rather than dealing directly with legislators in order to work out compromises, he appealed to the people to exert pressure on his colleagues. La Follette looked over the heads of legislators to address the galleries and the greater public. As a result, while he was often in disfavor with his colleagues, he was almost always popular among his constituency.

Throughout his career La Follette believed his primary rhetorical task was to educate the voters. As he remarked in his *Autobiography*,

I have always felt that the political reformer, like the engineer or the architect, must know that his foundations are right. To build the superstructure in advance of that is likely to be disastrous to the whole thing. He must not put the roof on before he gets the underpinning in. And the underpinning is education of the people.

La Follette believed in following the will of the people, but he realized that on some issues the public could be misinformed or deceived. In such cases, the public needed the proper education. After receiving this instruction, the people would see the truth and move to protect their rights and interests. Thus, La Follette characterized his rhetoric as essentially didactic rather than persuasive. In his mind education implied certain knowledge, and the entire thrust of his rhetoric was based on the concept of absolute truth. "Democracy is based upon knowledge," he wrote in his *Autobiography*:

It is of first importance that the people shall know about their government and the work of their public servants. 'Ye shall know the truth, and the truth shall make you free.' This I have always believed vital to self government.

Such a faith helps account for La Follette's devotion to evidence. "Facts count high everywhere," he said:

Whether the matter in hand is railroad regulation or the tariff, it is always a question of digging out the facts upon which to base your case. . . . Neither laws, nor opinions, nor even constitutions, will finally convince people: it is only the concrete facts of concrete cases.[9]

La Follette's rhetoric was consistent both in concept and technique. His refusal to compromise, his persistence, and his unwavering conviction are the keys to understanding both the successes and limitations of his political career. La Follette was undeniably a successful politician. He held public office for a combined total of thirty-four years. Time and again his political obituary was written in Wisconsin, but from 1900 to 1925 he dominated politics in his home state. While La Follette never obtained his ultimate goal of the presidency, he was an insistent voice of conscience in the Senate, and he made himself heard over the clamor of war. Although he sometimes committed rhetorical excesses, he did so out of a profound sense of responsibility. He believed that someone had to act forcefully if the country was to be saved from impending disaster. He fought with all his heart for the causes in which he believed, and even his opponents admired him for that. He died confident that the future would judge his record kindly and that the will of the people would indeed become the law of the land.

Notes

CHAPTER ONE

1. Robert M. La Follette, quoted in *Madison Democrat*, 10 May 1905.
2. Ernest J. Wrage, "Public Address: A Study in Social and Intellectual History," *Quarterly Journal of Speech* 33 (1947): 453-55.
3. Edwin Black, *Rhetorical Criticism: A Study in Method* (1965; rpt., Madison, Wis.: The University of Wisconsin Press, 1978), 26; Edwin Black, "The Second Persona," *Quarterly Journal of Speech* 56 (1970): 110.
4. David P. Thelen, *Robert M. La Follette and the Insurgent Spirit* (Boston: Little, Brown, and Company, 1976), 16.

CHAPTER TWO

1. Carroll P. Lahman, "Robert Marion La Follette as Public Speaker and Political Leader, 1855-1905," (Ph.D. diss., University of Wisconsin, 1939), 22, 27; Belle Case La Follette and Fola La Follette, *Robert M. La Follette*, 2 vols. (1953; rpt., New York: Hafner Publishing Company, 1971), I, 16, 19; David P. Thelen, *The Early Life of Robert M. La Follette, 1855-1884* (Chicago: Loyola University Press, 1966), 30; Franklin Higgins, quoted in Lahman, "Robert Marion La Follette," 22; Albert O. Barton, "Franklin Higgins, Bob's Early Teacher," *La Follette's Magazine*, February 1929, 29-30.
2. La Follette and La Follette, *Robert M. La Follette*, I, 25-26; Lahman, "Robert Marion La Follette," 46-47; Christopher Gorham, quoted in La Follette and La Follette, *Robert M. La Follette*, I, 26.
3. Lahman, "Robert Marion La Follette," 47-48, 57-60; Thelen, *Early Life*, 28, 31; La Follette and La Follette, *Robert M. La Follette*, I, 28. La Follette appeared on January 23, 1878, at Chapel rhetoricals to deliver an address titled "Tramps." Unfortunately, we do not have a manuscript of this speech. La Follette developed the tramp topic further on July 4, 1879, in

"Home and the State." See La Follette and La Follette, *Robert M. La Follette*, I, 31-32; Lahman, "Robert Marion La Follette," 71-72.

4. Thelen, *Early Life*, 36-39; La Follette and La Follette, *Robert M. La Follette*, I, 30.

5. Thelen, *Early Life*, 39; Lahman, "Robert Marion La Follette," 101-103; Alexander Berger, Letter to Carroll P. Lahman, 16 July 1938, quoted in Lahman, "Robert Marion La Follette," 102; A.N. Hitchcock, Letter to Carroll P. Lahman, 14 July 1938, quoted in Lahman, "Robert Marion La Follette," 103.

6. *The University Press*, 3 Oct. 1876; *The University Press*, 22 Feb., 5 May 1877; *The University Press*, 19 June 1876; *The University Press*, 25 May, 1877.

7. Thelen, *Early Life*, 39-40; La Follette and La Follette, *Robert M. La Follette*, I, 30.

8. Thelen, *Early Life*, 30; La Follette and La Follette, *Robert M. La Follette*, I, 30-31; Lahman, "Robert Marion La Follette," 67-68, 114-16; Belle Case La Follette, "Robert M. La Follette: College Orator," *La Follette's Magazine*, October 1927, 152; Berger, cited in Lahman, "Robert Marion La Follette," 115.

9. Lahman, "Robert Marion La Follette," 116-17; Robert M. La Follette, *La Follette's Autobiography: A Personal Narrative of Political Experiences* (1913; rpt., Madison: The University of Wisconsin Press, 1961), 16. For representative samples of Ingersoll's rhetoric see Robert G. Ingersoll, "Decoration Day Oration," "Speech at Indianapolis, September 21, 1876," and "Bob Ingersoll's Great Republican Speech," in *Complete Lectures of Col. R.G. Ingersoll* (n.p.: n.p., n.d.), n. pag.; Robert G. Ingersoll, "Speech at Cincinnati," "The Past Rises Before Me Like a Dream," and "About Farming in Illinois," in *The Ghosts and other Lectures* (Peoria, Ill., C.P. Farrell, Publisher, 1878), n. pag. Also see Lionel Crocker, "Robert Green Ingersoll's Influence on American Oratory," *Quarterly Journal of Speech* 24 (1938): 299-312.

10. *The University Press*, 19 June 1876; Thelen, *Early Life*, 32; *The University Press*, 3 April 1878; *Wisconsin State Journal* (Madison), 25 March 1878; *Madison Democrat*, 23 March 1878; La Follette and La Follette, *Robert M. La Follette*, I, 32; Lahman, "Robert Marion La Follette," 72-73.

11. Lahman, "Robert Marion La Follette," 69-70; Kemper Knapp, Letter to Carroll P. Lahman, quoted in Lahman, "Robert Marion La Follette," 69; Thelen, *Early Life*, 34-35; La Follette and La Follette, *Robert M. La Follette*, I, 44.

12. La Follette and La Follette, *Robert M. La Follette*, I, 34-35; Lahman, "Robert Marion La Follette," 74-81.

13. Lahman, "Robert Marion La Follette," 78-79; La Follette and La Follette, *Robert M. La Follette*, I, 34; Thelen, *Early Life*, 42-44; Belle Case La Follette, "Robert M. La Follette: College Orator," 152.

14. Robert M. La Follette, "Iago" (n.p.: n.p., [1879]), Pamphlet, State Historical Society of Wisconsin. The complete text of "Iago" is printed in Part II. "Iago" was published originally in pamphlet form. The back cover of the pamphlet bears the following note: "To the large number of friends whose kind words of congratulations were received immediately after the Inter-State Contest the within full text of the oration—Iago—is presented with the compliments of—R.M.L." The text of "Iago" also appeared in Charles Edgar Prather, ed., *Winning Orations of the Inter-State Oratorical Contests* (Topeka, Kan.: Charles Edgar Prather, 1891), 80-86. Parts of this analysis were drawn from my article "Discovering Rhetorical Imprints: La Follette, 'Iago,' and the Melodramatic Scenario," *Quarterly Journal of Speech* 71 (1985): 441-56.

15. Samuel Taylor Coleridge, *Coleridge's Shakespearean Criticism*, ed. Thomas Middleton Raysor (Cambridge: Harvard University Press, 1930), I, 49.

16. Emerson Hough, "La Follette of Wisconsin," *Chicago Daily Review*, quoted in Lahman, "Robert Marion La Follette," 84; Charles Van Hise, Letter to Alice M. Ring, 11 June 1879, quoted in Thelen, *Early Life*, 43; Lahman, "Robert Marion La Follette," 83-86.

17. Prather, *Winning Orations*, 73-77, 53-57, 48-52; Lahman, "Robert Marion La Follette," 79, 84.

18. Prather, *Winning Orations*, 53-57, 48-52.

19. Carroll P. Lahman interview with J.B. Simpson, in Lahman, "Robert Marion La Follette," 79; Lahman, "Robert Marion La Follette," 79, 91-93; Olin A. Curtis, "Satan and Mephistopheles," in Prather, *Winning Orations*, 57.

20. Reverend F.L. Kenyon, quoted in Pauline Grahame, "La Follette Wins," *The Palimpsest*, May 1931, 187-88; La Follette and La Follette, *Robert M. La Follette*, I, 35-36. For additional reactions to "Iago," see *Opinions of the Press: Mr. La Follette's Oratorical Victory* (Madison: The Madison Democrat, [1880]), Pamphlet, State Historical Society of Wisconsin.

21. James Bryce, *The American Commonwealth* (London: Macmillan, 1889), II, 652-53, 655.

22. La Follette and La Follette, *Robert M. La Follette*, I, 36; Thelen, *Early Life*, 44.

23. Thelen, *Early Life*, 45, 50. Ronald H. Carpenter has argued that "Iago" influenced the rhetoric of other people, most notably Frederick Jackson Turner. See Carpenter's "The Rhetorical Genesis of Style in the 'Frontier Hypothesis' of Frederick Jackson Turner," *Southern Speech Communication Journal* 37 (1972): 233-48.

24. Lahman, "Robert Marion La Follette," 109; Thelen, *Early Life*, 48-49; La Follette and La Follette, *Robert M. La Follette*, I, 36.

128 Robert M. La Follette, Sr.

25. For a detailed discussion of rhetorical imprints, see Carl R. Burgchardt, "Discovering Rhetorical Imprints: La Follette, 'Iago,' and the Melodramatic Scenario," *Quarterly Journal of Speech* 71 (1985): 441-56.

CHAPTER THREE

1. Belle Case and Fola La Follette, *Robert M. La Follette*, 2 vols. (1953; rpt., New York: Hafner Publishing Company, 1971), I, 42; Robert M. La Follette, "Home and the State," in *Sun Prairie Countryman*, 10 July 1879.
2. La Follette and La Follette, *Robert M. La Follette*, I, 42; *Sun Prairie Countryman*, 7 July 1879; *Wisconsin State Journal*, 6 July 1880; Carroll P. Lahman, "Robert Marion La Follette as Public Speaker and Political Leader, 1855-1905," (Ph.D. diss., University of Wisconsin, 1939), 144-45.
3. David P. Thelen, *The Early Life of Robert M. La Follette, 1855-1884* (Chicago: Loyola University Press, 1966), 52; *Opinions of the Press: Mr. La Follette's Oratorical Victory* (Madison: The Madison Democrat, [1880]), Pamphlet, State Historical Society of Wisconsin; *Wisconsin State Journal*, 16 Sept. 1880.
4. *Wisconsin State Journal*, 30 Sept., 7 Oct., 1880; *Madison Democrat*, 8 Oct. 1880; Lahman, "Robert Marion La Follette," 169, 174; Thelen, *Early Life*, 57-58, 65, 73-100.
5. La Follette and La Follette, *Robert M. La Follette*, I, 57; Robert M. La Follette, "Memorial Day Address," in *Madison Democrat*, 31 May 1884.
6. La Follette and La Follette, *Robert M. La Follette*, I, 57.
7. La Follette and La Follette, *Robert M. La Follette*, I, 59; Lahman, "Robert Marion La Follette," 187-88; Robert M. La Follette, "Acceptance Speech," in *Wisconsin State Journal*, 12 Sept. 1884.
8. *Wisconsin State Journal*, 10 Sept., 24 Oct. 1884; *Monroe Sun*, 18 Oct. 1884.
9. *Dodgeville Star*, 12 Sept. 1884; *Prairie du Chien Courier*, quoted in *Wisconsin State Journal*, 25 Sept. 1884.
10. Fred Greenbaum, *Robert Marion La Follette* (Boston: Twayne Publishers, 1975), 29-30; La Follette and La Follette, *Robert M. La Follette*, I, 60, 65, 68-69; Lahman, "Robert Marion La Follette," 202; *Wisconsin State Journal*, 27 Oct. 1886; Robert M. La Follette, 22 April 1886, *Cong. Rec.*, 49th Cong., 1st Sess., 3746-48; Robert M. La Follette, 6 May 1886, *Cong. Rec.*, 49th Cong., 1st Sess., 4243-44. The April 22 oration was considered La Follette's "maiden speech" in the House, even though his first speech was a memorial address for Joseph Rankin, delivered on March 25, 1886.
11. La Follette and La Follette, *Robert M. La Follette*, I, 69; Robert M. La Follette, "Oleomargarine," 2 June 1886, *Cong. Rec.*, 49th Cong., 1st Sess., App., 223-26. La Follette articulated similar concepts in his speech on

"Agricultural Experiment Stations," 25 Feb. 1887, *Cong. Rec.*, 49th Cong., 2d Sess., App., 147; Lahman, "Robert Marion La Follette," 221-22, 227-28.

12. Robert M. La Follette, "Interstate Commerce," 20 Jan. 1887, *Cong. Rec.*, 49th Cong., 2d Sess., App., 185, 187, 188. In February of 1889 La Follette spoke out against the practice of railroads controlling grain elevators along the major lines. See 6 Feb. 1889, *Cong. Rec.*, 50th Cong., 2d Sess., 1586.

13. Lahman, "Robert Marion La Follette," 233-34; La Follette and La Follette, *Robert M. La Follette*, I, 76-77.

14. Robert M. La Follette, 14 July 1888, *Cong. Rec.*, 50th Cong., 1st Sess., 6307-11. La Follette and La Follette, *Robert M. La Follette*, I, 76-78; Lahman, "Robert Marion La Follette," 236-37. Less than a week later, La Follette argued in favor of high protective tariffs for American tobacco. See Robert M. La Follette, 19 July 1888, *Cong. Rec.*, 50th Cong., 1st Sess., 6513-15.

15. Robert M. La Follette, 13 Feb. 1889, *Cong. Rec.*, 50th Cong., 2d Sess., 1866; Lahman, "Robert Marion La Follette," 238-40.

16. La Follette and La Follette, *Robert M. La Follette*, I, 79-81; Robert M. La Follette, 10 May 1890, *Cong. Rec.*, 51st Cong., 1st Sess., 4473-82. Lahman, "Robert Marion La Follette," 248-51.

17. Robert M. La Follette, "Proposed Federal Election Law," 2 July 1890, *Cong. Rec.*, 51st Cong., 1st Sess., App., 469; Lahman, "Robert Marion La Follette," 241.

18. Lahman, "Robert Marion La Follette," 251-52; Robert M. La Follette, "Original-Package Bill," 19 July 1890, *Cong. Rec.*, 51st Cong., 1st Sess., App., 518; La Follette and La Follette, *Robert M. La Follette*, I, 87-89.

19. *Wisconsin State Journal*, 16 Sept., 30 Oct. 1886; *Wisconsin State Journal*, 12 Oct., 7 Nov. 1888; Lahman, "Robert Marion La Follette," 221, 224-28, 245-46.

20. La Follette and La Follette, *Robert M. La Follette*, I, 87-89; Lahman, "Robert Marion La Follette," 260.

21. La Follette and La Follette, *Robert M. La Follette*, I, 90; Thelen, *Insurgent Spirit*, 14-15; Lahman, "Robert Marion La Follette," 260-65; *New York Tribune*, 8 Nov. 1890.

22. La Follette, "Home and the State"; La Follette, "Memorial Day Address"; La Follette, 22 April 1886, *Cong. Rec.*; La Follette, 13 Feb. 1889, *Cong. Rec.*; La Follette, 19 July 1888, *Cong. Rec.*; La Follette, "Original-Package Bill."

23. La Follette, "Oleomargarine," 225-26. This text is reproduced in Part II.

24. Robert M. La Follette, "Iago" (n.p.: n.p., [1879]), Pamphlet, State Historical Society of Wisconsin. This text is reproduced in Part II.

25. La Follette, 10 May 1890, *Cong. Rec.*, 4473-74.
26. La Follette, "Memorial Day Address"; La Follette, 13 Feb. 1889, *Cong. Rec.*, 1870-71; La Follette, 2 July 1890, *Cong. Rec.*, 468.
27. La Follette, "Oleomargarine," 223-26. Also see La Follette, 10 May 1890, *Cong. Rec.*, 4475; La Follette, 25 Feb. 1887, *Cong. Rec.*, 147.
28. La Follette, "Memorial Day Address." Also see La Follette, 10 May 1890, *Cong. Rec.*, 4475; La Follette, "Original-Package Bill," 518.
29. La Follette, "Interstate Commerce," 185-88; *Milwaukee Free Press*, 5 Nov. 1904; Robert M. La Follette, *La Follette's Autobiography: A Personal Narrative of Political Experiences* (1913; rpt., Madison: The University of Wisconsin Press, 1961), 52. Also see La Follette, 6 Feb. 1889, *Cong. Rec.*, 1586.
30. Robert M. La Follette, "Permanent Republican Clubs," *North American Review*, 146 (1888), 249. Robert M. La Follette, Speech on Republican Clubs, March 14, 1888, in *Wisconsin State Journal*, 15 March 1888; Robert M. La Follette, "Speech ca. 1890," La Follette Papers, State Historical Society of Wisconsin; La Follette, 13 Feb. 1889, *Cong. Rec.*, 1866, 1870; La Follette, "Proposed Federal Election Law," 468-69.
31. La Follette, 19 July 1888, *Cong. Rec.*, 6515.
32. La Follette, "Oleomargarine," 223-29. Also see La Follette, 22 April 1886, *Cong. Rec.*, 3746-47; La Follette, 13 Feb. 1889, *Cong. Rec.*, 1866.
33. La Follette, "Proposed Federal Election Law," 468; La Follette, 10 May 1890, *Cong. Rec.*, 4476-77.
34. La Follette, 10 May 1890, *Cong. Rec.*, 4478, 4481. Also see La Follette, 14 July 1888, *Cong. Rec.*, 6310-11.
35. La Follette, 14 July 1888, *Cong. Rec.*, 6309.

CHAPTER FOUR

1. Carroll P. Lahman, "Robert Marion La Follette as Public Speaker and Political Leader, 1855-1905," (Ph.D. diss., University of Wisconsin, 1939), 318-20; Belle Case and Fola La Follette, *Robert M. La Follette*, 2 vols. (1953; rpt., New York: Hafner Publishing Company, 1971), I, 95-97.
2. La Follette and La Follette, *Robert M. La Follette*, I, 97-98; *Milwaukee Sentinel*, 27 Oct., 29 Oct. 1891.
3. La Follette and La Follette, *Robert M. La Follette*, I, 99; David P. Thelen, *Robert M. La Follette and the Insurgent Spirit* (Boston: Little, Brown, and Company, 1976), 19; *Milwaukee Journal*, 4 Aug. 1897; Lahman, "Robert Marion La Follette," 324-26.
4. Thelen, *Insurgent Spirit*, 19-20; La Follette and La Follette, *Robert M. La Follette*, I, 103-104; Fred Greenbaum, *Robert Marion La Follette* (Boston: Twayne Publishers, 1975), 36.

5. Lahman, "Robert Marion La Follette," 329-34; *Dunn County News* (Menomonie), 4 Nov. 1892; *Wisconsin State Journal*, 26 Oct. 1892; *Evansville Review*, 25 Oct. 1892; *Chippewa Herald*, 4 Nov. 1892.

6. Thelen, *Insurgent Spirit*, 19-20; La Follette and La Follette, *Robert M. La Follette*, I, 106-107; Herbert F. Margulies, *The Decline of the Progressive Movement in Wisconsin: 1890-1920* (Madison: State Historical Society of Wisconsin, 1968), 24-29.

7. La Follette and La Follette, *Robert M. La Follette*, I, 107-109; Lahman, "Robert Marion La Follette," 348-61; Robert M. La Follette, Campaign Document, June 15, 1894, in Lahman, "Robert Marion La Follette," Appendix, 341-42; Albert O. Barton, *La Follette's Winning of Wisconsin (1894-1904)* (Des Moines, Iowa: The Homestead Company, 1922), 67.

8. La Follette and La Follette, *Robert M. La Follette*, I, 113-15; Robert M. La Follette, "Speech Seconding the Nomination of Henry Clay Evans of Tennessee," in Lahman, "Robert M. La Follette," Appendix, 32; *Whitewater Register*, 2 July 1896.

9. *Milwaukee Sentinel*, 2 July 1896; Lahman, "Robert Marion La Follette," 375-81; Thelen, *Insurgent Spirit*, 21.

10. Greenbaum, *Robert Marion La Follette*, 39-40; Robert M. La Follette, Campaign Letter, 1896, in Lahman, "Robert Marion La Follette," Appendix, 343; Lahman, "Robert Marion La Follette," 381-88; Margulies, *Decline*, 32; Thelen, *Insurgent Spirit*, 21.

11. Lahman, "Robert Marion La Follette," 388-95; Robert M. La Follette, Campaign Speech, Milwaukee, November 2, 1896, in *Milwaukee Sentinel*, 3 Nov. 1896; Greenbaum, *Robert Marion La Follette*, 40; La Follette and La Follette, *Robert M. La Follette*, I, 117-21.

12. Thelen, *Insurgent Spirit*, 21; Greenbaum, *Robert Marion La Follette*, 40-43; Lahman, "Robert Marion La Follette," 395-97, 401; Margulies, *Decline*, 35-36.

13. Margulies, *Decline*, 36; La Follette and La Follette, *Robert M. La Follette*, I, 119.

14. Lahman, "Robert Marion La Follette," 398; La Follette and La Follette, *Robert M. La Follette*, I, 120; Robert M. La Follette, "The Menace of the Political Machine," in *Milwaukee Sentinel*, 23 Feb. 1897. The complete text of this speech is printed in Part II.

15. *Milwaukee Sentinel*, 23 Feb. 1897; Lahman, "Robert Marion La Follette," 402-403; La Follette and La Follette, *Robert M. La Follette*, I, 120; Greenbaum, *Robert Marion La Follette*, 44.

16. Margulies, *Decline*, 37; La Follette and La Follette, *Robert M. La Follette*, I, 121-24; Greenbaum, *Robert Marion La Follette*, 44; Lahman, "Robert Marion La Follette," 407-408.

132 Robert M. La Follette, Sr.

17. The most widely available version of "The Dangers Threatening Representative Government" was delivered on September 24, 1897, at the state fair in Milwaukee and later published in *The State*, 24 June 1898.

18. *Wisconsin State Journal*, 7 July 1897; *Sauk County Democrat* (Baraboo), 2 Sept. 1897; *Milwaukee Journal*, 27 Aug. 1897; Greenbaum, *Robert Marion La Follette*, 44; Lahman, "Robert Marion La Follette," 404-405; *Milwaukee Journal*, 4 Sept. 1897; *Milwaukee Sentinel*, 10 Sept. 1897; *Milwaukee Journal*, 22 Sept. 1897; *Milwaukee Sentinel*, 25 Sept., 1 Oct. 1897; Milwaukee Journal, 2 Oct. 1897. La Follette's concern about being misquoted was to become a central issue in his career, particularly during the controversial period surrounding World War I.

19. B.J. Daly, quoted in Barton, *Winning*, 91-92.

20. *Milwaukee Journal*, 2 Oct. 1897.

21. *Milwaukee Journal*, 27 Aug. 1897; B.J. Daly, quoted in Barton, *Winning*, 91; *Milwaukee Journal*, 4 Sept. 1897.

22. *Milwaukee Sentinel*, 25 Sept. 1897; Thelen, *Insurgent Spirit*, 21-24; Margulies, *Decline*, 24-25.

23. Lahman, "Robert Marion La Follette," 403-404; Margulies, *Decline*, 40-41.

24. La Follette and La Follette, *Robert M. La Follette*, I, 125; Robert M. La Follette, "Primary Elections for the Nomination of All Candidates by Australian Ballot," in *The State*, 27 July 1900; Lahman, "Robert Marion La Follette," 489; See *Primary Elections for the Nominations of All Candidates by Australian Ballot* (n.p.: n.p., [1900]), Pamphlet, State Historical Society of Wisconsin.

25. La Follette and La Follette, *Robert M. La Follette*, I, 126; Lahman, "Robert Marion La Follette," 424; Robert M. La Follette, "An Address to the Republicans of Wisconsin" (n.p.: n.p., [1898]), Pamphlet, Robert M. La Follette Papers, State Historical Society of Wisconsin.

26. Lahman, "Robert Marion La Follette," 431-38; Greenbaum, *Robert Marion La Follette*, 46; Thelen, *Insurgent Spirit*, 29-30.

27. *Republican State Platform of 1898*, in Lahman, "Robert Marion La Follette," Appendix, 352; Barton, *Winning*, 136-37; Margulies, *Decline*, 43-44.

28. La Follette and La Follette, *Robert M. La Follette*, I, 129-30; Margulies, *Decline*, 44-45; Lahman, "Robert Marion La Follette," 443-44; Barton, *Winning*, 138.

29. Greenbaum, *Robert Marion La Follette*, 47-48; Lahman, "Robert Marion La Follette," 448-49, 453-54.

30. La Follette and La Follette, *Robert M. La Follette*, I, 131; Lahman, "Robert Marion La Follette," 452-53; Robert M. La Follette, "Campaign Announcement of 1900," in *Milwaukee Daily News*, 16 May 1900.

31. Greenbaum, *Robert Marion La Follette*, 48-49; La Follette and La Follette, *Robert M. La Follette*, I, 132; Thelen, *Insurgent Spirit*, 31.

32. Lahman, "Robert Marion La Follette," 459-60; Robert M. La Follette, "Acceptance Speech of 1900," Manuscript, La Follette Papers, State Historical Society of Wisconsin, 6. Also see, *Milwaukee Sentinel*, 9 Aug. 1900.

33. Margulies, *Decline*, 48; La Follette and La Follette, *Robert M. La Follette*, I, 133-34.

34. Robert M. La Follette, Campaign Speech, Milwaukee, September 19, 1900, in *Milwaukee Sentinel*, 20 Sept. 1900.

35. Lahman, "Robert Marion La Follette," 472-74; Barton, *Winning*, 160; *Milwaukee Sentinel*, 4 Nov. 1900; La Follette and La Follette, *Robert M. La Follette*, I, 135.

36. Barton, *Winning*, 163-64; Lahman, "Robert Marion La Follette," 474; La Follette and La Follette, *Robert M. La Follette*, I, 135; Thelen, *Insurgent Spirit*, 31.

37. Robert M. La Follette, "Memorial Day Address," in *Madison Democrat*, 31 May 1884.

38. For other examples of this, see La Follette, "Representative Government" and La Follette, "Primary Elections for the Nomination of All Candidates by Australian Ballot."

39. Robert M. La Follette, "Iago" (n.p.: n.p., [1879]), Pamphlet, State Historical Society of Wisconsin. The text of this speech is printed in Part II. Portions of this analysis were drawn from my article "Discovering Rhetorical Imprints: La Follette, 'Iago,' and the Melodramatic Scenario," *Quarterly Journal of Speech* 71 (1985): 448.

40. Also see La Follette, "Representative Government."

41. La Follette's speech of May 10, 1890, on the McKinley tariff is a good example of a previous address that relied extensively on the device of contrast (10 May 1890, *Cong. Rec.*, 51st Cong., 1st Sess., 4473-74).

42. See La Follette, "Primary Elections" and La Follette, "Representative Government," for other examples.

43. La Follette, "Representative Government."

44. La Follette, "Representative Government"; La Follette, "Acceptance Speech of 1900," 4, 6. When La Follette's loyalty was questioned during World War I, he used the same tactic of redefinition. He argued that vocal dissent was the highest kind of loyalty to the United States.

45. La Follette, "Representative Government."

46. La Follette, "Primary Elections."

47. La Follette and La Follette, *Robert M. La Follette*, I, 131; Greenbaum, *Robert Marion La Follette*, 48.

134 Robert M. La Follette, Sr.

CHAPTER FIVE

1. Albert O. Barton, *La Follette's Winning of Wisconsin (1894-1904)* (Des Moines, Iowa: The Homestead Company, 1922), 166-68; Belle Case La Follette and Fola La Follette, *Robert M. La Follette* (1953; rpt., New York: Hafner Publishing Company, 1971), I, 137-38; Robert M. La Follette, "First Inaugural Address," in 10 Jan. 1901, *Senate Journal*, State of Wisconsin, 45th Sess., 56, 16, 34-35, 31-38, 19-31, 47-49, 38-41, 49-50.
2. Herbert F. Margulies, *The Decline of the Progressive Movement in Wisconsin: 1890-1920* (Madison: State Historical Society of Wisconsin, 1968), 51; *Milwaukee Journal*, 10 Jan. 1901; Barton, *Winning*, 169.
3. Barton, *Winning*, 170-73; La Follette and La Follette, *Robert M. La Follette*, I, 138-39, 142; Carroll P. Lahman, "Robert Marion La Follette as Public Speaker and Political Leader, 1855-1905," (Ph.D. diss., University of Wisconsin, 1939), 534-55; Emanuel L. Philipp, *Political Reform in Wisconsin*, ed. Stanley P. Caine and Roger W. Wyman (Madison: State Historical Society of Wisconsin, 1973), 27-29.
4. La Follette and La Follette, *Robert M. La Follette*, I, 142; Lahman, "Robert Marion La Follette," 566-74; Barton, *Winning*, 177-78; Robert M. La Follette, "Dog-Tax Veto," in 2 May 1901, *Assembly Journal*, State of Wisconsin, 45th Sess., 1084.
5. Lahman, "Robert Marion La Follette," 574-75; La Follette and La Follette, *Robert M. La Follette*, I, 142-43; Barton, *Winning*, 179.
6. Barton, *Winning*, 173-74; *Wisconsin State Journal*, 4 May 1901. Robert M. La Follette, "Veto Message," in 10 May 1901, *Senate Journal*, State of Wisconsin, 45th Sess., 1026, 1027-35.
7. 11 May 1901, *Senate Journal*, State of Wisconsin, 45th Sess., 1062; Lahman, "Robert Marion La Follette," 562-64; *Milwaukee Sentinel* and (Milwaukee) *Evening Wisconsin*, quoted in *Wisconsin State Journal*, 11 May 1901.
8. Philipp, *Political Reform*, 45; La Follette and La Follette, *Robert M. La Follette*, I, 144.
9. La Follette and La Follette, *Robert M. La Follette*, I, 146-48; Robert M. La Follette, "Address to Farmers' Institute," in *Voters' Hand-Book* (Milwaukee: Milwaukee Free Press, 1902), Pamphlet, State Historical Society of Wisconsin, 117-18; Robert M. La Follette, Campaign Speech, Grand Rapids, June 4, 1902, in *Milwaukee Free Press*, 5 June 1902; Robert M. La Follette, Campaign Speech, Blue Mounds, July 4, 1902, in *Milwaukee Free Press*, 5 July 1902; *Milwaukee Daily News*, 20 March 1902; *Milwaukee Journal*, 20 March 1902; *Milwaukee Sentinel*, 20 March 1902; *Milwaukee Free Press*, 21 March 1902.

10. Margulies, *Decline*, 64; Lahman, "Robert Marion La Follette," 641-42; Barton, *Winning*, 200-01, 207-08; *Wisconsin State Journal*, 17 July 1902.

11. *Wisconsin State Journal*, 17 July 1902; *Milwaukee Free Press*, 18 July 1902; Robert M. La Follette, "Acceptance Speech," July 16, 1902, in *Republican Platform and Gov. La Follette's Acceptance Speech* (n.p.: n.p., [1902]), Pamphlet, State Historical Society of Wisconsin, n. pag. The text of this speech is reproduced in Part II.

12. *Wisconsin State Journal*, 17 July 1902; *Milwaukee Free Press*, 18 July 1902; *Milwaukee Journal*, 17 July 1902; Lahman, "Robert Marion La Follette," 648-49. Also see, *Milwaukee Sentinel*, 18 July 1902.

13. Lahman, "Robert Marion La Follette," 653, 658-60; *Milwaukee Sentinel*, 1 Oct. 1902; Robert M. La Follette, Campaign Speech, Milwaukee, September 30, 1902, in *Governor La Follette on National and State Issues* (Milwaukee: Allied Printing, [1902]), Pamphlet, State Historical Society of Wisconsin, 1-29. 27, 11-12, 29.

14. *Milwaukee Sentinel*, 1 Oct. 1902; *Milwaukee Journal*, 1 Oct. 1902; *Wisconsin State Journal*, 1 Oct. 1902; Barton, *Winning*, 217-30; Lahman, "Robert Marion La Follette," 672-75. For a more detailed account of the election campaign, see *Milwaukee Free Press*, 10-13 Oct., 16 Oct., 27 Oct., 2 Nov. 1902.

15. Lahman, "Robert Marion La Follette," 703-704; Fred Greenbaum, *Robert Marion La Follette* (Boston: Twayne Publishers, 1975), 56; Thelen, *Insurgent Spirit*, 38-39.

16. La Follette and La Follette, *Robert M. La Follette*, I, 157; Lahman, "Robert Marion La Follette," 731; Robert M. La Follette, "Second Inaugural Address," in *Message of Robert M. La Follette, Governor of Wisconsin, January 15, 1903* (Madison: Democrat Printing Co., State Printer, 1903), Pamphlet, State Historical Society of Wisconsin, 1-98.

17. Lahman, "Robert Marion La Follette," 740; La Follette and La Follette, *Robert M. La Follette*, I, 157; La Follette, "Second Inaugural Address," 24-25.

18. La Follette, "Second Inaugural Address," 34, 55-56, 25-26, 52.

19. Lahman, "Robert Marion La Follette," 746-48; *Milwaukee Daily News*, 16 Jan. 1903; *Wisconsin State Journal*, 15 Jan. 1903; *Milwaukee Sentinel*, 16 Jan. 1903.

20. *Milwaukee Journal*, 26 March 1903; Lahman, "Robert Marion La Follette," 750-60; La Follette and La Follette, *Robert M. La Follette*, I, 159-60; Thelen, *Insurgent Spirit*, 39.

21. Lahman, "Robert Marion La Follette," 760-62; Robert M. La Follette, Special Message of April 23, 1903, in 28 April 1903, *Senate Journal*, State of Wisconsin, 46th Sess., 848-50; *Wisconsin State Journal*, 24 April 1903.

136 Robert M. La Follette, Sr.

22. La Follette and La Follette, *Robert M. La Follette*, I, 158; Lahman, "Robert Marion La Follette," 762-63; Robert M. La Follette, Special Message of April 28, 1903, in *State Regulation of Railroad Rates: Special Message of Robert M. La Follette, Governor of Wisconsin* (Madison: Democrat Printing Company, State Printer, 1903), Pamphlet, State Historical Society of Wisconsin, 25, 107, 12; *Milwaukee Sentinel*, 30 April 1903; Resolution of Protest, quoted in Lahman, "Robert Marion La Follette," 767.

23. Lahman, "Robert Marion La Follette," 767-69; Robert M. La Follette, Special Message of May 7, 1903, in 8 May 1903, *Senate Journal*, State of Wisconsin, 46th Sess., 1006-1009; La Follette and La Follette, *Robert M. La Follette*, I, 159.

24. La Follette and La Follette, *Robert M. La Follette*, I, 157-58; Thelen, *Insurgent Spirit*, 40; Lahman, "Robert Marion La Follette," 769, 776; Emanuel Philipp, *Political Reform*, 177; Robert M. La Follette, quoted in Barton, *Winning*, 262; *Wisconsin State Journal*, 27 April 1903.

25. Barton, *Winning*, 276-77; Lahman, "Robert Marion La Follette," 785-89; La Follette and La Follette, *Robert M. La Follette*, I, 165-68; *Milwaukee Sentinel*, 26 Sept. 1903; *Milwaukee Free Press*, 28 June, 19 July, 31 July 1903; *Madison Democrat*, 19 July 1903; Thelen, *Insurgent Spirit*, 41; Robert M. La Follette, "Hamlet: The World's Greatest Tragedy," Manuscript, La Follette Papers, State Historical Society of Wisconsin, 5, 8, 12.

26. La Follette, "Hamlet," 38, 36-37.

27. Lahman, "Robert Marion La Follette," 789-802; Philipp, *Political Reform*, 178; Barton, *Winning*, 281-82; *Madison Democrat*, 28 Aug. 1903; *Wisconsin State Journal*, 8 Sept. 1903; *Milwaukee Sentinel*, 25 Sept. 1903; *Milwaukee Journal*, 1 Oct. 1903; *Milwaukee Free Press*, 3 Sept., 5 Sept., 6 Sept., 10 Sept., 24 Sept., 1 Oct. 1903.

28. Barton, *Winning*, 281-82; *Milwaukee Journal*, 1 Oct. 1903.

29. Lahman, "Robert Marion La Follette," 802-807; Barton, *Winning*, 289.

30. Lahman, "Robert Marion La Follette," 813, 823-24; *Wisconsin State Journal*, 7 Aug. 1903; Barton, *Winning*, 293-95.

31. Lahman, "Robert Marion La Follette," 816-17, 808; Barton, *Winning*, 335.

32. Robert M. La Follette, *Granger Legislation and State Control of Railway Rates* (n.p.: n.p., [1904]), Pamphlet, State Historical Society of Wisconsin, 24, 18-20, 6, 3.

33. *Mt. Horeb Times*, quoted in *Milwaukee Free Press*, 6 Feb. 1904; *Wood County Reporter*, 19 April 1904; Barton, *Winning*, 312-15; Lahman, "Robert Marion La Follette," 810-11, 832-33; *Milwaukee Free Press*, 23 April, 24 April, 4 May 1904; *Milwaukee Sentinel*, 4 May 1904; Campaign Speech, Milwaukee, April 22, 1904, in *Milwaukee Free Press*, 23 April 1904; Campaign

Speech, La Crosse, April 22, 1904, Manuscript, La Follette Papers, State Historical Society of Wisconsin.

34. Lahman, "Robert Marion La Follette," 846, 853, 858; Robert M. La Follette, "Acceptance Speech," May 19, 1904, in *Speech of Gov. La Follette Accepting the Nomination* (Milwaukee: Keystone Press, [1904]), Pamphlet, State Historical Society of Wisconsin, 7.

35. Lahman, "Robert Marion La Follette," 878-82; Barton, *Winning*, 392, 400-01; La Follette and La Follette, *Robert M. La Follette*, I, 183-84; Margulies, *Decline*, 66-67.

36. Lahman, "Robert Marion La Follette," 830-31, 836; Margulies, *Decline*, 70; La Follette and La Follette, *Robert M. La Follette*, I, 172-73; Thelen, *Insurgent Spirit*, 41-42; Robert M. La Follette, Campaign Speech, Milwaukee, November 4, 1904, in *Milwaukee Free Press*, 5 Nov. 1904.

37. La Follette and La Follette, *Robert M. La Follette*, I, 172-73; Robert M. La Follette, *La Follette's Autobiography* (Madison: University of Wisconsin Press, 1961), 142-43.

38. La Follette and La Follette, *Robert M. La Follette*, I, 183-84; Barton, *Winning*, 431-51; Lahman, "Robert Marion La Follette," 919-20; Thelen, *Insurgent Spirit*, 44-45; Greenbaum, *Robert Marion La Follette*, 62-63; Margulies, *Decline*, 79.

39. Lahman, "Robert Marion La Follette," 954-55; Robert M. La Follette, "Third Inaugural Address," January 12, 1905, in *Message of Governor Robert M. La Follette to the Wisconsin Legislature, Regular Session, 1905* (n.p.: n.p., 1905), Document Department, State Historical Society of Wisconsin, 78, 22, 72-73, 96; La Follette and La Follette, *Robert M. La Follette*, I, 187-88.

40. La Follette, "Third Inaugural Address," 45, 65.

41. Lahman, "Robert Marion La Follette," 957-62; La Follette and La Follette, *Robert M. La Follette*, I, 189.

42. Robert M. La Follette, "Speech Accepting Election to the United States Senate," in 25 Jan. 1905, *Senate Journal*, State of Wisconsin, 47th Sess., 171-73.

43. *Milwaukee Daily News*, 17 June 1905; Lahman, "Robert Marion La Follette," 992-93, 986-87, 973-75; La Follette and La Follette, *Robert M. La Follette*, I, 191-92; *Milwaukee Journal*, 19 May 1905.

44. La Follette and La Follette, *Robert M. La Follette*, I, 193-94; Lahman, "Robert Marion La Follette," 1002-1005; Robert Stuart MacArthur, "Chautauqua Assemblies and Political Ambitions," *The World To-day*, October 1905, 1075-76; Charles L. Wagner and Charles W. Bentley, quoted in Lahman, "Robert Marion La Follette," 1102-1103.

45. Lahman, "Robert Marion La Follette," 1006-1008, 1010-11, 1014-20; La Follette and La Follette, *Robert M. La Follette*, I, 197-98; Robert M. La Follette, "Message to the Wisconsin Legislature," December 5, 1905, in

138 Robert M. La Follette, Sr.

Message of Governor Robert M. La Follette to the Wisconsin Legislature, Special Session, 1905 (n.p.: n.p., [1905]), Pamphlet, State Historical Society of Wisconsin, 4, 18, 31; Robert M. La Follette, "Message Read to the Legislature Announcing Decision to Resign as Governor, December 5, 1905," in *Milwaukee Free Press*, 6 Dec. 1905.

46. La Follette, "Veto Message," May 10, 1901, 1032. Also see "Acceptance Speech," July 16, 1902.

47. La Follette, Campaign Speech, Blue Mounds, July 4, 1902.

48. La Follette, "Acceptance Speech," July 16, 1902; La Follette, Campaign Speech, Milwaukee, April 22, 1904.

49. Robert M. La Follette, Campaign Speech, Plymouth, September 2, 1903, in *Milwaukee Free Press*, 3 Sept. 1903. Also see manuscript marked "Plymouth" in La Follette Papers, State Historical Society of Wisconsin.

50. La Follette, "Farmers' Institute," 118; La Follette, "Acceptance Speech," July 16, 1902.

51. La Follette, *Granger Legislation*, 19, 24.

52. La Follette, "Acceptance Speech," May 19, 1904, 7-8.

53. La Follette, Campaign Speech, Grand Rapids, June 4, 1902; La Follette, Campaign Speech, Blue Mounds, July 4, 1902; La Follette, "Acceptance Speech," July 16, 1902.

54. La Follette, "Veto Message," May 10, 1901, 1028-29, 1032. Also see La Follette, "Acceptance Speech," July 16, 1902.

55. La Follette, "Second Inaugural Address," 25-26, 51-52. Also see La Follette, Campaign Speech, Milwaukee, November 4, 1904.

56. La Follette, Campaign Speech, Milwaukee, April 22, 1904; La Follette, Campaign Speech, Milwaukee, November 4, 1904.

57. La Follette, Campaign Speech, Milwaukee, April 22, 1904.

58. La Follette and La Follette, *Robert M. La Follette*, I, 191-92.

CHAPTER SIX

1. Belle Case La Follette and Fola La Follette, *Robert M. La Follette*, 2 vols. (1953; rpt., New York: Hafner Publishing Company, 1971), I, 202-204; Fred Greenbaum, *Robert Marion La Follette* (Boston: Twayne Publishers, 1975), 69-71; David P. Thelen, *Robert M. La Follette and the Insurgent Spirit* (Boston: Little, Brown and Company, 1976), 56.

2. La Follette and La Follette, *Robert M. La Follette*, I, 204-205; Greenbaum, *Robert Marion La Follette*, 72; Robert M. La Follette, "Regulation of Railroad Rates," 23 April 1906, *Cong. Rec.*, 59th Cong., 1st Sess., 5688.

3. La Follette, "Regulation of Railroad Rates," 5708, 5710-11, 5688-89, 5720, 5693, 5714, 5722, 5684, 5688, 5705. For similar speeches on railroad rate regulation, see Robert M. La Follette, 12 April 1910, *Cong. Rec.*, 61st

Cong., 2d Sess., 4549-64; Robert M. La Follette, 29 April 1910, *Cong. Rec.*, 61st Cong., 2d Sess., 5563-66; Robert M. La Follette, 26 May 1910, *Cong. Rec.*, 61st Cong., 2d Sess., 6896-6909; Robert M. La Follette, 31 May 1910, *Cong. Rec.*, 61st Cong., 2d Sess., 7139-44; Robert M. La Follette, 3 June 1910, *Cong. Rec.*, 61st Cong., 2d Sess., 7372-74.

4. Thelen, *Insurgent Spirit*, 62-63; La Follette and La Follette, *Robert M. La Follette*, I, 239-40; Greenbaum, *Robert Marion La Follette*, 77.

5. La Follette and La Follette, *Robert M. La Follette*, I, 240-43; Thelen, *Insurgent Spirit*, 63-64; Robert M. La Follette, "Amendment of National Banking Laws," 17 March 1908, *Cong. Rec.*, 60th Cong., 1st Sess., 3434-53; 19 March 1908, *Cong. Rec.*, 60th Cong., 1st Sess., 3566-78; 24 March 1908, *Cong. Rec.*, 60th Cong., 1st Sess., 3793-3800.

6. La Follette, "Amendment of National Banking Laws," 17 March 1908, *Cong. Rec.*, 3434-35, 3449, 3452; 19 March 1908, *Cong. Rec.*, 3569, 3574; 24 March 1908, *Cong. Rec.*, 3795; 19 March 1908, *Cong. Rec.*, 3566; 17 March 1908, *Cong. Rec.*, 3451; 24 March 1908, *Cong. Rec.*, 3795, 3799; 19 March 1908, *Cong. Rec.*, 3574.

7. La Follette and La Follette, *Robert M. La Follette*, I, 244-45; Greenbaum, *Robert Marion La Follette*, 78; Thelen, *Insurgent Spirit*, 64.

8. La Follette and La Follette, *Robert M. La Follette*, I, 245-56; Greenbaum, *Robert Marion La Follette*, 78-79; Thelen, *Insurgent Spirit*, 64-65; Robert M. La Follette, 29 May 1908, *Cong. Rec.*, 60th Cong., 1st Sess., 7161-7201; Robert M. La Follette, 30 May 1908, *Cong. Rec.*, 60th Cong., 1st Sess., 7221-26.

9. Thelen, *Insurgent Spirit*, 65.

10. Thelen, *Insurgent Spirit*, 69-72; La Follette and La Follette, *Robert M. La Follette*, I, 272-75.

11. Robert M. La Follette, 9 June 1909, *Cong. Rec.*, 61st Cong., 1st Sess., 3013-28; Robert M. La Follette, 11 June 1909, *Cong. Rec.*, 61st Cong., 1st Sess., 3126-27; La Follette, 9 June 1909, *Cong. Rec.*, 3022.

12. La Follette and La Follette, *Robert M. La Follette*, I, 275-76; Greenbaum, *Robert Marion La Follette*, 87-88.

13. La Follette and La Follette, *Robert M. La Follette*, I, 278; Greenbaum, *Robert Marion La Follette*, 89; Robert M. La Follette, 5 Aug. 1909, *Cong. Rec.*, 61st Cong., 1st Sess., 4954; Thelen, *Insurgent Spirit*, 74; La Follette, 9 June 1909, *Cong. Rec.*, 3013. For similar tariff arguments, see Robert M. La Follette, 21 July 1911, *Cong. Rec.*, 62d Cong., 1st Sess., 3139-53; Robert M. La Follette, 27 July 1911, *Cong. Rec.*, 62d Cong., 1st Sess., 3264-67; Robert M. La Follette, 15 Aug. 1911, *Cong. Rec.*, 62d Cong., 1st Sess., 3943-46, 3951-55; Robert M. La Follette, 19 Aug. 1911, *Cong. Rec.*, 62d Cong., 1st Sess., 4183-90.

14. La Follette and La Follette, *Robert M. La Follette*, I, 211-12, 215-16, 230-37, 260-62; Greenbaum, *Robert Marion La Follette*, 73-74; Thelen, *Insurgent Spirit*, 57-58, 61-62. For a version of La Follette's Chautauqua speeches from this period, see "Representative Government," delivered in Indiana, 1907, Manuscript, in La Follette Papers, Library of Congress.

15. La Follette and La Follette, *Robert M. La Follette*, I, 212, 215-16, 218-19; Thelen, *Insurgent Spirit*, 57-59, 67; Robert M. La Follette, *La Follette's Autobiography: A Personal Narrative of Political Experiences* (1913; rpt., Madison: The University of Wisconsin Press, 1961), 142-43; Robert M. La Follette, quoted in La Follette and La Follette, *Robert M. La Follette*, I, 236.

16. Greenbaum, *Robert Marion La Follette*, 82; La Follette and La Follette, *Robert M. La Follette*, I, 263, 265; *La Follette's Weekly Magazine*, 9 Jan. 1909, 1; Thelen, *Insurgent Spirit*, 67-68.

17. La Follette and La Follette, *Robert M. La Follette*, I, 299-300, 305-309; Greenbaum, *Robert Marion La Follette*, 96-97; Thelen, *Insurgent Spirit*, 76-78.

18. Thelen, *Insurgent Spirit*, 80-82; La Follette and La Follette, *Robert M. La Follette*, I, 312, 314, 316-19; Greenbaum, *Robert Marion La Follette*, 98-99; Robert M. La Follette, "The National Progressive Republican League Declaration of Principles," La Follette Papers, Library of Congress; Robert M. La Follette, "The Will of the People Is the Law of the Land," *La Follette's Magazine*, 8 Oct. 1910, 7-9.

19. Greenbaum, *Robert Marion La Follette*, 79, 100-103; Thelen, *Insurgent Spirit*, 66-67, 87-88; La Follette and La Follette, *Robert M. La Follette*, I, 257-59, 320-35, 349-69.

20. La Follette and La Follette, *Robert M. La Follette*, I, 341, 348, 369; Thelen, *Insurgent Spirit*, 88; Greenbaum, *Robert Marion La Follette*, 104; La Follette, *Autobiography*, 71-137, 159-83.

21. La Follette and La Follette, *Robert M. La Follette*, I, 370-72, 376-81, 383, 387-95; Thelen, *Insurgent Spirit*, 89-90; Greenbaum, *Robert Marion La Follette*, 108.

22. Thelen, *Insurgent Spirit*, 90-91; Greenbaum, *Robert Marion La Follette*, 108-109; La Follette and La Follette, *Robert M. La Follette*, I, 398-400.

23. La Follette and La Follette, *Robert M. La Follette*, I, 400-403; Greenbaum, *Robert Marion La Follette*, 109-10; Thelen, *Insurgent Spirit*, 91. Later on, La Follette published a revised manuscript of the Philadelphia speech. This was not the speech that he actually delivered but an ideal version. See "The Undermining of Democracy," Philadelphia, February 12, 1912, in La Follette Papers, Library of Congress. The ideal version also appeared as an appendix to La Follette, *Autobiography*, 322-42.

24. La Follette and La Follette, *Robert M. La Follette*, I, 404-409, 417; Greenbaum, *Robert Marion La Follette*, 110-11; Thelen, *Insurgent Spirit*, 91-92.

25. La Follette and La Follette, *Robert M. La Follette*, I, 425-28; Greenbaum, *Robert Marion La Follette*, 111-12; Thelen, *Insurgent Spirit*, 93-94; Robert M. La Follette, Campaign Speech, Valley City, North Dakota [Normal School], March 13, 1912, Manuscript, La Follette Papers, Library of Congress, 1.

26. La Follette, Valley City [Normal School], 2, 5, 8, 11, 12, 12-13, 13.

27. *The Minneapolis Sunday Tribune*, 17 March 1912; La Follette and La Follette, *Robert M. La Follette*, I, 427-35; Greenbaum, *Robert Marion La Follette*, 112; Thelen, *Insurgent Spirit*, 94.

28. La Follette and La Follette, *Robert M. La Follette*, I, 436-41, 444-47, 450; Thelen, *Insurgent Spirit*, 95-96; Greenbaum, *Robert Marion La Follette*, 117-18.

29. La Follette, *Autobiography*, 204-207, 218-19, 222, 249, 259-60, 265, 270, 276, 306, 314.

30. Greenbaum, *Robert Marion La Follette*, 125-27, 138, 141; Thelen, *Insurgent Spirit*, 100; La Follette and La Follette, *Robert M. La Follette*, I, 472-82, 484-85, 522-23, 529-30, 533-34; Robert M. La Follette, 16 May 1913, *Cong. Rec.*, 63d Cong., 1st Sess., 1596-99; Robert M. La Follette, 8 Sept. 1913, *Cong. Rec.*, 63d Cong., 1st Sess., 4446-58; Robert M. La Follette, 13 June 1913, *Cong. Rec.*, 63d Cong., 1st Sess., 1992; Robert M. La Follette, 31 July 1913, *Cong. Rec.*, 63d Cong., 1st Sess., 2951; Robert M. La Follette, 21 Oct. 1913, *Cong. Rec.*, 63d Cong., 1st Sess., 5714-21; Robert M. La Follette, 23 Oct. 1913, *Cong. Rec.*, 63d Cong., 1st Sess., 5781-83.

CHAPTER SEVEN

1. Belle Case La Follette and Fola La Follette, *Robert M. La Follette*, 2 vols. (1953; rpt., New York: Hafner Publishing Company, 1971), I, 517-19; David P. Thelen, *Robert M. La Follette and the Insurgent Spirit* (Boston: Little, Brown and Company, 1976), 128; Fred Greenbaum, *Robert Marion La Follette* (Boston: Twayne Publishers, 1975), 147-48; Robert M. La Follette, "La Follette Peace Resolution," 8 Feb. 1915, *Cong. Rec.*, 63d Cong., 3d Sess., 3254; Robert M. La Follette, "Proposed International Peace Conference," 12 Feb. 1915, *Cong. Rec.*, 63d Cong., 3d Sess., 3631-33.

2. Arthur S. Link, *Woodrow Wilson and the Progressive Era, 1910-1917* (New York: Harper and Row, 1963), 176, 179, 190, 211, 214; La Follette and La Follette, *Robert M. La Follette*, I, 550-53, 557-60, 575-78; Thelen, *Insurgent Spirit*, 128-31; Robert M. La Follette, "On Right of Petition," 27 Jan. 1916, *Cong. Rec.*, 64th Cong., 1st Sess., 1619; Robert M. La Follette, "Armed Merchant Vessels," 10 March 1916, *Cong. Rec.*, 64th Cong., 1st Sess.,

3886-91; Robert M. La Follette, 20 July 1916, *Cong. Rec.*, 64th Cong., 1st Sess., 11,330-47.

3. La Follette and La Follette, *Robert M. La Follette*, I, 578-83; Thelen, *Insurgent Spirit*, 122-24; *Wisconsin State Journal*, 7 Oct., 5 Nov. 1916. These speeches were probably similar to La Follette's "Washington Birthday Message," February 22, 1916, Pamphlet, La Follette Papers, Library of Congress. La Follette announced his candidacy for president of the United States in this speech, but he gathered little support outside of Wisconsin and soon abandoned the effort. See La Follette and La Follette, *Robert M. La Follette*, I, 562-71. Another campaign speech from 1916 is La Follette's "On Peace," Mt. Vernon, Wisconsin, Arbor Day, Manuscript, La Follette Papers, Library of Congress.

4. La Follette and La Follette, *Robert M. La Follette*, I, 584-85; Greenbaum, *Robert Marion La Follette*, 151-52; Thelen, *Insurgent Spirit*, 124.

5. La Follette and La Follette, *Robert M. La Follette*, I, 601-25; Thelen, *Insurgent Spirit*, 133-34; Greenbaum, *Robert Marion La Follette*, 155-56.

6. Woodrow Wilson, quoted in *New York Times*, 5 March 1917; Greenbaum, *Robert Marion La Follette*, 156; La Follette and La Follette, *Robert M. La Follette*, I, 626-32; Thelen, *Insurgent Spirit*, 134; *Literary Digest*, 17 March 1917, 691-92; *Cincinnati Post*, quoted in La Follette and La Follette, *Robert M. La Follette*, I, 629.

7. La Follette and La Follette, *Robert M. La Follette*, I, 636-57; Thelen, *Insurgent Spirit*, 134-35; Greenbaum, *Robert Marion La Follette*, 156-58; Robert M. La Follette, 8 March 1917, *Cong. Rec.*, 65th Cong., Special Sess., 40-45; Robert M. La Follette, 4 April 1917, *Cong. Rec.*, 65th Cong., 1st Sess., 223-34.

8. La Follette, 4 April 1917, *Cong. Rec.*, 224-34; La Follette and La Follette, *Robert M. La Follette*, I, 665-68.

9. Greenbaum, *Robert Marion La Follette*, 160; La Follette and La Follette, *Robert M. La Follette*, II, 731-49, 756-59; Thelen, *Insurgent Spirit*, 135-38; Robert M. La Follette, 27 April 1917, *Cong. Rec.*, 65th Cong., 1st Sess., 1354-64; Robert M. La Follette, War Aims Resolution, 11 Aug. 1917, *Cong. Rec.*, 65th Cong., 1st Sess., 5956; Robert M. La Follette, 21 Aug. 1917, *Cong. Rec.*, 65th Cong., 1st Sess., 6201-10; Robert M. La Follette, 23 Aug. 1917, *Cong. Rec.*, 65th Cong., 1st Sess., 6273-79; *New York World*, 14 Aug. 1917; Atlee Pomerene, quoted in *New York Times*, 13 Aug. 1917. For other speeches that develop and extend these positions, see Robert M. La Follette, 1 Sept. 1917, *Cong. Rec.*, 65th Cong., 1st Sess., 6503-19; Robert M. La Follette, 3 Sept. 1917, *Cong. Rec.*, 65th Cong., 1st Sess., 6523-34; Robert M. La Follette, 10 Sept. 1917, *Cong. Rec.*, 65th Cong., 1st Sess., 6853-61.

10. La Follette, 20 July 1916, *Cong. Rec.*, 11,330, 11,332, 11,339, 11,345; La Follette, "Proposed International Peace Conference," 3632-33; La

Follette, "On Right of Petition," 1619; La Follette, 21 Aug. 1917, *Cong. Rec.*, 6202-05, 6208-09; La Follette, 23 Aug. 1917, *Cong. Rec.*, 6273, 6279; La Follette, 1 Sept. 1917, *Cong. Rec.*, 6503; La Follette, 10 Sept. 1917, *Cong. Rec.*, 6861.

11. La Follette, 20 July 1916, *Cong. Rec.*, 11,336-37. Also see La Follette, "Proposed International Peace Conference," 3632-33; La Follette, 27 April 1917, *Cong. Rec.*, 1360.

12. La Follette, "Armed Merchant Vessels," 10 March 1916, *Cong. Rec.*, 3887-88; La Follette, 27 April 1917, *Cong. Rec.*, 1354, 1360.

13. La Follette, 8 March 1917, *Cong. Rec.*, 41; La Follette, 10 Sept. 1917, *Cong. Rec.*, 6854-61, 6858.

14. La Follette, "Peace Conference," 12 Feb. 1915, *Cong. Rec.*, 3631-32; La Follette, "Armed Merchant Vessels," 3887-89; La Follette, 8 March 1917, *Cong. Rec.*, 41-43; La Follette, 27 April 1917, *Cong. Rec.*, 1356-59; La Follette, 20 July 1916, *Cong. Rec.*, 11,330-36; La Follette, 21 Aug. 1917, *Cong. Rec.*, 6202.

15. La Follette, "Proposed International Peace Conference," 3631-33; La Follette, "On Right of Petition," 1619; La Follette, "Armed Merchant Vessels," 3886; La Follette, 20 July 1916, *Cong. Rec.*, 11,338, 11,342; La Follette, 4 April 1917, *Cong. Rec.*, 225; La Follette, 27 April 1917, *Cong. Rec.*, 1361, 1364.

16. La Follette, 4 April 1917, *Cong. Rec.*, 224, 226; La Follette, 27 April 1917, *Cong. Rec.*, 1357-58, 1360, 1364; La Follette, 21 Aug. 1917, *Cong. Rec.*, 6203; La Follette, "On Right of Petition," 1619.

17. La Follette, "Proposed International Peace Conference," 3631-32; La Follette, 27 April 1917, *Cong. Rec.*, 1355; La Follette, 20 July 1916, *Cong. Rec.*, 11330, 11339; La Follette, 21 Aug. 1917, *Cong. Rec.*, 6202, 6208-09; La Follette, 23 Aug. 1917, *Cong. Rec.*, 6273, 6279; La Follette, 1 Sept. 1917, *Cong. Rec.*, 6503; La Follette, 3 Sept. 1917, *Cong. Rec.*, 6525; La Follette, 21 Aug. 1917, *Cong. Rec.*, 6209.

18. La Follette and La Follette, *Robert M. La Follette*, II, 762-69; H.C. Peterson and Gilbert C. Fite, *Opponents of War, 1917-1918* (Madison: University of Wisconsin Press, 1957), 67-69; Robert M. La Follette, "St. Paul Speech," Manuscript, La Follette Papers, Library of Congress. Three days later, La Follette delivered a speech on his War Aims Resolution in Toledo, Ohio. See Manuscript in La Follette Papers, Library of Congress.

19. La Follette and La Follette, *Robert M. La Follette*, II, 769-70, 776-77, 780-81; Thelen, *Insurgent Spirit*, 141; Peterson and Fite, *Opponents of War*, 69-70.

20. La Follette and La Follette, *Robert M. La Follette*, II, 783-88; Thelen, *Insurgent Spirit*, 141-42. Robert M. La Follette, "Free Speech and the Right of Congress to Declare the Objects of the War," 6 Oct. 1917, *Cong. Rec.*, 65th

144 Robert M. La Follette, Sr.

Cong., 1st Sess., 7878-86. An edited text of this speech is reproduced in Part II. Also, the subsequent analysis of La Follette's October 6 speech is drawn from my article "Apology as Attack: La Follette *vs.* Robinson on Freedom of Speech," in *Oratorical Encounters: Selected Studies and Sources of Twentieth-Century Political Accusations and Apologies*, ed. Halford Ross Ryan (Westport: Greenwood Press, 1988), 1-16.

21. Frank Kellogg, 6 Oct. 1917, *Cong. Rec.*, 65th Cong., 1st Sess., 7886-88; Joseph T. Robinson, 6 Oct. 1917, *Cong. Rec.*, 65th Cong., 1st Sess., 7888-93; Albert Fall, 6 Oct. 1917, *Cong. Rec.*, 65th Cong., 1st Sess., 7893-95; Thelen, *Insurgent Spirit*, 142; La Follette and La Follette, *Robert M. La Follette*, II, 789-90; Nevin Emil Neal, "A Biography of Joseph T. Robinson" (Ph.D. diss., University of Oklahoma, 1958), 154-55.

22. La Follette and La Follette, *Robert M. La Follette*, II, 791; La Follette, "Free Speech," 7895. Outside of the Senate, La Follette did deny that he had said, "We had no grievance against Germany." See La Follette and La Follette, *Robert M. La Follette*, II, 772-75; "What Sen. La Follette Said and What Newspapers Say He Said," *La Follette's Magazine*, November 1917, 6.

23. B.L. Ware and Wil Linkugel, "They Spoke in Defense of Themselves: On the Generic Criticism of Apologia," *Quarterly Journal of Speech* 59 (1973): 280.

24. For examples of how La Follette used this technique of redefinition in Wisconsin, see Robert M. La Follette, "The Dangers Threatening Representative Government," in *The State*, 24 June 1898.

25. The *St. Louis Republic*, 7 Oct. 1917, quoted in Neal, "A Biography of Joseph T. Robinson," 155; La Follette and La Follette, *Robert M. La Follette*, II, 791; Thelen, *Insurgent Spirit*, 143.

26. Thomas W. Ryley, *A Little Group of Willful Men* (Port Washington: Kennikat Press, 1975), 174-75; Peterson and Fite, *Opponents of War*, 71-72; La Follette and La Follette, *Robert M. La Follette*, II, 795-816, 874-86, 910-11, 927-31; Greenbaum, *Robert Marion La Follette* 159-73; Thelen, *Insurgent Spirit*, 125-54.

27. Robinson, 6 Oct. 1917, *Cong. Rec.*, 7888-90, 7892-93.

28. La Follette and La Follette, *Robert M. La Follette*, II, 966-71; Greenbaum, *Robert Marion La Follette*, 180-81; Robert M. La Follette, "Wilson's Broken Pledges," *La Follette's Magazine*, July 1919, 102.

29. Robert M. La Follette, 16 Oct. 1919, *Cong. Rec.*, 66th Cong., 1st Sess., 7011.

30. Robert M. La Follette, 29 Oct. 1919, *Cong. Rec.*, 66th Cong., 1st Sess., 7673.

31. Robert M. La Follette, 6 Nov. 1919, *Cong. Rec.*, 66th Cong., 1st Sess., 8007-10, 8008.

32. Robert M. La Follette, 13 Nov. 1919, *Cong. Rec.*, 66th Cong., 1st Sess., 8429-30.

33. Robert M. La Follette, 18 Nov. 1919, *Cong. Rec.*, 66th Cong., 1st Sess., 8727-28.

34. La Follette and La Follette, *Robert M. La Follette*, II, 982-83.

35. Thelen, *Insurgent Spirit*, 150; La Follette and La Follette, *Robert M. La Follette*, II, 984.

36. See, in particular, La Follette, "Proposed International Peace Conference," 3631-33.

CHAPTER EIGHT

1. Belle Case and Fola La Follette, *Robert M. La Follette*, 2 vols. (1953; rpt., New York: Hafner Publishing Company, 1971), II, 985-86; David P. Thelen, *Robert M. La Follette and the Insurgent Spirit* (Boston: Little, Brown, and Company, 1976), 158-61.

2. La Follette and La Follette, *Robert M. La Follette*, II, 986-88; Thelen, *Insurgent Spirit*, 159; Robert M. La Follette, "Railroad Control," 13 Dec. 1919, *Cong. Rec.*, 66th Cong., 2d Sess., 502-29; 20 Dec. 1919, *Cong. Rec.*, 66th Cong., 2d Sess., App., 8746-61.

3. La Follette, 13 Dec. 1919, *Cong. Rec.*, 504, 511, 510, 525-27, 509; La Follette and La Follette, *Robert M. La Follette*, II, 988. Also see La Follette, 20 Dec. 1919, *Cong. Rec.*, App., 8747, 8749, 8753.

4. La Follette and La Follette, *Robert M. La Follette*, II, 991, 993; Fred Greenbaum, *Robert Marion La Follette* (Boston: Twayne Publishers, 1975), 171-72; Thelen, *Insurgent Spirit*, 160.

5. La Follette and La Follette, *Robert M. La Follette*, II, 995-97; Greenbaum, *Robert Marion La Follette*, 189; Thelen, *Insurgent Spirit*, 163; Oswald Garrison Villard, "The 'Unbossed' Republican Convention," *The Nation*, 19 June 1920, 821; *New York Times*, 11 June 1920.

6. Greenbaum, *Robert Marion La Follette*, 189-90; La Follette and La Follette, *Robert M. La Follette*, II, 998-1000, 1004, 1011-13; Thelen, *Insurgent Spirit*, 164.

7. La Follette and La Follette, *Robert M. La Follette*, II, 1016-17.

8. Robert M. La Follette, Campaign Speech, Milwaukee, October 21, 1920, Manuscript, La Follette Papers, Library of Congress, 14, 20, 7, 54; *Milwaukee Journal*, 22 Oct. 1920.

9. La Follette and La Follette, *Robert M. La Follette*, II, 1022-23; Robert M. La Follette, "Partial Payments of Guaranty Under the Esch-Cummins Law," 21 Feb. 1921, *Cong. Rec.*, 66th Cong., 3d Sess., App., 4602-20; *New York Times*, 27 March 1921; (Madison) *Capital Times*, 26 March 1921.

10. La Follette and La Follette, *Robert M. La Follette*, II, 1025-26; quoted in Thelen, *Insurgent Spirit*, 180; Robert M. La Follette, "Speech to the People's Reconstruction League," March 25, 1921, Madison, in *Wisconsin State Journal*, 26 March 1921.

11. La Follette and La Follette, *Robert M. La Follette*, II, 1028-29, 1033-35; Robert M. La Follette, 25 May 1921, *Cong. Rec.*, 67th Cong., 1st Sess., 1745; Robert M. La Follette, 29 Sept. 1921, *Cong. Rec.*, 67th Cong., 1st Sess., 5868.

12. La Follette and La Follette, *Robert M. La Follette*, II, 1037-38; Robert M. La Follette, "Michigan Senatorial Election," 12 Jan. 1922, *Cong. Rec.*, 67th Cong., 2d Sess., App., 13550, 13552; Robert M. La Follette, 22 March 1922, *Cong. Rec.*, 67th Cong., 2d Sess., 4235.

13. La Follette and La Follette, *Robert M. La Follette*, II, 1028-30, 1033-39.

14. La Follette and La Follette, *Robert M. La Follette*, II, 1041-50; Thelen, *Insurgent Spirit*, 175.

15. Robert M. La Follette, "Naval Oil Reserves," 28 April 1922, *Cong. Rec.*, 67th Cong., 2d Sess., 6045; La Follette and La Follette, *Robert M. La Follette*, II, 1050.

16. La Follette and La Follette, *Robert M. La Follette*, II, 1055-56; Thelen, *Insurgent Spirit*, 173; Robert M. La Follette, "Address Before Annual Convention of American Federation of Labor, Cincinnati, June 14, 1922," in 21 June 1922, *Cong. Rec.*, 67th Cong., 2d Sess., 9075-82. The speech also appears in *Capital Times*, 29 June 1922.

17. Robert M. La Follette, "American Federation of Labor," 9077, 9081-82.

18. *New York Times*, 15 June 1922; Nicholas Murray Butler, "Abstract of Address at the Annual Banquet of the New Jersey State Bar Association," 19 June 1922, *Cong. Rec.*, 67th Cong., 2d Sess., 8931-32; La Follette and La Follette, *Robert M. La Follette*, II, 1057; Greenbaum, *Robert Marion La Follette*, 192-93.

19. Thelen, *Insurgent Spirit*, 170-71; Greenbaum, *Robert Marion La Follette*, 193; La Follette and La Follette, *Robert M. La Follette*, II, 1058-59.

20. Robert M. La Follette, "Congress Betrays Peoples' Interests," *La Follette's Magazine*, July 1922, 100-104; *Milwaukee Journal*, 18 July 1922; La Follette and La Follette, *Robert M. La Follette*, II, 1059; *Capital Times*, 18 July 1922.

21. La Follette and La Follette, *Robert M. La Follette*, II, 1060; Greenbaum, *Robert Marion La Follette*, 193.

22. Greenbaum, *Robert Marion La Follette*, 193; La Follette and La Follette, *Robert M. La Follette*, II, 1061.

23. *Wisconsin State Journal*, 20 Oct., 4 Nov. 1922; *Capital Times*, 20 Oct., 24 Oct., 30 Oct., 3 Nov., 4 Nov., 1922; La Follette and La Follette, *Robert M. La Follette*, II, 1061-65; Greenbaum, *Robert Marion La Follette*, 194; Thelen, *Insurgent Spirit*, 171-72; *New York Times*, 19 Nov. 1922; *Raleigh News and Observer*, quoted in *Literary Digest*, 23 Sept. 1922, 12.

24. La Follette and La Follette, *Robert M. La Follette*, II, 1069, 1073-87.

25. La Follette and La Follette, *Robert M. La Follette*, II, 1092-94; Robert M. La Follette, "Edwin Denby, Secretary of the Navy," 11 Feb. 1924, *Cong. Rec.*, 68th Cong., 1st Sess., 2233.

26. La Follette and La Follette, *Robert M. La Follette*, II, 1094; Thelen, *Insurgent Spirit*, 179; Clinton W. Gilbert, *"You Takes Your Choice"* (New York: G.P. Putnam's Sons, 1924), 104-105.

27. La Follette, "Railroad Control," 13 Dec. 1919, *Cong. Rec.*, 502-504, 509-11, 513-15, 528-29; La Follette, "Congress Betrays Peoples' Interests," 103-104; La Follette, Campaign Speech, Milwaukee, October 21, 1920, 2; La Follette, "Naval Oil Reserves," 6047. Also see La Follette, "Esch-Cummins Law," 4602; La Follette, "Michigan Senatorial Elections," 13550-52.

28. La Follette, "American Federation of Labor," 9077-78, 9081.

29. Thelen, *Insurgent Spirit*, 180-83, 187; La Follette and La Follette, *Robert M. La Follette*, II, 1095-96, 1107-13, 1116; *New York Times*, 6 April 1924; Robert M. La Follette, "Statement and Platform of Robert M. La Follette, July 4, 1924," (Chicago: La Follette Progressive Headquarters, 1924), Pamphlet, La Follette Papers, Library of Congress, 20-24; Greenbaum, *Robert Marion La Follette*, 213-14; Kenneth Campbell MacKay, *The Progressive Movement of 1924* (New York: Columbia University Press, 1947), 132-33.

30. La Follette, "Statement and Platform," 6-7, 13, 14, 14-15, 15, 16-17.

31. La Follette and La Follette, *Robert M. La Follette*, II, 1115-21; Thelen, *Insurgent Spirit*, 184; *New York Times*, 15 Sept., 16 Sept., 28 Sept., 24 Oct. 1924; Charles Dawes, quoted in *Milwaukee Sentinel*, 20 Aug. 1924. See also *Milwaukee Sentinel*, 12 Sept. 1924.

32. La Follette and La Follette, *Robert M. La Follette*, II, 1121-24; Greenbaum, *Robert Marion La Follette*, 217; Thelen, *Insurgent Spirit*, 185-86.

33. La Follette and La Follette, *Robert M. La Follette*, II, 1125; *New York Times*, 19 Sept. 1924; *New York Evening Journal*, 2 Sept. 1924, quoted in La Follette and La Follette, *Robert M. La Follette*, II, 1125.

34. La Follette and La Follette, *Robert M. La Follette*, II, 1125-26, 1136; Robert M. La Follette, "Labor Day Address," September 1, 1924, Washington, D.C., Manuscript, La Follette Papers, Library of Congress. The text of this speech is reproduced in Part II.

35. La Follette and La Follette, *Robert M. La Follette*, II, 1126; Robert M. La Follette, quoted in *Capital Times*, 29 Sept. 1924; Robert M. La Follette, quoted in La Follette and La Follette, *Robert M. La Follette*, II, 1136.

36. La Follette and La Follette, *Robert M. La Follette*, II, 1127-46; Thelen, *Insurgent Spirit*, 188-89; MacKay, *Progressive Movement*, 156-59.

37. La Follette and La Follette, *Robert M. La Follette*, II, 1146-47; *Capital Times*, 3 Nov. 1924; *Wisconsin State Journal*, 3 Nov. 1924; Robert M. La Follette, quoted in La Follette and La Follette, *Robert M. La Follette*, II, 1146-47.

38. Robert M. La Follette, Campaign Speech, Kansas City, October 13, 1924, Manuscript, La Follette Papers, Library of Congress, 1, 1-2, 3, 3-4.

39. La Follette, Kansas City, 6; Robert M. La Follette, Campaign Speech, Des Moines, October 15, 1924, Manuscript, La Follette Papers, Library of Congress, 19.

40. La Follette, Kansas City, 7-8; Robert M. La Follette, Campaign Speech, Syracuse, October 24, 1924, Manuscript, La Follette Papers, Library of Congress, 9.

41. La Follette, Syracuse, 18-19; La Follette, "Labor Day Address," 1.

42. Robert M. La Follette, Campaign Speech, Pittsburgh, October 31, 1924, Manuscript, La Follette Papers, Library of Congress, 11-12, 19, 17.

43. Greenbaum, *Robert Marion La Follette*, 217-18; Thelen, *Insurgent Spirit*, 191-92.

44. Thelen, *Insurgent Spirit*, 189-90; Greenbaum, *Robert Marion La Follette*, 218; La Follette and La Follette, *Robert M. La Follette*, II, 1148; MacKay, *Progressive Movement*, 249.

45. Thelen, *Insurgent Spirit*, 191-92; La Follette and La Follette, *Robert M. La Follette*, II, 1147.

46. Thelen, *Insurgent Spirit*, 189-90; Greenbaum, *Robert Marion La Follette*, 218; MacKay, *Progressive Movement*, 252, 159-60.

47. Robert M. La Follette, "Forward Progressives for Campaign of 1926," *La Follette's Magazine*, November 1924, 165.

48. Quoted in La Follette and La Follette, *Robert M. La Follette*, II, 1174.

CHAPTER NINE

1. Robert M. La Follette, "Iago" (complete text is in Part II); Robert M. La Follette, "Oleomargarine Speech" (complete text is in Part II); Robert M. La Follette, "Amendment of National Banking Laws," 17 March 1908, *Cong. Rec.*, 60th Cong., 1st Sess., 3449; Robert M. La Follette, "Address before Annual Convention of American Federation of Labor, Cincinnati, June 14, 1922," 21 June 1922, *Cong. Rec.*, 67th Cong., 2d Sess., 9081. Parts of this chapter were previously published in "Discovering Rhetorical Imprints: La Follette, 'Iago,' and the Melodramatic Scenario," *Quarterly Journal of Speech* 71 (1985): 444-52.

2. La Follette, "Iago"; La Follette, "Oleomargarine Speech"; La Follette, "The Menace of the Political Machine" (complete text is in Part II); Robert M. La Follette, "Veto Message," in 10 May 1901, *Senate Journal*, State of Wisconsin, 45th Sess., 1026-28; La Follette, "Amendment of National Banking Laws," 3451-52; Robert M. La Follette, 20 July 1916, *Cong. Rec.*, 64th Cong., 1st Sess., 11,330, 11,338; La Follette, "American Federation of Labor," 9078.

3. La Follette, 20 July 1916, *Cong. Rec.*, 11,330, 11,339.

4. It is also obviously impossible to prove with certainty that an invisible enemy does exist. However, it is generally easier for an accuser to create doubts in the minds of an audience than it is for a defender to offer reassurances of innocence.

5. La Follette, "Iago."

6. George E. Mowry, *The Era of Theodore Roosevelt and the Birth of Modern America, 1900-1912* (New York: Harper Torchbooks, 1962), 294; Herbert F. Margulies, *The Decline of the Progressive Movement in Wisconsin: 1890-1920* (Madison: State Historical Society of Wisconsin, 1968), 25; Russell B. Nye, *Midwestern Progressive Politics* (East Lansing: Michigan State University Press, 1959), 7-16, 30, 197-204, 222-24; Gordon F. Hostettler, "The Public Speaking of Robert M. La Follette," in *American Public Address: Studies in Honor of Albert Craig Baird*, ed. Loren Reid (Columbia, Missouri: University of Missouri Press, 1961), 113-14, 119-20; Carroll P. Lahman, "Robert M. La Follette," in *A History and Criticism of American Public Address*, ed. William Norwood Brigance (New York: Russell and Russell, 1960) II, 943-44.

7. Richard Hofstadter, "The Paranoid Style in American Politics," in *The Paranoid Style in American Politics and Other Essays* (New York: Vintage Books, 1967), 4, 7, 9, 39.

8. David P. Thelen, *Robert M. La Follette and the Insurgent Spirit* (Boston: Little, Brown, and Company, 1976), 46.

9. Robert M. La Follette, *La Follette's Autobiography: A Personal Narrative of Political Experiences* (1913; rpt., Madison, The University of Wisconsin Press, 1961), 104, 29, 19. Also see Belle Case La Follette and Fola La Follette, *Robert M. La Follette* (1953; rpt., New York: Hafner Publishing Company, 1971), II, 1039-40.

II
SELECTED SPEECHES

Iago

Iowa City, Iowa, May 7, 1879

Shakespeare's Iago personifies two constituents of mind—*intellect* and *will*. These alone are the springs of his action, the source of his power. What he lacks in emotion he has gained in intellectual acuteness, but the result is deformity. The character is not *un*natural; it is fiendishly natural. His reasoning power is abnormally developed; but he has no feeling, no sympathy, no affection, no fear. His is the cold passion of intellect, whose icy touch chills the warm life in all it reaches. He is an intellectual athlete, and is unceasing in his mental gymnastics. His contempt for all good is supreme; his greatest crime is his greatest pleasure; and his own hypocrisy gladdens and intoxicates him. Whatever is most mean, whatever is most hard, whatever is vilely atrocious and dangerously difficult, he seizes with greedy glee. Skeptical of all virtue, to him love is lechery, truth-telling stupid goodness, and lying a daring to be ingenious.

The emotions are the native soil of moral life. From the feelings are grown great ethical truths, one by one, forming at last the grand body of the moral law. But Iago is emotionally a cipher, and his poverty of sentiment and wealth of intellect render him doubly dangerous. Here we have the key to his character—he is possessed of an inflexible will, of an intellect, pungent, subtle, super-sensual. He not only knows more than he feels, he knows everything, feels nothing.

The other characters of the tragedy of Othello—a tragedy which Macaulay pronounced Shakespeare's greatest—are but puppets, moving at the will of this master. He reads them at a glance, by a flash of instinct. He wastes no words on Roderigo other than to make the "fool his purse." But upon Othello he plays with more subtlety, and infinitely greater zest. Upon him he exercises his crafty ingenuity; and the "double knavery," the "How? how?" whets him keen. Now flashes forth the invisible lightning of his malignant mind, and woe to all virtue within its reach. Now we see his character in all its artful cunning, all its devilish cruelty. With what marvelous skill he makes his first attack! He does nothing in the common way. His methods have the merit of originality. He does not assail Desdemona's virtue with a well-conned story, but is seemingly surprised into an exclamation, appearing to utter his suspicions by the merest accident. And when he has engaged Othello's ear, note his matchless cunning; he comes and goes, and comes and goes again, with his ingenious inuendos; changing like the chameleon, quick to take his cue from the Moor, yet craftily giving direction to the other's thoughts; cursing Cassio with his protestations of love, and damning Desdemona while joining in a benediction to her honesty. The "constant, loving, noble nature," of the Moor changes quickly under the "almost superhuman art" of Iago; but too well he knows the human mind to gorge it with suspicion; and, with every dose of poison, gives just a little antidote. With pious self-accusation, he says, "'tis my nature's plague to spy into abuses;" and, "oft my jealousy shapes faults that are not;" but carefully adds, "it were not for your quiet nor your good to let you know my thoughts;" and is equally careful to tell them; smothering with one hand all suspicion of his perfidy, and kindling with the other the consuming fires of the Moor's jealousy.

Iago's manner of practicing on Othello is only matched by the means he employs. Like the genuine devil, he destroys the entire household—not through some unguarded vice, but through its very virtues. He sets all goodness by the ears. The strength of the Moor's affection is made a fatal weakness; and, more than this the very medium of all their misery is she,

> Of spirit so still and gentle that her motion
> Blushed at herself.

Iago and Desdemona! Strange, unspeakable union of opposites! Weird harmony of discords! Sombre mingling of a smile and a sneer! O the poet whose genius could compound these elements without an explosion! O this "unequal contest between the powers of grossness and purity!" That Desdemona, whose childlike nature is a divine fusion of innocence and chastity, should be played off against a moral outlaw, a being whose livery is "heavenly shows" and whose logic is the "divinity of hell," is a juxtaposition appalling, fascinating! 'Tis Diana in the talons of a Harpy. That virtue should be "turned into pitch," that "out of goodness" should be made "the net to enmesh them all," that innocence should become the instrument of the infernal, is a "moral antithesis" that preludes the oncoming of chaos. And it comes like the quick night and consummates the tragedy; while over all, in sullen silence, gloats this imp of darkness.

Somewhere, Thomas Carlyle has said, "there are depths in man that go the length of the lowest Hell, as there are heights that reach highest Heaven;" but Iago is a magnet with only one pole which ever points toward the infernal. Why is it, then, that this character does not disgust us? Why do we follow his intricate windings with such intense interest? Why do we tolerate him? We find the answer in his great intellect. This is the core of his character—abstract intellectuality united to volitional force, devoid of all morality, divorced from all feeling. He is hardly human, yet he sounds humanity like a philosopher. He is wanting in ethical parts; yet he makes the nicest moral distinctions. He is a fraction, yet greater than a unit; a part, yet more than the whole. He is a paradox. In his deep schemes, we nearly forget the villain. His triumph over all obstacles pins the attention to his intellectual powers. He is "instinct with thought." This redeems him to us as a subject, and yields another explanation for what has been termed his "little trace of conscience." His self-questionings, his subtle sophisms, his cataclysm of reasons, are not the weak protest of a moral part, but the logical outcome of a sleepless intellect. He is emphatically a being of reasons. He will do nothing except he furnish to himself the "why!" It is not that he requires these reasons as a "whetstone for his revenge," it is not that his "resolution is too much for his conscience," but rather that he revels in reasons, that his hungry mind will have its food. He "suspects the lusty Moor," and fears "Cassio with his night-cap, too," on occasion; not that he dreads to destroy either without some motive, but because his mental constitution demands a reason for all things. Schlegel defines wickedness as "nothing but selfishness designedly unconscientious;" but Iago makes no effort to deceive himself, for he says:

> When devils will their blackest sins put on,
> They do suggest at first with heavenly shows
> As I do now.

He does not care to justify himself, except as an intellectual satisfaction. He desires no moral vindication. In fact he commits crime merely for crime's sake, and there is no sin that he will not claim as his own. Think of it! a being who clutches at wickedness with all the greed of a miser. Thoroughly passionless, coldly intellectual, he is forced into the self confession that he is no libertine; yet fearful lest the admission has cost him one hellish trait, he quickly adds that he stands "accountant for as great a sin." This is a moral defiance sublimely hideous, but hardly reconcilable in a being with even a "little trace of conscience." Were there a single golden thread of moral sense to knit him to the good in humanity, it would shine forth when Desdemona—whose only offence against him is that she is pure—sinks under his cursed cunning. But it is a quality he feels not, knows not; and what Coleridge calls *"the motive-hunting of a motiveless malignity;"* this constant combing of his wits for reasons, is simply a service performed at the mandate of his craving intellect.

These are the premises from which, as a conclusion, we deduce Iago—a character without a conscience.

Mark the "steep inequality" between him and Richard III: The Duke of Gloster, born with teeth, a twisted body, and a majestic mind, cuts his way through those of his own flesh, to a throne. Malignant and artful, hypocritical and heartless, he "seems a saint when most he plays the devil." Monster, he stands apart from men; he is "like himself alone," and he stalks along his bloody course, a solitary creation. Brave, he has the audacity to defy destiny, the impudent confidence to enter the lists against the Unknown. But hidden away somewhere in his black soul is a germ of conscience disguised as superstitious fear,—a germ of conscience which starts forth when that towering will is off guard; coming in the thin substance of a dream, yet so terrible that the remorseful "drops hang on his trembling flesh." Here is his humanity, his mortal weakness; and through this the "all-powerful and ever-watchful Nemesis" hurls her lance, barbed to the shaft with retribution. Pursued by croaking phantoms, scourged by the invisible lash of violated conscience, he flings himself into the conflict, and with a royal flourish, in perfect keeping with his character, closes the tragedy. His death satisfies the equation of right.

Richard and Iago possess some qualities in common: both have mighty intellects; both are wily, cunning, crafty; both dissimulators, both actors. But farther that [sic] this they are profoundly unlike. Richard III is more humanly terrible; Iago more devilishly perfect. Richard loves nothing human; Iago hates everything good. Richard is arrogant, passionate, powerful, violent; Iago egotistical, cold, cynical, sly. Richard is fire; Iago ice. Richard III is more objective; Iago more subjective. Richard would pulverize the universe; Iago would like to reverse the order of things. In point of satanical finish Iago is Richard—and more. Richard III murders many, and sweats with horror; Iago few, and forgets remorse. Richard III mounts the throne of England on a score of dead bodies; Iago wins the throne of Hell in three strides. The conscience of Richard wakes from its swoon; Iago has no conscience. Richard III is a monstrosity; Iago a psychological contradiction.

We offer Iago then as Shakespeare's conception of the "Evil Principle." And how perfect the creation. In the whole course of his crime, he betrays never a weakness, never a check of conscience—nothing to mar the elegant symmetry of his fiendishness. From the time he lays down the postulate that "I am not what I am" till he attains his infernal majority, he is the same refined, pitiless, sarcastic devil. He is often surprised, but is never disconcerted. He plans, but it is because he likes the mental exercise. It has been said that "deep rogues take all their villainy *a priori*; that they do not construct plans in anticipation." Iago's carefully perfected schemes would seem to rebuke this philosophy were it not that they appear, rather, meat for his mind, than directions for his diabolisms. Indeed it is in those unpremised scenes where the occasion fails to fit his plans, where all the odds are arrayed against him, that he achieves the greatest triumph. This is nothing short of Stygian skill; and it is just here that he attains the dignity of a devil. That dignity would have been sacrificed in his death. By all the principles of dramatic tragedy, Othello is his fit executioner. Significant fact! we are only promised that his "punishment shall torment him much and hold him long." This is to appease the moral demand, and in its vagueness the poet seeks to avoid a decline in tragic intensity. This we offer as the ethical and aesthetical reason for the indefiniteness thrown about Iago's fate by the dramatist. He had pushed his creation to the verge of the finite, punishment was demanded, none could be devised which would requite him.

The full course of tragedy, the mighty sweep of its changing scenes must yield an apt sequence, a sublime completeness, else it fails in its aim. Schiller says: "Life is great only as a means of accomplishing the moral law; and nothing is sublimer than a criminal yielding his life because of the morality he has violated." With the single exception of Iago, Shakespeare has availed himself of this principle. The thane of Cawdor tops all his murders with his own head; Lady Macbeth bleaches in death the "damned spot" from her unclean hand; Richard III seals with his own blood, on Bosworth field the sublime in his career; but Iago is just beyond the reach of death and we can fancy him disappearing in the darkness of which he is a part.

There are two fitnesses in a villain's death—the moral fitness and the tragic fitness. The one, the ethical satisfaction at the inevitable recoil of the broken moral law; the other, the grandeur of a *finale*. To condense into one moment the whole of life, to put a fiat on existence, to engulf a soul in the awful immensity of its own acts—this is sublime. But to have conceived and brought forth a being so super-physical, so positively devilish, so intensely infernal, that his death would be bathos—this is genius.

And this is Iago. The polished, affable, attendant; the boon companion; the supple sophist, the nimble logician; the philosopher, the moralist—the scoffing demon; the goblin whose smile is a stab and whose laugh is an infernal sneer; who has sworn eternal vengeance on virtue everywhere; who would turn cosmos into chaos. This compound of wickedness and reason, this incarnation of intellect, this tartarean basilisk is the logical conclusion in a syllogism whose premises are "Hell and Night." He is a criminal climax: endow him with a single supernatural quality and he stands among the devils of fiction supreme.

Oleomargarine

Washington, D.C., June 2, 1886

Mr. CHAIRMAN: I have waited till the close of this discussion hoping that gentlemen whose eminent abilities and long service give them the prerogative to instruct us on constitutional questions would present to this body fully their views and the authorities upon those questions, to the end that we should be aided in our work here and that the same should become a part of the record of this legislation.

It has been from the first maintained by the enemies and apparently conceded by the friends of this measure that it must masquerade through the House as a bill to raise revenue, and that no other constitutional defense can be found for it.

I have noticed that those who favor a tax so high as to practically prohibit the manufacture of oleomargarine, as well as those who favor one so low as to barely recompense the Government for its supervision, although in either case no revenue could possibly be collected, have, when pressed by the sharp questioning of the gentleman from Georgia [Mr. Hammond], been driven to take refuge behind the lines of the bill. When asked if either a prohibitory tax or one just paying the collecting would yield revenue, of course answer is made that it would not. When asked if we need an increase in revenue at this time, answer is made that we do not. When asked whether it is a proper use of constitutional power to levy a tax when revenue is not needed, answer is made that it is not. Then, driven to extremes, it is said that "this appears to be a revenue bill, that it will go out as a revenue bill, that it will have to be interpreted as a revenue tax, and that the motives of members can not be questioned."

While this may answer the forms of lawful legislation, it is nevertheless a pretty severe strain on the conscience. And, sir, if there is any other constitutional warrant which primarily may move in laying a tax other than the naked purpose to raise revenue it is important that it be asserted in this discussion and with any authority supporting it made a part of the history of this proceeding.

It has to me seemed singular that the arguments made against this measure, and in no instance disguised, should not have renewed the contest along the line dividing protection and a tariff for revenue only; but the friends of the American system have apparently seen in this issue no call for application of the principles to which they are committed. And yet all the arguments which have been advanced against the constitutionality of this bill during the discussion are the same that have always been made against protective and prohibitory duties.

The gentleman from Georgia [Mr. Hammond] cited as one of the principal authorities supporting his view of the unconstitutionality of this measure a portion of Mr. Webster's speech against the tariff, delivered at Faneuil Hall in 1820, long before he changed his views on that subject; and the argument of the distinguished chairman of the Judiciary Committee [Mr. Tucker] in his speech against this bill a few days ago was exactly in line with that which has always been advanced against protective and prohibitory duties.

Compare the summation of the argument against this use of the taxing power which Mr. Story gives in section 963 of his work on the Constitution, as the views of the strict constructionist, with that of the gentleman from Virginia in the speech referred to. The one says, "The power to lay taxes is a power exclusively given to raise revenue;" the other says, "Congress has the power to lay the tax on oleomargarine" (but for what purpose?) "to raise revenue." The one says, "When revenue is wanted for constitutional purposes the power to lay taxes may be applied; but when revenue is not wanted it is not a proper means for any constitutional end;" the other says, "Can you use that as a weapon to destroy some industry that is not within your power, merely because you have that weapon to use, for the purpose of raising revenue?" Both would concede that incidental benefits might lawfully go with the tax, but both would contend that the right to lay the tax could never be exercised for any other purpose than to raise revenue, no matter how much that purpose might be for the common defense and general welfare.

And so I say that the argument offered here to show the unconstitutionality of this bill is the argument which has always been made when the use of the taxing power was employed primarily for purposes other than revenue. In applying to this question the same reasoning on which rests the constitutional authority for all protective tariff, and thus invoking at least half of the great names of history to its support, I have the sanction of high constitutional authority. Mr. Story, as I have quoted, says in his chapter on the "Power of Congress to tax," that though the argument which he gives for an against the constitutional authority to tax for other purposes than to raise revenue is given as applied to the protection of manufactures, still, as the learned author himself says, "the argument is equally applicable to all other cases when revenue is not the object."

If it be true, then, that we do not at this time need to increase our revenues, and if it be likewise true that the primary object of this bill be not to gather revenue, the question addressed to the legislative conscience is, Has Congress the authority to tax primarily for purposes other than revenue?

I turn directly to section 964, Story on the Constitution, and though instead of asserting dogmatically his own views on this controverted question he gives the best reasoning upon both sides, I think no lawyer on this floor can read it all without coming to the conclusion that the opinion of the able commentator himself was that the power there given to tax can be exercised in any way for the common good.

Mr. HAMMOND: That is, on the commerce clause.

Mr. LA FOLLETTE: No, sir; it is not on the commerce clause. I am reading from chapter 14, the title of which is "Taxes," and which is devoted exclusively to the consideration of the clause: "Congress shall have power to lay and collect taxes, duties, imposts, and excises, to pay the debts and provide for the common defense and general welfare of the United States; but all duties, imposts, and excises shall be uniform throughout the United States."

The learned commentator devotes most of this chapter to the consideration of the question to which we seek an answer. Has Congress the power to tax for purposes other than revenue? Admonishing us not to commit the fallacy of the gentlemen who oppose this bill and assume the very point which must be proved—that is, that the power to lay taxes is limited to revenue only—he says:

> It will not do to assume that the clause was intended solely for the purpose of raising revenue, and then argue, that being so, the power can not be constitutionally applied to any other purposes. The very point in controversy is whether it is restricted to purposes of revenue. That must be proved and can not be assumed as the basis of reasoning.
>
> The language of the Constitution is: "Congress shall have power to lay and collect taxes, duties, imposts, and excises." If the clause had stopped here and remained in this absolute form, there could not have been the slightest doubt on the subject. The absolute power to lay taxes includes the power in every form in which it may be used, and for every purpose to which the legislature may choose to apply it. This results from the very nature of such an unrestricted power. *A fortiori*, it might be applied by Congress to purposes for which nations have been accustomed to apply it. Now, nothing is more clear, from the history of commercial nations, than the fact that the taxing power is often, very often, applied for other purposes than revenue.
>
> It is often applied as a regulation of commerce. It is often applied as a virtual prohibition upon the importation of particular articles, for the encouragement and protection of domestic products and industry; for the support of agriculture, commerce, and manufactures; for retaliation upon foreign monopolies and injurious restrictions; for mere purposes of state policy and domestic economy; sometimes to banish a noxious article of consumption; sometimes as a bounty upon an infant manufacture, or agricultural product; sometimes as a temporary restraint of trade; sometimes as a suppression of particular employments; sometimes as a prerogative power to destroy competition and secure a monopoly to the Government!

If, then, the power to lay taxes, being general, may embrace and in the practice of nations does embrace all these objects, either separately or in combination, upon what foundation does the argument rest which assumes one object only, to the exclusion of all the rest; which insists, in effect, that because revenue may be one object, therefore it is the sole object of the power; which assumes its own construction to be correct because it suits its own theory, and denies the same right to others entertaining a different theory?

Mr. Story nowhere lays it down that the power to tax is general, but he says the limitations are found in the same clause of the Constitution. The exact extent of this limitation as construed by the commentator, in the language of section 922, where he sums up his conclusions on the proper grammatical construction of this clause, is as follows:

A power to lay taxes for any purposes whatsoever is a general power; a power to lay taxes for certain specified purposes is a limited power; a power to lay taxes for the common defense and general welfare of the United States is not in common sense a general power. It is limited to those objects. It can not constitutionally transcend them. If the defense proposed by a tax be not in the common defense of the United States, if the welfare be not general, but special or local, as contradistinguished from national, it is not within the scope of the Constitution. If the tax be not proposed for the common defense or general welfare, but for other objects, wholly extraneous (as, for instance, for propagating Mahometism among the Turks or giving aids and subsidies to a foreign nation to build palaces for its kings or erect monuments to its heroes), it would be wholly indefensible upon constitutional principles.

In other words, the reading which he says seems supported by the best reasoning, and that which he maintains throughout his commentaries, is that—"Congress shall have power to lay and collect taxes, duties, imposts, and excises [in order] to pay the debts, and to provide for the common defense and general welfare."

And then continuing the reasoning says:

Is raising revenue the only proper mode to provide for the common defense and general welfare? May not the general welfare, in the judgment of Congress, be, in given circumstances, as well provided for, nay, better provided for, by prohibitory duties, or by encouragements to domestic industry of all sorts?

If the common defense or general welfare can be promoted by laying taxes in any other manner than for revenue, who is at liberty to say that Congress can not constitutionally exercise the power for such a purpose? No one has the right to say that the common defense and general welfare can never be promoted by laying taxes except for revenue.

[Here the hammer fell.]

Mr. TUCKER: If I can be recognized I will yield my time to the gentleman from Wisconsin [Mr. La Follette].

Mr. LA FOLLETTE: I thank the gentleman.

Mr. Chairman, in further support of the view that Congress has the constitutional right to tax for purposes other than revenue, I would call the attention of the House to the following words, found in an exhaustive report from the Committee on Manufactures, made May 23, 1832:

> To pay the debts of the United States was the first of the objects for which by the Constitution of the United States the power to lay and collect taxes, duties, imposts, and excises was conferred upon Congress; to provide for the common defense and general welfare was the second object; and these expressions, broad and comprehensive in their import, far from being without meaning in the intention of the founders of the Constitution, embraced the great purposes for which the Constitution itself was formed. They are introduced in that solemn preamble, by which the whole people of the United States, speaking in the first person, "We, the people of the United States," announce the great purposes for which they do ordain and establish this Constitution; they are emphatically repeated in the eighth section of the first article, containing the grants to Congress of power; and they are not only grants of power but trusts to be executed, duties to be discharged for the common defense and general welfare of the Union; to provide for that common defense and general welfare were obligations imposed upon the organized body upon whom the power was conferred of laying and collecting taxes, duties, imposts, and excises for effecting the purpose—obligations not less imperious than that of paying the debts of the Union. To provide for the common defense and general welfare is the duty, the irremissible duty of the Congress; the power to levy duties, taxes, imposts, and excises is the means with which they are invested for the execution of the trust. The non-user of the power is a violation of the trust—a violation as culpable as would have been the neglect or refusal to levy taxes for the payment of the public debt. That the intention of the people was to confer the power in great amplitude is apparent not only from the greatness of the purpose to be accomplished and from the generality of the terms in which the power is conferred, not only from the emphatic repetition of the terms in which the objects of the Constitution are announced in the preamble, but from the anxious use of all the words by which the contributions of taxation can be levied—taxes, duties, imposts, and excises.
>
> The argument which denies the power of Congress to levy duties for the protection of domestic manufactures pronounces unconstitutional two of the first acts by which Congress exercised their powers—acts among the most memorable, among the most beneficent exercises of power which have rendered the Constitution itself a blessing to the nation. It expunges from the Constitution the grant of power to provide for the common defense.

The above language from this able report does not mean, as has been contended by the opponents of this bill, that Congress can levy a tax so as to discriminate against certain articles only when revenue is needed. It means that Congress has constitutional authority to lay a tax for the general welfare even though there be not the slightest necessity for revenue, as is shown by the following paragraph from the same report:

To pay the debts of the nation was an object of more immediate urgency than even that of providing for the common defense. It was to enable the nation itself to do justice to others. To provide for the common defense was the discharge of a debt which the nation owed itself—a debt of wider scope, of deeper import, of more permanent duration. The power of levying money to pay the debts was a power limited by the consummation of its object. The power of contracting further debts was conferred by another grant. The exercise of these powers would, in its nature, be occasional and temporary; that of providing for the common defense was permanent and unceasing, a debt still paying, still to owe, and limited in its duration only by that of the existence of the nation itself. The payment of the debts is about to be consummated. The power of levying duties, taxes, imposts, and excises for that purpose is about to be extinguished in its own fulfillment. There being no debts to be paid, the power of levying taxes for their payment will for the time cease to exist; but that of providing for the common defense will remain, not merely unimpaired but acquiring fresh strength and more impressive weight from the accomplishment of the nation's liberation from debt, swelling and expanding with the increase and expansion of the population and wealth to be defended, and destined to enlarge its dimensions and gather accumulating weight and intensity to a period coeval with the destined existence of the Federal Union.

The author of this report was John Quincy Adams. As might have been expected, it called down upon him the denunciation of those narrow constructionists of the Constitution who assumed then as now that the power to tax for the general welfare meant to tax for revenue only with incidental protection.

The Congressional Librarian informs me that the masterly defense of the position taken in this report, made by Mr. Adams subsequently in a letter to Mr. Speaker Stevenson, July 11, 1832, could only be found after several days' search in an old copy of the National Intelligencer. Such an exhaustive exposition, from such a source, on the construction of this clause of the Constitution ought to be rescued and put in enduring form; and as the whole argument is directly applicable to this discussion I shall append the entire letter to my remarks when published in the RECORD.

Although Mr. Cooley in his work on Constitutional Principles is authority against the use of the taxing power, except for purposes of revenue, we find in his recent work on taxation the following: "On the other hand, one purpose of taxation sometimes is to discourage a business and perhaps to put it out of existence without any idea of protection attending the burden. This has been avowedly the purpose in the case of some Federal taxes."

Mr. STRUBLE: And he cites authorities.

Mr. LA FOLLETTE: Yes, sir; he cites Veazie Bank *vs.* Fenno; but I am bound to say that the opinion of the court in that case, standing alone, may seem scarcely broad enough to warrant Mr. Cooley's general conclusion.

But in the license-tax cases (5 Wall., 462) the court said:

The power of Congress to tax is a very extensive power. It is given in the Constitution with only one exception and only two qualifications. Congress can not tax exports, and it must impose direct taxes by the rule of apportionment and indirect taxes by the rule of uniformity. Thus limited, and thus only, it reaches every subject and may be exercised at discretion.

Chief-Justice Marshall, in McCulloch *vs.* State of Maryland (4 Wheat., 316), says that—"The power to tax involves the power to destroy."

And in Collector *vs.* Day (11 Wall., 113) we find the Supreme Court giving precisely the same construction to the case of Veazie Bank *vs.* Fenno that Mr. Cooley gives on the page from which I have just read in the following language: "But we are referred to the Veazie Bank *vs.* Fenno in support of this power of taxation. That case furnishes a strong illustration of the position taken by the Chief-Justice in McCulloch *vs.* Maryland, namely, 'that the power to tax involves the power to destroy.'"

If, then, the power to tax involves the power to destroy when given without limitations, and if the only limitations fixed by the Constitution is "to pay the debts and provide for the common defense and general welfare," then does it not follow that the tax even when laid to destroy might be for the general welfare, and if so would it not be clearly constitutional?

But it has been said in this discussion that "we can not do indirectly what we have not the authority to do directly, that we have no express authority to prohibit and therefore we can not rightfully use any other power to prohibit." But if we have granted to us a power which by its very nature, as the Supreme Court say, involves the power to destroy—that is, to prohibit—and if, at the same time, there is given with that power an express direction that we shall use it to accomplish the general welfare, and if it manifestly appears that by using this power which involves the right to destroy, if necessary, to obey the mandate to provide for and secure the general welfare, are we then, I ask you, doing anything by an indirection? Are we then acting without authority? Indeed, are we not obeying the Constitution and performing strictly and within its very terms the trust committed to us?

In the practices of this Government from the beginning has not this very construction been, I ask you, adopted in practice? Hamilton in his report on manufactures in 1791, said: "That of duties equivalent to prohibitions there are examples in the laws of the United States," and he advised the further application of the same principle. So, too, Jefferson, in 1793, recommended in his report on commercial restrictions the use of the same power within narrower limits—nevertheless the direct application of the same principle. Of Mr. Jefferson's expressed views John Quincy Adams said: "That Mr. Jefferson had no doubt of the power of Congress to protect the native interests not only by taxation, but by prohibition, has been amply proved, and particularly by one of his messages to Congress."

Probably in the whole history of this people no more liberal construction was ever made of this clause than that given by President Jefferson in the acquisition of Louisiana. Mr. Adams tells us that upon the passage of the act taking possession of Louisiana and for the government thereof this very paragraph of the Constitution was cited by Mr. Rodney, of Delaware, a distinguished lawyer and statesman and the ardent friend and supporter of Mr. Jefferson's administration, as containing the grant of power by which Congress was authorized to make the acquisition. In this instance the object of laying a tax of fifteen millions was not primarily to get revenue to meet the expenses of Government, but was first and foremost for the common defense and general welfare.

Here, though accomplished by one and the same act, it became necessary first to create by the power, given in this clause a necessity for revenue, before there could be any right, in the narrow view, to lay the tax; and this power of providing for the common defense and general welfare moved first in the mind of the legislator, drawing after it as secondary that which it is now claimed on the other side must be the prime essential to any legislation before the tax is laid.

If the repeated enactment of laws under the construction of the Constitution contended for by these eminent authorities and their ready acceptance and approval by the people can give interpretation to a particular clause, this question is in that sense *res adjudicata*.

Should it be claimed that protective and prohibitory taxes, such as have been laid from time to time since the adoption of the Constitution, must find their warrant in the clause giving Congress the power to regulate commerce and not in the clause we are considering, then to claim this is to claim that under the power to regulate commerce you have the right by implication to use the taxing power for another object than revenue; for an object which must prevent revenue being derived; but that under the clause giving directly the power to lay taxes you can only lay them to raise revenue. Is that satisfactory reasoning to any gentleman here? Employing the exact language given in Story:

> If Congress may, in any or all of these cases (in cases where laid to prohibit), lay taxes, then, as revenue constitutes upon the very basis of reasoning no object of the taxes, is it not clear that the enumerated powers (as the power to regulate commerce) require the power to lay taxes to be more extensively construed than for purposes of revenue? It would be no answer to say that the power of taxation, though in its nature only a power to raise revenue, may be resorted to as an implied power to carry into effect these enumerated powers in any effectual manner. That would be to contend that an express power to lay taxes is not coextensive with an implied power to lay taxes; that when the express power is given it means a power to raise revenue only, but when it is implied it no longer has any regard to this object.

And Mr. Adams, in the letter to Mr. Speaker Stevenson, before referred to, touching the power to lay protective or prohibitory taxes, says:

So far as I am able to judge of the force of language the derivation of the power, from the duty to provide for the common defense and general welfare, is more direct, more immediate, less needing a winding staircase of argumentation to come to the result than its derivation from the power to regulate commerce.

There is, then, gentlemen, both strong reasoning and high authority to say that the power to tax is the power to tax whenever it subserves the general welfare.

But you say this is a dangerous power. Is it then more dangerous, if this power to tax for the general welfare is claimed as a right, than is the power (which gentlemen concede we have) to tax ostensibly for the purpose of raising revenue, but with the real purpose of literally taxing out of existence? In either case the only remedy lies in the relation of the legislator to his constituents. And in adopting the broad language, placing the power to tax in the hands of Congress for the high purpose of the general welfare—the common good—under the wise system of frequent revision by the people through the recurring elections, was not the safest check, guard, and protection provided which human foresight could devise?

Resting on the broad ground that Congress has the power to tax for the general welfare, the objection which has been made that this measure, seeking in part as it does to protect the people from a fraudulent and unwholesome article of food, is an interference with the so-called police power of the States ceases to exist.

Instances are not wanting where the authority of the State and Federal powers overlap each other in accomplishing the objects of government. Because the police powers of the State may be employed within the State to subserve the interests and well-being of its citizens, it has never been held that the General Government could not in the exercise of other and different powers delegated to it accomplish the same results for the whole people.

If Congress in the exercise of some of its lawful powers, such as that to tax or to regulate commerce, happens to accomplish the same results which States might accomplish by the police power, it can not be maintained that it is excluded from using the powers delegated to it by the Constitution. And because it effects the same or better results in dealing at the same time with the same subject by no means makes the exercise of the power it employs a police power. The character of the power is not changed because the result it secures is the same as that which the State attempts to secure by a different power.

To construe the authorities as laying down any other doctrine is entirely to misapprehend their meaning. In the License-tax cases (5 Wall., 462) Chief-Justice Chase says: "That the recognition by the acts of Congress of the power and right of the States to tax, control, or regulate any business carried on within their limits is entirely consistent with an intention on the part of Congress to tax such business for national purposes."

The question then which presents itself to every man here is, Will this measure minister to the general good, to the national welfare? If its benefits are merely local and special and not general, then we have no warrant, no right to enact it into a law. These reasons address themselves to the legislative judgment exclusively, our judgment being ever subject to approval or disapproval, to stand or fall before that great tribunal, the people of this country.

Nearly one-half of all the people of this country are engaged in and directly dependent upon agriculture. The vital forces of every other business, I care not what its character, are drawn from and nourished by it. From the standpoint of economics purely and upon the strictest business principles the interests of agriculture are the interests of this Government. No other pursuit so universally and profoundly concerns every other citizen of the Republic—no other calling known to civilized man, where so entirely and completely the interests of one is the interest of all.

There are other considerations which are worthy the thought of those charged in part with the duties of government. Favored by the character of our institutions, almost all of the farm land in this country is held and owned by the men who cultivate it. Ownership of soil means ownership of home, and I tell you, that government whose people build and own their own homes, lays broadest and deepest its foundations and bargains most surely and happily with time. Such homes, no matter how humble, are pledges of the perpetuity of the nation. Our little modest homes scattered over this land, reared by those who live in them, are the pillars of strength which lift this government above other nations of the civilized world. And it is well for us to remember here as elsewhere that the poorest home is just as great an element of strength to the state as the costliest mansion. To the state, to the government, there is no difference.

Now, sir, these rural homes are built on small margins. They are maintained only by industry and frugality. Every factor of strength and support about them is important to comfortable, decent existence.

Sir, I know something of life upon the farm; I know the value of the little things in the economical system, in the sparing, cautious management practiced there. I know how the small things are used to fill up and round out the seasons as they go. There is little that can be safely spared.

I know, sir, the vital, the absolutely vital importance of the dairy to the maintenance not only of the home comforts, the sweetening of the home life, but its great value to that which makes the home possible—the farm itself. It is the one important element in almost the only system which can be adopted upon the small farms to sustain their soil and preserve their producing properties. To foreclose the farmer from this essential branch of his business is to greatly narrow the limits of his industry, lessen the number of farm products, and force overproduction in the few produced with all its consequent disasters to commerce and trade.

It is too late in this discussion to go into figures, nor is it necessary. The dairy interest and all that it carries with it is in a distressing condition. It has been driven to the wall and is to-day fighting for a place to stand. It is set upon from all sides by an unseen foe. It is struck from behind. It is taken in ambush. It can make no defense.

Ah! but you say, "This is competition, and are you going to apply the taxing power to settle differences of competition between domestic industries?" I answer that is not the question presented here. We face a new situation in history. Ingenuity, striking hands with cunning trickery, compounds a substance to counterfeit an article of food. It is made to look like something it is not; to taste and smell like something it is not; to sell for something it is not, and so deceive the purchaser. It follows faithfully two rules: "Miss no opportunity to deceive;" "At all times put money in thy purse." It obeys no laws.

The evidence, undisputed, is that there enters into its composition a large number of substances which singly, or in combination, are unwholesome, poisonous, and either directly or indirectly destructive of human life.

It is no longer a question with the citizen anywhere, from ocean to ocean, whether he would prefer to eat it. He is forced to eat it. This monstrous product of greed and hypocrisy makes its way into the home and onto the table of every consumer. It is as powerful and irresistible as vicious ingenuity can make it. It is as pitiless as a plague. It wants only one thing: it wants your money—it does not care for your life.

Talk about competition! Why, gentlemen, stop and think! There can be no competition except where there is rivalry. Competition implies two or more persons or things or employments—two or more entities—each with an individuality, a character, an identity of its own, in common strife for the same object. But there can, from the very nature of things, be no competition between a substance and its counterfeit. The sole object in making one substance in imitation of another, for purposes of sale, is to avoid competition.

It is time that this idle talk about interference with the competition of two industries should cease. The purpose of this bill is to insure competition. Here is a villainous device for making money lawlessly and subtilely, eating the heart out of an industry which is to this Government what blood is to the body. It is not only striking prostrate the agricultural industry, but it accomplishes this by cheating and defrauding the balance of the people—the great body of consumers out of both money and health. It spares no one.

All legislation attempted by, or within the reach of the States is impotent to deal with this monster. If there was ever a time in the history of this Government when the essence of the great protection principles should be applied—when this body was solemnly commanded to use its delegated powers for the general good, this is the hour.

I shall vote for this bill.

The Menace of the Political Machine

Chicago, February 22, 1897

Mr. President, Gentlemen of the Faculty, Students of the University of Chicago, Ladies and Gentlemen: In accepting the invitation of your distinguished president to address you, I fully realize the difficulties of the situation. Situated as you are in an atmosphere of investigation and research, surrounded by the most eminent living exponents of the highest thought on every subject of learning, I could scarcely hope to interest you in any attempt at a historical and philosophical review, such as the day suggests. I therefore turn the thought aside and speak to you upon a practical question of the hour. After all, we can share in no higher commemoration of this occasion than to render an account of the stewardship committed to us by the Father of our country. This brings me to ask you to consider here to-day the political machine, its evolution in our political history, and its menace to representative government.

In every democracy men will affiliate with one or the other of two great political parties. The ballot must determine which party shall administer government, enact new legislation, adjust the laws to all the complex social relations of life, to all the complicated business transactions of millions of human beings with order and justice. The ballot can achieve the kind of administration desired, establish the economic and financial policies essential, only through the election of men of integrity and ability, embodying the ideas expressed in the ballot. That the voter may be thoroughly informed upon the question involved, and upon the men to be chosen as the representatives of his convictions, there should be the widest discussion and the most searching investigation. Every means which contributes to this end is an aid to good government. Here, then, is the open field for the highest work of political organization—the work preliminary to the selection of candidates.

INDIVIDUAL RESPONSIBILITY

The fundamental principle of a republic is individual responsibility. The responsibility is personal at the point in our political system where the citizen comes in direct contact with the system itself. This is the initial point of all legislation, all administration. In all the activities preliminary to the primary, and in the primary itself, the citizen is an elementary force in government. Here the voter can lay his hand directly upon the shoulder of the public servant and point the way he should go. But this ends with the adjournment of the primary or caucus. From that moment the citizen, in a representative democracy, under a caucus, delegate and convention system, does not again come in direct personal touch with the work either of legislation or administration. How essential, then, if he is to be a factor in government, that he take part, and intelligently too, in this fundamental work. If there be failure here, there is failure throughout. If through inattention or indifference, through mistake or misrepresentation, through trickery or fraud, or "fine work," the minority control in the caucus, the laws will be made and executed by the agent of the minority and the first principle of our government fails.

To enlist the interest of every individual, encourage research, stimulate discussion of measures and of men, prior to the time when the voter should discharge this primary duty of citizenship, offers political organization opportunity for the highest public service. Teaching the principles of the party, reviewing political history, discussing pending and proposed legislation, investigating the fitness of candidates for office, quickening the sense of obligation and personal responsibility in all the duties of citizenship, commanding the continuous, intelligent, personal interest of the individual voter—and when the campaign is on conducting the canvass—these are the legitimate functions of political organization.

Such organizations cannot be used as a political machine for individuals or factions. Whenever such organizations are maintained political slates are shattered and political bargains fail of consummation. Cliques, rings, machines thrive upon the citizen's indifference to the plain duties of representative government.

There is no likeness or similitude between political organization that appeals to every voter in the party and a machine that appeals only to the most skilled and unscrupulous workers of the party.

That a political organization can exist without degenerating into a political machine; that it can serve the cause of good government, sometimes in defiance of the machine, is very recent political history.

PEOPLE'S TRIUMPH OVER THE MACHINE

It is well known that, for a long time prior to the last Republican National convention, the conditions then prevailing throughout the country were such as to occasion a widespread and profound interest in the selection of a Republican candidate for the presidency. It is well known that this interest centered upon Maj. McKinley. It is well known that the political machine in every state where it controlled party organization cooperated to defeat his nomination. The ensuing contest was one of the most interesting in American politics, and well illustrates the distinction I would make, between machine politics designed to control in defiance of the desires of a majority, and legitimate political organization which seeks only a fair and honest expression of the people's will.

The admitted choice of nine-tenths of his party, without wise leadership and perfected organization, Maj. McKinley would have been defeated. The time and opportunity were ripe for a victory over the worst elements in the party. The people were in earnest and ready, but the field covered a continent, and it was a prodigious undertaking to marshal the masses, untrained in the arts of political management, against the disciplined veterans of the machine; to force the contest out into the open field; to leave no opportunity for surprise or betrayal; to make every politician wear his colors and declare his choice.

There were other candidates of high merit and distinguished public service, but owing to existing conditions their support was chiefly local or sectional.

Hard pressed the machine resorted to the usual plan of dividing the people by inspiring the candidacy of a favorite son, in each of as large a number of states as possible. Failing in this the last desperate trick was attempted, of securing delegates nominally for McKinley but in fact for any candidate to defeat McKinley. This expedient was promptly met by instructing delegates to vote in convention for the people's choice. And the convention which finally assembled at St. Louis in June, 1896, simply recorded the result determined months before.

Since the appearance of the machine in politics this is the most notable instance of its defeat. It brings with it a lesson for this hour. Probably not twice in a generation would the experience of the people be of such a character, be so general and extend over such a period of time, as to make the members of one party so unitedly of one mind, so fused together in one mass. Never before was the power of machine influence so strongly shown in concerted movement over such a wide field of action. From the control of great cities and great states, of legislatures and of seats in the United States senate—unless speedily arrested, it is manifest that ultimately the machine will acquire supreme control of government. Right-minded, thoughtful, patriotic men observe the rapid and almost irresistible advance of this era of misrule with serious apprehension and misgiving.

EVOLUTION OF POPULAR REPRESENTATION

Whence came this menace to the Republic established by Washington and his followers? What is its evolution in our political life?

There was no place in the beginning for the machine. The simple plan provided at the outset was to assemble the people of a district and to select one of their number to represent them. This at least brought together the more prominent citizens and insured the choice of those for public life who would represent their constituencies, in conformity with the views of the founders of representative government—that is, a representative government through representative men. These representative men were expected to maintain their independence of thought and action, rather than reflect the opinions of those whom they represented. Our forefathers were a little distrustful of a too immediate participation in political control by the people unaccustomed to self-government. The judgment of the few was regarded as safer and wiser than the untested judgment of the many. The growth of the government they planned very soon overran their most abundant caution, and always in the direction of a more pronounced democracy.

The hasty intervention of congress in the nomination of the president, and—with the prompt emasculation of the Electoral college—in the election of the president as well, all in violation of the letter and spirit of the constitution, were causes early moving to a larger depository of power with the people.

Along with popular development, came competition and contest for the distinctions of public service. With opportunities of wider choice the people began to demand a more exact reflection of their own views by their representatives. The representative now came in fact to be regarded as the servant of the people. This did not preclude leadership. While in one direction there was a tendency toward the loss of individuality in an identification of the representative with his constituency, in another there was a larger field for the higher talents of creative statesmanship in marking out public policy and moulding public opinion to its adoption. But whether originating with the people or the representative, the time came finally when they demanded that he represent their ideas—either by reflecting their opinions, or by furnishing them with a better set of opinions.

This was progress along the lines of pure democracy. It marked an advance of the people, the assertion of the individual as a political factor.

The development of the individual in government called for instrumentalities which would enable him to make the government feel the full weight of his personality.

THE CAUCUS AND THE CONVENTION

It is here that we note the appearance of the caucus and convention. The complicated system of caucuses, to select delegates to attend conventions, to select other delegates to attend nominating conventions to choose candidates to be voted for at the general elections, was never thought of by the framers of the constitution, and no provision whatever was made with reference to it. Except in two states the caucus and convention plan was unheard of for nearly a generation following the constitution. And it was not until after 1840 that it became an established part of our system of American politics. It was devised to give the people a direct voice in self government. It has sustained general and complete transformation. The voice still seems the voice of the people, but, alas, it has become the edict of the machine.

On the 19th of November, thirty-three years ago, a great concourse of people gathered on a Pennsylvania hillside and overran the cleared wheat fields adjoining. All about them were the fresh evidences of mighty conflict—leveled fences, demolished buildings, dismounted guns, trees torn and blasted, and on every side the newly turned earth in broken billows, marked the places where rested the uncounted dead. A tall form towered above the multitude, and all eyes were turned toward a face, plain and careworn to sadness. A deeper stillness fell upon them, as those immortal words were borne to their expectant ears, on that gray November day:

We here highly resolve that these dead shall not have died in vain; that this nation, under God, shall have a new birth of freedom and that the government of the people, by the people, and for the people, shall not perish from the earth.

"The government of the people, by the people, and for the people." It was reserved for this highest product of the American Republic—this embodied spirit of all the nobility and simplicity, all the wisdom and sentiment, all the courage and patience, all the serious earnestness and quaint humor, all the fear of God and faith in the plain people, in American character to immortalize at once the profoundness and most philosophical, yet simplest and most popular definition of American democracy ever uttered. How dear to us then were those words! How deeply they laid hold of our national life! What sacrifices we were freely making for that kind [of] government! How ready were we to give our fortunes, mortgage our future, march our brave men to battle, blot out our individual homes and hopes, clothe the dead in glory and the living in mourning—all to preserve a government of the people, by the people, and for the people! Who then would have believed that before a generation of time should pass this would gradually become a government of the people, by the machine, and for the machine?

PEOPLE TOO BUSY FOR POLITICS

It was but natural that a sense of deep security should follow the successful termination of the war for the Union. The government which had withstood rebellion had nothing to fear in peace. There remained but to restore the waste places, revive dominant industries, return to the shops and farms, and quicken the halting pace of trade and commerce. Nothing required the good citizen's attention but the material affairs of the nation. The fires never went out in the furnaces, the factories ran day and night, invention awoke like a young giant from his sleep, the merchant drove his bargains, the lawyer was busy with his briefs, the scholar shut himself in his study, the farmer was early and late in his fields, the music of industry and prosperity filled the land. Few men had time for the small affair of politics. To turn aside from the hot pursuit of fortune, to ignore the pressing calls in one's profession, to let business go for politics, was not to be considered for one moment. It came to be regarded as a great personal sacrifice, entitling one to much commendation for public spirit, to close the office and shop and factory and store for a single day that the votes might be cast and counted.

After a time changes came in to disturb the even flow of business prosperity. Something was wrong somewhere. Surely the fault must be with the administration; and it occurred to the good citizen to inquire who had been attending to the business of government all these years.

DOCTRINE OF PRACTICAL POLITICS PROCLAIMED

When the business man, the scholar, the farmer, the artisan, awoke to the importance of participating in municipal, state and federal politics, they were amazed to find that a new force occupied the field and assumed the right to control. This new force sneered at their ideas as theoretical, and proclaimed the doctrine of practical politics. They were indignant. This government belonged to the people. Every man had equal rights, equal responsibilities and should have equal voice in making and executing the laws. The people were in the majority, they would not submit to dictation by a mere political cabal. They would contest the field with the practical politicians. The merchant left his store, the workman his bench, the farmer his harvest fields, and came forth to assert the sacred rights of a majority. At the close of the day they found themselves beaten at every point, and not one of them could tell how it occurred. They certainly had an overwhelming majority, but there had been misunderstanding, confusion and defeat. The majority could spare but the day from business; the practical politician found it profitable to give it his entire time. The proceeding was new to the majority; the practical politician understood every detail. The majority was embarrassed with a multitude of counsel; the practical politicians obeyed one voice. The majority was as inefficient as a mob; the practical politicians were as effective as the "Old Guard."

Again and again, season after season, the majority went out blindly to defeat the practical politicians, but always with the same result. For a long time the business of manipulating the caucuses and the conventions had been left to the practical politician, and he had become very expert. He matured and perfected a system. It produced results with mathematical certainty. It was always in operation. It had acquired the trick of perpetual motion.

THE MODERN POLITICAL MACHINE

This is the modern political machine. It is impersonal, irresponsible, extra-legal. The courts offer no redress for the rights it violates, the wrongs it inflicts. It is without conscience and without remorse. It has come to be enthroned in American politics. It rules caucuses, names delegates, appoints committees, dominates the councils of the party, dictates nominations, makes platforms, dispenses patronage, directs state administrations, controls legislatures, stifles opposition, punishes independence, and elects United States senators. In the states where it is supreme, the edict of the machine is the only sound heard, and outside it is easily mistaken for the voice of the people. If some particular platform pledge is necessary to the triumph of the hour, the platform is so written and the pledge violated without offering excuse or justification. If public opinion be roused to indignant protest, some scapegoat is put forward to suffer vicariously for the sins of the machine, and subsequently rewarded for his service by the emoluments of machine spoils. If popular revolt against the machine sweeps over the state on rare occasions and the machine finds itself hard pressed to maintain its hold on party organization, control conventions, and nominate its candidates—when threats and promises fail—the "barrel" is not wanting until the way is cleared.

AGENCIES BY WHICH IT CONTROLS

The agencies by which it executes its will are many. The types of its big wheels and little wheels, its pinions and cogs, are only too familiar and recognizable. The sharp, shifty man whose absence of other occupations gives leisure for anticipation and execution of necessary details—the manager for a county or a congressional district, as befits the measure of his abilities; his pay, promotion either within the machine or as one of its candidates for official station; the local agent who disburses the campaign fund and takes out his own tithing; the "heeler" who expects only a cash per diem, and a friendly recognition useful in the time of his occasional collision with the law; a section of the press with its goal an office and its certainty a slice of the campaign money; the broken down political hack, whom not even the power of the machine can force upon the people and who must seek a place by sycophantic obeisance to the machine managers and the whole servile, conscienceless crew who—

> Crook the pregnant hinges of the knee,
> Where thrift may follow fawning.

They serve in a multitude of places. To one is assigned the duty of quietly passing the word for the caucus work; to another the important position of presiding at the caucus, of recognizing only machine motions and declaring them carried at all hazards; to another the duty of moving with great alacrity the election of delegates slated; to another the artful mission of posing as the leader of the opposition; to another that he shall make the timely motion to adjourn; to another the delicate responsibility of "seeing" delegates at the convention "alone"; to another, who is gifted by nature for the service, the traveling commission of visiting candidates for the legislature and diplomatically offering some pecuniary "encouragement" in their canvass, as the "party leaders consider it very important that the Hon. Richard Roe should be elected to the United States senate"; to another the pleasant business of calling upon certain brethren of the press, and suggesting about what is likely to happen in the next convention and in the next legislature—thus affording the opportunity to publish the fact, that there is a "growing sentiment" for this man and for that measure— and so on to the end. Every man is placed over the state and every line is laid, every duty assigned. And behind this instrument of evil sit in conference and command the few choice spirits who touch the springs by which the modern juggernaut is set in motion.

ABUSES WHICH IT HAS DEVELOPED

The wrongs inflicted by the machine do not end with the appropriation of offices. It does not secure the offices for salaries primarily. The salary is merely an incident. Government by the machine is machine despotism. It administers the laws through its agents, after its own interpretation. It is independent of the people, and fears no reckoning. In extreme cases where it becomes necessary to meet arraignment it has its own press to parry or soften the blow. Having no constituency to serve, it serves itself. The machine is its own master. It owes no obligation and acknowledges no responsibility.

Its legislatures make the laws by its schedule. It names their committees. It suppresses bills inimical to its interests, behind the closed doors of its committee rooms. It suppresses debate by a machine rule and the ready gavel of a pliant speaker. It exploits measures with reform titles, designed to perpetuate machine control. It cares for special interests and takes tribute from its willing subjects, the private corporations. There was a time when the corporation lobbyist was an important functionary, and the mercenary legislator a factor with whom it was necessary to make terms. The perfected political machine is fast superseding the lobbyist. The corporation now makes terms direct with the machine and the lobbyist now attends upon the legislature to look after details and spy upon the action of members.

The private corporation is a source of large income to the machine, for it is everywhere present to-day. The individual is rapidly disappearing from the business world, and nearly all of the business of the country to-day is transacted by private corporations. Artificial light, fuel, the food we eat, the clothes we wear, the medicine measured out to us in sickness, indeed nearly everything which ministers to man's comfort or nourishes life, passes under corporate control before it reaches the consumer. And the corporation with its special franchise, its special power, its special exemptions, its exclusive privilege, is ever present and always well cared for in the machine legislature.

DESPOTISM DISPLACES DEMOCRACY

But it is not in its bad legislation, not yet in its vicious administration of the laws, that the political machine is most to be apprehended. The work of a bad legislature may be undone, its unjust laws repealed, the stain of its record purged from the statutes.

In so far as the public is concerned with the individuals it may be of small consequence what particular set of men fill the offices this year or next. Individuals count for but little. The ambitions of men contending for personal supremacy vex the passing hour and are forgotten. But one thing, however, does remain as part of every victory achieved for machine men by machine methods. It goes to the very life of the state itself that its laws shall be made and administered by those constitutionally chosen to represent the majority. Control by the machine is without exception the rule of the minority. Every machine victory is the triumph of despotism over democracy. Within its reach and scope every such victory destroys representative government. Its acts are as essentially treasonable to the fundamental principles of this Republic as was the assault on Fort Sumter. Grave danger lies not in waiting for this Republic, to destroy its life or change its character by force of arms. The shock and heat of collision will ever rouse and solidify patriotic citizenship in defense of American liberty. It is the insidious, creeping, progressive encroachment that presents the greatest peril.

The machine—this invisible empire, does its work so quietly. There is no explosion, no clash of arms, no open rebellion, but a sly covert nullification of the highest law of the land. It incurs none of the risks of armed assault, escapes the personal dangers and swift public retribution provoked by organized violence and intimidation. So long as the methods were the methods of Boss Tweed it was more notorious but infinitely less dangerous. It would in time go down beneath the overpowering weight of decent loyal public condemnation. But when adroit, skilled, talented men, schooled in practical politics, devised a system that had in the beginning the semblance of serving its party but mastered it instead; that openly lauded allegiance to party principle and artfully violated every principle of honor; that had its secret agents in every community and its cunning operatives in every caucus; that fooled the citizen by the tricks of legerdemain; that with a handful of unscrupulous men manipulated caucuses, defeated majorities, debauched politics, and drove thousands of good citizens away from the primaries to stay—then indeed was the danger to the Republic greatly augmented. But more than all this, when they worked into the political thought and life of people by the thousands, young and old, ignorant men and educated, the pernicious, monstrous doctrine, that the violation of the sacred principle of representative government, the spirit and letter of the Constitution, is highly commendable if it is only successful, that the American citizen's ballot, his defense, his power, his hope, his prophesy, is the legitimate, rightful, spoil and plunder of the political machine—then they corrupted the very springs of national life, and polluted them in their courses as they flow on to meet the coming generations.

WHAT SHALL WE DO TO BE SAVED?

What, then, shall we do to be saved?

Waste no more time in vain sermons on the duty of attending the caucus. It is too late for that. Except at long intervals, when in a sort of frenzy the citizen strikes at the machine shackles, men can no longer be drafted into caucus attendance. They have seen the game before. They know the dice are loaded. They are no longer indifferent to their duties, nor ignorant of the situation. They well understand that their only part in government is to vote the ticket prepared for them, and bear the machine rule of their own party or the machine rule of the other party. They know they do not get the kind of government they vote for, but they do the best they can. They still attend the elections. They are as vitally interested in good government as ever. They are only waiting to find the way to achieve it. Here is our final safety. Here is the ultimate overthrow of the machine.

If we provide the same safeguards, the same certainty, the same facility for expressing and executing the will of the people at the primaries as now prevail at the elections, we shall have the same general interest, the same general participation in the one as in the other.

Aye, more than this; if we guarantee the American citizen a full voice in the selection of candidates and shaping the policy of his party and the administration of government incident thereto, then shall we invest not only the primaries but the elections as well, with an abiding interest for him, extending beyond the day of the primary, the day of the election, the weeks of the campaign; then indeed shall we make the primary and the election of vastly deeper significance, appealing in a new way to his deliberate judgment, his patriotism, and his personal responsibility.

Disinterested consideration of a few plain facts that govern the situation points the remedy. As our government has developed it is surely as important to the state that the citizen be protected in the exercise of his choice of candidates as in the election of candidates to office.

SAFEGUARDS ABOUT THE NOMINATIONS

It is as much the interest and as plainly the duty of the state to as carefully perfect and guard a system of nominating candidates as it perfects and guards the system of electing them.

The reformation effected in our elections by the Australian voting system should inspire us with confidence in advancing the lines of attack. Recall for one moment the change wrought wherever the Australian system has been adopted. Formerly the polling place was the scene of wrangling, dispute, disorder, often of violence and collision; weak men were badgered, corrupt men were bought. The employer often followed his men to the ballot box, voting them in a body, and the political boss was always present. Today the voter, freed from all annoyances, all espionage, all intimidation, goes alone into the quiet of the election booth and exercises his right without fear of punishment or hope of reward, other than his own conscience affords and the general good secures. Here rich and poor, employer and employed, meet on the same level. That which had become a mere theory under the old plan of voting is transformed into an assured fact under the new, and the state maintains in this place the quality of its citizens before the law.

Is there any good reason why a plan so successful in securing a free, honest ballot and fair count in the election, will not work equally well in the nomination of candidates?

CAUCUS AND CONVENTION SYSTEM INHERENTLY BAD

It is idle to talk of reforming the caucus. The machine, in some instances, already anticipating the danger of the destruction of this foundation of machine control, under the mask of caucus reform, is seeking to satisfy public interest and save all the elements of the caucus essential to machine manipulation and supremacy.

The caucus, delegate, and convention system is inherently bad. It invites to manipulation, scheming, trickery, corruption and fraud. Even if the caucus were fairly conducted, the plan, of which it is a part, removes the nomination too far from the voter. Every transfer of delegated power weakens responsibility, until finally, by the time it is lodged in the hands of a nominating convention, the sense of responsibility has been lost in transit, unless it has been ticketed through by instructions from its original source. And even then all along the journey, from the primary to the convention, the confidential agents of the machine are introducing delegates to the mysteries of "gold brick" and "three card" political schemes.

The convention under the most favorable conditions is anything but a deliberative body. Its work is hurried and business necessarily transacted in confusion. There is great excitement. It is the storm center of a political tempest. There are rumors and roor-backs, challenges and denials. There is no time for investigation and no opportunity to distinguish the real issue from the false issue. Charges are withheld and "sprung" in the convention purposely to avoid disapproval and mislead delegates. And the dark horse is ever in reserve, waiting a favorable opportunity to take the convention unawares. These are the most favorable conditions which we can hope to have prevail in and about the convention under the present system. Add to this all the corruption, which comes with machine domination of a convention, and you have political disaster and political crime as a result.

If after long suffering and misrepresentation the people by tremendous and united effort could succeed in defeating and even destroying the machine, the opportunity offered by the caucus and convention plan would simply restore the old or build up a new machine in its place.

A PRIMARY ELECTION THE REMEDY

No, No! Beginning the work in the state, put aside the caucus and the convention. They have been and will continue to be prostituted to the service of corrupt organization. They answer no purpose further than to give respectable form to political robbery. Abolish the caucus and the convention. Go back to the first principles of democracy. Go back to the people. Substitute for both the caucus and the convention a primary election—held under all the sanctions of law which prevail at the general elections—where the citizen may cast his vote directly to nominate the candidate of the party with which he affiliates, and have it canvassed and returned just as he cast it.

Provide a means of placing the candidates in nomination before the primary, and forestall the creation of a new caucus system, back of the primary election.

Provide a ballot for the primary election and print on it the names of all candidates for nomination who have previously filed preliminary nomination papers with a designated official.

Provide that no candidate for nomination shall be entitled to have his name printed on the primary election ticket who shall not have been called out as a candidate by the written request of a given percentage of the vote cast at the preceding election in the district, county or state in which he is proposed as a candidate; in the same manner that judicial candidates are now called out in many states.

Provide for the selection of a committee to represent the party organization and promulgate the party platform by the election at the primary of a representative man from the party for each county in the state.

Under severe penalties for violation of the law, prohibit electioneering in or about the election booth, punish bribery or the attempt to bribe, and protect fully the canvass and return of the votes cast.

Do this and the knell of the political machine has sounded in the state.

Then every citizen will share equally in the nomination of the candidates of his party and attend primary elections, as a privilege as well as duty. It will no longer be necessary to create an artificial interest in the general election to induce voters to attend. Intelligent, well-considered judgment will be substituted for unthinking enthusiasm, the lamp of reason for the torchlight. The voter will not require to be persuaded that he has an interest in the election. He will know that he has. The nominations of the party will not be the result of "compromise" or impulse, or evil design—the "barrel" and the machine, but the candidates of the majority honestly and fairly nominated.

To every generation some important work is committed. If this generation will destroy the political machine, will emancipate the majority from its enslavement, will again place the destinies of this nation in the hands of its citizens, then, "Under God, this government of the people, by the people and for the people shall not perish from the earth."

Governor La Follette's Speech of Acceptance

Madison, July 16, 1902

Gentlemen,—I am informed by your committee of my nomination for governor of the state of Wisconsin, by the Republican party which you represent here in convention. I accept the nomination with a deep sense of the honor which is conferred and of the duty which is imposed. I am grateful for the approval of the acts of the administration by the Republican party for which you are authorized to speak, and to which you have given strong expression here today. Called for a second time to represent the Republican party as its candidate for governor, permit me through you to convey my profound appreciation to your constituents for this evidence of their continued confidence.

PARTY THAT KEEPS THE FAITH

When William McKinley was officially notified of his renomination for the presidency, he was able to say that faith with the public had been kept; that the pledges made to the people by the Republican party had been redeemed. It has been the proud boast of the party from Lincoln to Roosevelt that its obligations were always honored. A citizen of this country could at any time ascertain the lines upon which the Republican party would legislate by consulting its platform declarations. It never equivocated; it never dodged; it never straddled. In plain terms it presented its promises. In good faith it redeemed them.

Political platforms must be upheld if political parties are to be maintained. Their declarations are the expression of the deliberate judgment, the consensus of opinion, the common intent, the generally accepted and well understood policy of the party on important issues.

PLATFORM PLEDGES SACRED

Platform pledges express the convictions of the party and are the inducements offered by the party for the votes of the people. They are the party's promise to do specific things. They are the voter's guide in determining with what party he will affiliate. They constitute a written contract deliberately entered into with every man who casts his vote for the candidate of his party. Neither the party nor the official representative of the party can with honor change or repudiate that contract. The candidate who is unwilling to be bound by the platform of the party has no moral or political right to accept a party nomination. If having accepted a nomination he finds that he is not in accord with the pledges of his party, if he cannot carry out its promises as an official, if he decides to be independent of platform obligations, he is then in honor bound so to announce, at once to withdraw as a party candidate and stand, if at all, upon his individual declaration as a candidate for office independent of party support.

These propositions require no argument. They are the unwritten but unchangeable law of political ethics. They enforce themselves between the candidate and the party, the official and the public.

YET THEY HAVE BEEN BROKEN

That the platform promises of the Republican party have been broken and its honor stained in Wisconsin, no man is permitted truthfully to deny. After years of discussion of just and equal taxation and nominations by direct vote, no party platform pledged to those issues could have been adopted unanimously two years ago, unless that platform proclaimed the will of the Republican party. That many legislators remained loyal to the party and faithful to their constituents for the enactment of these pledges into law, battling for the right and steadfastly endeavoring to hold the party erect in honor, will never be forgotten by the people of Wisconsin.

Opposition to that platform sought to justify itself upon the plea that the pledges were not well understood and did not represent the real sentiment of the party. That claim will not be made again. For eighteen months the debate has been on. If the arguments have not always been addressed to reason, if the discussion has not always been parliamentary, at least the lines have been clearly drawn and the count fairly made.

NO MORE MISUNDERSTANDING

There can be no misunderstanding as to the Republican platform of 1902. Whatever difference of opinion individuals may have heretofore entertained, as Republicans they must now acquiesce in the expressed will of the party. It has spoken in no uncertain voice for the enactment of these platform declarations into law in twenty-four of the thirty-three senate districts and seventy-four of the one hundred assembly districts of the state. It has proclaimed by overwhelming majority, from Lake Superior to the Illinois line, that its promises shall now be made good to the last letter.

CHIEF JUSTICE RYAN'S WARNING

Twenty-nine years ago, before a cultured audience in the assembly chamber of the capitol, Chief Justice Ryan made a warning forecast. I see him now as then,—his bowed figure, his transparent face, his luminous eyes, through which, undimmed with age, shone the genius of one of the great intellects of the last century. Again I hear his vibrant voice across almost a generation of time:

There is looming up a new and dark power. I cannot dwell upon the signs and shocking omens of its advent. The accumulation of individual wealth seems to be greater than it ever has been since the downfall of the Roman empire. And the enterprises of the country are aggregating vast corporate combinations of unexampled capital, boldly marching, not for economic conquests only, but for political power. We see their colors, we hear their trumpets, we distinguish the sound of preparation in their camps. For the first time really in our politics, money is taking the field as an organized power. It is unscrupulous, arrogant, and overbearing. Already, here at home, one great corporation has trifled with the sovereign power and insulted the state. There is grave fear that it and its great rival have confederated to make partition of the state and share it as spoils. Wealth has its rights. Industrious wealth has its honors. These it is the duty of the law to assert and protect, though wealth has great power of self protection and influence beyond the limits of integrity. But money as a political influence is essentially corrupt; it is one of the most dangerous to free institutions; by far the most dangerous to the free and just administration of the law. It is entitled to fear, if not to respect. The question will arise, and arise in your day, though perhaps not fully in mine:—Which shall rule—wealth or men; which shall lead—money or intellect; who shall fill public stations—educated and patriotic free men, or the feudal serfs of corporate capital?

OUR GRAVEST DANGER

How prophetic his words!

The gravest danger menacing republican institutions to-day is the over-balancing control of city, state, and national legislatures by the wealth and power of public-service corporations. This is not more marked with one political party when in power than with another. It deals with public officials. It makes no political distinctions. It cannot be cured by denunciation. it cannot be defended by the cry of "purist" or "populist" or "demagogue." It goes directly to the root of government. It threatens to sap the life of American citizenship. The voter elects the candidate; the corporation controls the official.

It leaves the citizen the semblance of power which is actually exercised against him.

IT CALLS FOR COURAGE

The problem presented is a momentous one. It calls for no appeal to passion or prejudice or fear. It calls for courage and patriotism and self-sacrifice. It calls for solution. Shall the American people become servants instead of masters of their boasted material progress and prosperity,—victims of the colossal wealth this free land has fostered and protected? Surely our great cities, our great states, our great nation, will not helplessly surrender to this most insidious enemy which is everywhere undermining official integrity and American institutions. Surely the party of Abraham Lincoln which abolished slavery, which kept the United States undivided upon the map of the world, will not abandon its traditions, its memories, its hopes, and become the instrument of injustice and oppression. It will do its plain duty now, as it did in that greatest epoch of the country's history. It will meet the issues with rectitude and unfaltering devotion, strong in the faith of ultimate triumph.

CONTEST NOT YET FULLY WON

Gentlemen of the convention, the contest for equal and just taxation and nominations by direct vote is not yet completely won. The nomination which you have just tendered me is the unmistakable, the emphatic demand of the republican party for the prompt enactment of these laws. But between that expressed will and the ripening of these measures into law, there are caucuses and conventions for the nomination of candidates for the senate and assembly. When the legislature convenes there are the same forces to be met and contended with that led to the undoing of the last legislature. I appeal to you, and through you to the people of the state, to be vigilant to the last hour. Do not relax your efforts until this good work is finished. Let no man be named for the legislature who is not fully in accord with the Republican platform. Name only men who are willing to go on record for this legislation, who are free from all entanglements or complications that may force them to vote contrary to desire and conscience. Wherever senators or assemblymen already have been nominated, let them openly and publicly proclaim their position with respect to these issues. This is equally the right of the party and the public.

Gentlemen, the contest through which we have just passed strengthens the pillars of government by the people and for the people. It teaches the sacredness of public obligation. It elevates moral standards in public life.

ALL ELSE TO BE FORGOTTEN

These are lessons which we should cherish. Let all else of this contest be forgotten. It does not signify who began it, or why it was begun. It has been decided. Let that suffice. I do not treasure one personal injury or lodge in memory one personal insult. With individuals I have no quarrel and will have none. The span of my life is too short for that. But so much as it pleases God to spare unto me I shall give, whether in the public service or out of it, to the contest for good government.

Every pledge of the platform which you have adopted here to-day has my unqualified approval, and, if elected, I shall, in so far as the direction of public affairs is committed to me, faithfully strive to carry out those pledges.

I accept a renomination firm in the resolution to discharge every duty that devolves upon me conscientiously, sustained by the abiding conviction that the Republican party will redeem its pledges and press on to other victories.

If again chosen chief executive of this commonwealth, it will be my highest endeavor personally, and with the aid of my associates in office and the co-operation of the legislative department, to give to the people of Wisconsin an efficient and economic state government, honestly administered in a spirit of justice to all men and to all interests.

Free Speech and the Right of Congress to Declare the Objects of the War

Washington, D.C., October 6, 1917

Mr. LA FOLLETTE: Mr. President, I rise to a question of personal privilege.

I have no intention of taking the time of the Senate with a review of the events which led to our entrance into the war except in so far as they bear upon the question of personal privilege to which I am addressing myself.

Six Members of the Senate and 50 Members of the House voted against the declaration of war. Immediately there was let loose upon those Senators and Representatives a flood of invective and abuse from newspapers and individuals who had been clamoring for war, unequaled, I believe, in the history of civilized society.

Prior to the declaration of war every man who had ventured to oppose our entrance into it had been condemned as a coward or worse, and even the President had by no means been immune from these attacks.

Since the declaration of war the triumphant war press has pursued those Senators and Representatives who voted against war with malicious falsehood and recklessly libelous attacks, going to the extreme limit of charging them with treason against their country.

This campaign of libel and character assassination directed against the Members of Congress who opposed our entrance into the war has been continued down to the present hour, and I have upon my desk newspaper clippings, some of them libels upon me alone, some directed as well against other Senators who voted in opposition to the declaration of war.

One of these newspaper reports most widely circulated represents a Federal judge in the State of Texas as saying, in a charge to a grand jury—I read the article as it appeared in the newspaper and the headline with which it is introduced:

DISTRICT JUDGE WOULD LIKE TO TAKE A SHOT AT TRAITORS IN CONGRESS

[By Associated Press leased wire.]

Houston, Tex., October 1, 1917.

Judge Waller T. Burns, of the United States district court, in charging a Federal grand jury at the beginning of the October term to-day, after calling by name Senators STONE of Missouri, HARDWICK of Georgia, VARDAMAN of Mississippi, GRONNA of North Dakota, GORE of Oklahoma, and LA FOLLETTE of Wisconsin, said:

"If I had a wish, I would wish that you men had jurisdiction to return bills of indictment against these men. They ought to be tried promptly and fairly, and I believe this court could administer the law fairly; but I have a conviction, as strong as life, that this country should stand them up against an adobe wall to-morrow and give them what they deserve. If any man deserves death, it is a traitor. I wish that I could pay for the ammunition. I would like to attend the execution, and if I were in the firing squad I would not want to be the marksman who had the blank shell."

The above clipping, Mr. President, was sent to me by another Federal judge, who wrote upon the margin of the clipping that it occurred to him that the conduct of this judge might very properly be the subject of investigation. He enclosed with the clipping a letter, from which I quote the following:

I have been greatly depressed by the brutal and unjust attacks that great business interests have organized against you. It is a time when all the spirits of evil are turned loose. The Kaisers of high finance, who have been developing hatred of you for a generation because you have fought against them and for the common good, see this opportunity to turn the war patriotism into an engine of attack. They are using it everywhere, and it is a day when lovers of democracy, not only in the world, but here in the United States, need to go apart on the mountain and spend the night in fasting and prayer. I still have faith that the forces of good on this earth will be found to be greater than the forces of evil, but we all need resolution. I hope you will have the grace to keep your center of gravity on the inside of you and to keep a spirit that is unclouded by hatred. It is a time for the words, "with malice toward none and charity for all." It is the office of great service to be a shield to the good man's character against malice. Before this fight is over you will have a new revelation that such a shield is yours.

If this newspaper clipping were a single or exceptional instance of lawless defamation, I should not trouble the Senate with a reference to it. But, Mr. President, it is not.

In this mass of newspaper clippings which I have here upon my desk, and which I shall not trouble the Senate to read unless it is desired, and which represent but a small part of the accumulation clipped from the daily press of the country in the last three months, I find other Senators, as well as myself, accused of the highest crimes of which any man can be guilty—treason and disloyalty—and, sir, accused not only with no evidence to support the accusation, but without the suggestion that such evidence anywhere exists. It is not claimed that Senators who opposed the declaration of war have since that time acted with any concerted purpose either regarding war measures or any others. They have voted according to their individual opinions, have often been opposed to each other on bills which have come before the Senate since the declaration of war, and, according to my recollection, have never all voted together since that time upon any single proposition upon which the Senate has been divided.

I am aware, Mr. President, that in pursuance of this general campaign of vilification and attempted intimidation, requests from various individuals and certain organizations have been submitted to the Senate for my expulsion from this body, and that such requests have been referred to and considered by one of the committees of the Senate.

If I alone had been made the victim of these attacks, I should not take one moment of the Senate's time for their consideration, and I believe that other Senators who have been unjustly and unfairly assailed, as I have been, hold the same attitude upon this that I do. *Neither the clamor of the mob nor the voice of power will ever turn me by the breadth of a hair from the course I mark out for myself, guided by such knowledge as I can obtain and controlled and directed by a solemn conviction of right and duty.*

But, sir, it is not alone Members of Congress that the war party in this country has sought to intimidate. The mandate seems to have gone forth to the sovereign people of this country that they must be silent while those things are being done by their Government which most vitally concern their well-being, their happiness, and their lives. To-day and for weeks past honest and law-abiding citizens of this country are being terrorized and outraged in their rights by those sworn to uphold the laws and protect the rights of the people. I have in my possession numerous affidavits establishing the fact that people are being unlawfully arrested, thrown into jail, held incommunicado for days, only to be eventually discharged without ever having been taken into court, because they have committed no crime. Private residences are being invaded, loyal citizens of undoubted integrity and probity arrested, cross-examined, and the most sacred constitutional rights guaranteed to every American citizen are being violated.

It appears to be the purpose of those conducting this campaign to throw the country into a state of terror, to coerce public opinion, to stifle criticism, and suppress discussion of the great issues involved in this war.

I think all men recognize that in time of war the citizen must surrender some rights for the common good which he is entitled to enjoy in time of peace. *But, sir, the right to control their own Government according to constitutional forms is not one of the rights that the citizens of this country are called upon to surrender in time of war.*

Rather in time of war the citizen must be more alert to the preservation of his right to control his Government. He must be most watchful of the encroachment of the military upon the civil power. He must beware of those precedents in support of arbitrary action by administrative officials, which excused on the plea of necessity in war time, become the fixed rule when the necessity has passed and normal conditions have been restored.

More than all, the citizen and his representative in Congress in time of war must maintain his right of free speech. More than in times of peace it is necessary that the channels for free public discussion of governmental policies shall be open and unclogged. I believe, Mr. President, that I am now touching upon the most important question in this country to-day—and that is the right of the citizens of this country and their representatives in Congress to discuss in an orderly way frankly and publicly and without fear, from the platform and through the press, every important phase of this war; its causes, the manner in which it should be conducted, and the terms upon which peace should be made. The belief which is becoming widespread in this land that this most fundamental right is being denied to the citizens of this country is a fact the tremendous significance of which, those in authority have not yet begun to appreciate. I am contending, Mr. President, for the great fundamental right of the sovereign people of this country to make their voice heard and have that voice heeded upon the great questions arising out of this war, including not only how the war shall be prosecuted but the conditions upon which it may be terminated with a due regard for the rights and the honor of this Nation and the interests of humanity.

I am contending for this right because the exercise of it is necessary to the welfare, to the existence, of this Government, to the successful conduct of this war, and to a peace which shall be enduring and for the best interest of this country.

Suppose success attends the attempt to stifle all discussion of the issues of this war, all discussion of the terms upon which it should be concluded, all discussion of the objects and purposes to be accomplished by it, and concede the demand of the war-mad press and war extremists that they monopolize the right of public utterance upon these questions unchallenged, what think you would be the consequences to this country not only during the war but after the war?

RIGHT OF PEOPLE TO DISCUSS WAR ISSUES

Mr. President, our Government, above all others, is founded on the right of the people freely to discuss all matters pertaining to their Government, in war not less than in peace, for in this Government the people are the rulers in war no less than in peace. It is true, sir, that Members of the House of Representatives are elected for two years, the President for four years, and the Members of the Senate for six years, and during their temporary official terms these officers constitute what is called the Government. But back of them always is the controlling sovereign power of the people, and when the people can make their will known, the faithful officer will obey that will. Though the right of the people to express their will by ballot is suspended during the term of office of the elected official, nevertheless the duty of the official to obey the popular will continues throughout his entire term of office. How can that popular will express itself between elections except by meetings, by speeches, by publications, by petitions, and by addresses to the representatives of the people? Any man who seeks to set a limit upon those rights, whether in war or peace, aims a blow at the most vital part of our Government. And then as the time for election approaches and the official is called to account for his stewardship—not a day, not a week, not a month, before the election, but a year or more before it, if the people choose—they must have the right to the freest possible discussion of every question upon which their representative has acted, of the merits of every measure he has supported or opposed, of every vote he has cast and every speech that he has made. And before this great fundamental right every other must, if necessary, give way, for in no other manner can representative government be preserved.

Mr. President, what I am saying has been exemplified in the lives and public discussion of the ablest statesmen of this country, whose memories we most revere and whose deeds we most justly commemorate. I shall presently ask the attention of the Senate to the views of some of these men upon the subject we are now considering.

Closely related to this subject of the right of the citizen to discuss war is that of the constitutional power and duty of the Congress to declare the purposes and objects of any war in which our country may be engaged. The authorities which I shall cite cover both the right of the people to discuss the war in all its phases and the right and the duty of the people's representatives in Congress to declare the purposes and objects of the war. For the sake of brevity, I shall present these quotations together at this point instead of submitting them separately. [La Follette then quoted extensively from Henry Clay, Abraham Lincoln, Charles Sumner, Daniel Webster, and Tom Corwin.]

. . . .

Lincoln, Webster, Clay, Sumner—what a galaxy of names in American history! They all believed and asserted and advocated in the midst of war that it was the right—the constitutional right—and the patriotic duty of American citizens, after the declaration of war and while the war was in progress, to discuss the issues of the war and to criticize the policies employed in its prosecution and to work for the election of representatives opposed to prolonging war.

The right of Lincoln, Webster, Clay, Sumner to oppose the Mexican War, criticize its conduct, advocate its conclusion on a just basis, is exactly the same right and privilege as that possessed by every Representative in Congress and by each and every American citizen in our land to-day in respect to the war in which we are now engaged. Their arguments as to the power of Congress to shape the war policy and their opposition to what they believed to be the usurpation of power on the part of the Executive are potent so long as the Constitution remains the law of the land.

English history, like our own, shows that it has ever been the right of the citizen to criticize and, when he thought necessary, to condemn the war policy of his Government. [La Follette quoted John Bright, Lloyd-George, the Duke of Grafton, Charles Fox, and Edmund Burke.]

. . . .

Mr. President, I have made these quotations from some of the leading statesmen of England to show that the principle of free speech was no new doctrine born of the Constitution of the United States. Our Constitution merely declared the principle. It did not create it. It is a heritage of English-speaking peoples, which has been won by incalculable sacrifice, and which they must preserve so long as they hope to live as free men. I say without fear of contradiction that there has never been a time for more than a century and a half when the right of free speech and free press and the right of the people to peaceably assemble for public discussion have been so violated among English-speaking people as they are violated to-day throughout the United States. To-day, in the land we have been wont to call the free United States, governors, mayors, and policemen are preventing or breaking up peaceable meetings called to discuss the questions growing out of this war, and judges and courts, with some notable and worthy exceptions, are failing to protect the citizens in their rights.

It is no answer to say that when the war is over the citizen may once more resume his rights and feel some security in his liberty and his person. As I have already tried to point out, now is precisely the time when the country needs the counsel of all its citizens. In time of war even more than in time of peace, whether citizens happen to agree with the ruling administration or not, these precious fundamental personal rights—free speech, free press, and right of assemblage so explicitly and emphatically guaranteed by the Constitution should be maintained inviolable. There is no rebellion in the land, no martial law, no courts are closed, no legal processes suspended, and there is no threat even of invasion.

But more than this, if every preparation for war can be made the excuse for destroying free speech and a free press and the right of the people to assemble together for peaceful discussion, then we may well despair of ever again finding ourselves for a long period in a state of peace. With the possessions we already have in remote parts of the world, with the obligations we seem almost certain to assume as a result of the present war, a war can be made any time overnight and the destruction of personal rights now occurring will be pointed to then as precedents for a still further invasion of the rights of the citizen. This is the road which all free governments have heretofore traveled to their destruction, and how far we have progressed along it is shown when we compare the standard of liberty of Lincoln, Clay, and Webster with the standard of the present day.

This leads me, Mr. President, to the next thought to which I desire to invite the attention of the Senate, and that is the power of Congress to declare the purpose and objects of the war, and the failure of Congress to exercise that power in the present crisis.

POWER OF CONGRESS TO DECLARE OBJECTS OF WAR

For the mere assertion of that right, in the form of a resolution to be considered and discussed—which I introduced August 11, 1917—I have been denounced throughout this broad land as a traitor to my country.

Mr. President, we are in a war the awful consequences of which no man can foresee, which, in my judgment, could have been avoided if the Congress had exercised its constitutional power to influence and direct the foreign policy of this country.

On the 8th day of February, 1915, I introduced in the Senate a resolution authorizing the President to invite the representatives of the neutral nations of the world to assemble and consider, among other things, whether it would not be possible to lay out lanes of travel upon the high seas and through proper negotiation with the belligerent powers have those lanes recognized as neutral territory, through which the commerce of neutral nations might pass. This, together with other provisions, constituted a resolution, as I shall always regard it, of most vital and supreme importance in the world crisis, and one that should have been considered and acted upon by Congress.

I believe, sir, that had some such action been taken the history of the world would not be written at this hour in the blood of more than one-half of the nations of the earth, with the remaining nations in danger of becoming involved.

I believe that had Congress exercised the power in this respect, which I contend it possesses, we could and probably would have avoided the present war.

Mr. President, I believe that if we are to extricate ourselves from this war and restore this country to an honorable and lasting peace, the Congress must exercise in full the war powers entrusted to it by the Constitution. I have already called your attention sufficiently, no doubt, to the opinions upon this subject expressed by some of the greatest lawyers and statesmen of the country, and I now venture to ask your attention to a little closer examination of the subject viewed in the light of distinctly legal authorities and principles.

CONSTITUTIONAL PROVISIONS INVOLVED

Section 8, Article I, of the Constitution provides: "The Congress shall have the power to lay and collect taxes, duties, imposts, and excises to pay the debts and provide for the common defense and general welfare of the United States."

In this first sentence we find that no war can be prosecuted without the consent of the Congress. No war can be prosecuted without money. There is no power to raise the money for war except the power of Congress. From this provision alone it must follow absolutely and without qualification that the duty of determining whether a war shall be prosecuted or not, whether the people's money shall be expended for the purpose of war or not rests upon the Congress, and with that power goes necessarily the power to determine the purposes of the war, for if the Congress does not approve the purposes of the war, it may refuse to lay the tax upon the people to prosecute it.

Again, section 8 further provides that Congress shall have power—

To declare war, grant letters of marque and reprisal, and make rules concerning captures on land and water;

To raise and support armies, but no appropriation of money to that use shall be for a longer term than two years;

To provide and maintain a Navy;

To make rules for the government and regulation of the land and naval forces;

To provide for calling forth the militia to execute the laws of the Union, suppress insurrection, and repel invasion;

To provide for organizing, arming, and disciplining the militia, and for governing such part of them as may be employed in the service of the United States, reserving to the States, respectively, the appointment of the officers and the authority of training the militia according to the discipline prescribed by Congress.

In the foregoing grants of power, which are as complete as language can make them, there is no mention of the President. Nothing is omitted from the powers conferred upon the Congress. Even the power to make the rules for the government and the regulation of all the national forces, both on land and on the sea, is vested in the Congress.

Then, not content with this, to make certain that no question could possibly arise, the framers of the Constitution declared that Congress shall have power—"To make all laws which shall be necessary and proper for carrying into execution the foregoing powers, and all other powers vested by this Constitution in the Government of the United States, or in any department or officer thereof."

We all know from the debates which took place in the constitutional convention why it was that the Constitution was so framed as to vest in the Congress the entire war-making power. The framers of the Constitution knew that to give to one man that power meant danger to the rights and liberties of the people. They knew that it mattered not whether you call the man king or emperor, czar or president, to put into his hands the power of making war or peace meant despotism. It meant that the people would be called upon to wage wars in which they had no interest or to which they might even be opposed. It meant secret diplomacy and secret treaties. It meant that in those things, most vital to the lives and welfare of the people, they would have nothing to say. The framers of the Constitution believed that they had guarded against this in the language I have quoted. They placed the entire control of this subject in the hands of the Congress. And it was assumed that debate would be free and open, that many men representing all the sections of the country would freely, frankly, and calmly exchange their views, unafraid of the power of the Executive, uninfluenced by anything except their own convictions, and a desire to obey the will of the people expressed in a constitutional manner.

Another reason for giving this power to the Congress was that the Congress, particularly the House of Representatives, was assumed to be directly responsible to the people and would most nearly represent their views. The term of office for a Representative was fixed at only two years. One-third of the Senate would be elected each two years. It was believed that this close relation to the people would insure a fair representation of the popular will in the action which the Congress might take. Moreover, if the Congress for any reason was unfaithful to its trust and declared a war which the people did not desire to support or to continue, they could in two years at most retire from office their unfaithful Representatives and return others who would terminate the war. It is true that within two years much harm could be done by an unwise declaration of war, especially a war of aggression, where men were sent abroad. The framers of the Constitution made no provision for such a condition, for they apparently never contemplated that such a condition would arise.

Moreover, under the system of voluntary enlistment, which was the only system of raising an army for use outside the country of which the framers of the Constitution had any idea, the people could force a settlement of any war to which they were opposed by the simple means of not volunteering to fight it.

The only power relating to war with which the Executive was entrusted was that of acting as Commander in Chief of the Army and Navy and of the militia when called into actual service. This provision is found in section 2 of Article II, and is as follows: "The President shall be Commander in Chief of the Army and Navy of the United States and of the militia of the several States when called into the actual service of the United States."

Here is found the sum total of the President's war powers. After the Army is raised he becomes the General in Command. His function is purely military. He is the General in Command of the entire Army, just as there is a general in command of a certain field of operation. The authority of each is confined strictly to the field of military service. The Congress must raise and support and equip and maintain the Army which the President is to command. Until the Army is raised the President has no military authority over any of the persons that may compose it. He can not enlist a man, or provide a uniform, or a single gun, or pound of powder. The country may be invaded from all sides and except for the command of the Regular Army, the President, as Commander in Chief of the Army, is as powerless as any citizen to stem the tide of the invasion. In such case his only resort would be to the militia, as provided in the Constitution. Thus completely did the fathers of the Constitution strip the Executive of military power.

It may be said that the duty of the President to enforce the laws of the country carries with it by implication control over the military forces for that purpose, and that the decision as to when the laws are violated, and the manner in which they should be redressed, rests with the President. This whole matter was considered in the famous case of Ex parte Milligan (4 Wall., 2). The question of enforcing the laws of the United States, however, does not arise in the present discussion. *The laws of the United States have no effect outside the territory of the United States.* Our Army in France or our Navy on the high seas may be engaged in worthy enterprises, but they are not enforcing the laws of the United States, and the President derives from his constitutional obligation to enforce the laws of the country no power to determine the purposes of the present war.

The only remaining provision of the Constitution to be considered on the subject is that provision of Article II, section 2, which provides that the President—"Shall have power by and with the consent of the Senate to make treaties, *providing two-thirds of the Senate present concur.*"

This is the same section of the Constitution which provides that the President "shall nominate, and by and with the advice and consent of the Senate, shall appoint ambassadors, other public ministers, consuls, judges of the Supreme Court," and so forth.

Observe, the President under this constitutional provision gets no authority to declare the purposes and objects of any war in which the country may be engaged. It is true that a treaty of peace can not be executed except the President and the Senate concur in its execution. If a President should refuse to agree to terms of peace which were proposed, for instance, by a resolution of Congress, and accepted by the parliament of an enemy nation against the will, we will say, of an emperor, the war would simply stop, if the two parliaments agreed and exercised their powers respectively to withhold supplies; and the formal execution of a treaty of peace would be postponed until the people could select another President. It is devoutly to be hoped that such a situation will never arise, and it is hardly conceivable that it should arise with both an Executive and a Senate anxious, respectively, to discharge the constitutional duties of their office. But if it should arise, under the Constitution, the final authority and the power to ultimately control is vested by the Constitution in the Congress. The President can no more make a treaty of peace without the approval not only of the Senate but of two-thirds of the Senators present than he can appoint a judge of the Supreme Court without the concurrence of the Senate.

A decent regard for the duties of the President, as well as the duties of the Senators, and the consideration of the interests of the people, whose servants both the Senators and the President are, requires that the negotiations which lead up to the making of peace should be participated in equally by the Senators and by the President. For Senators to take any other position is to shirk a plain duty; is to avoid an obligation imposed upon them by the spirit and letter of the Constitution and by the solemn oath of office each has taken.

PRECEDENTS AND AUTHORITIES

As might be expected from the plain language of the Constitution, the precedents and authorities are all one way. I shall not attempt to present them all here, but only refer to those which have peculiar application to the present situation. [La Follette cited reference works on the Constitution and a number of congressional precedents.]

. . . .

Since the Constitution vests in Congress the supreme power to determine when and for what purpose the country will engage in war and the objects to attain which the war will be prosecuted, it seems to me to be an evasion of a solemn duty on the part of the Congress not to exercise that power at this critical time in the Nation's affairs. The Congress can no more avoid its responsibility in this matter than it can in any other. As the Nation's purposes in conducting this war are of supreme importance to the country, it is the supreme duty of Congress to exercise the function conferred upon it by the Constitution of guiding the foreign policy of the Nation in the present crisis.

A minor duty may be evaded by Congress, a minor responsibility avoided without disaster resulting, but on this momentous question there can be no evasion, no shirking of duty of the Congress, without subverting our form of government. If our Constitution is to be changed so as to give the President the power to determine the purposes for which this Nation will engage in war, and the conditions on which it will make peace, then let that change be made deliberately by an amendment to the Constitution proposed and adopted in a constitutional manner. It would be bad enough if the Constitution clothed the President with any such power, but to exercise such power without constitutional authority can not long be tolerated if even the forms of free government are to remain. We all know that no amendment to the Constitution giving the President the powers suggested would be adopted by the people. We know that if such an amendment were to be proposed it would be overwhelmingly defeated.

The universal conviction of those who yet believe in the rights of the people is that the first step toward the prevention of war and the establishment of peace, permanent peace, is to give the people who must bear the brunt of war's awful burden more to say about it. The masses will understand that it was the evil of a one-man power exercised in a half dozen nations through the malevolent influences of a system of secret diplomacy that plunged the helpless peoples of Europe into the awful war that has been raging with increasing horror and fury ever since it began and that now threatens to engulf the world before it stops.

No conviction is stronger with the people to-day than that there should be no future wars except in case of actual invasion, unless supported by a referendum, a plebiscite, a vote of ratification upon the declaration of war before it shall become effective.

And because there is no clearness of understanding, no unity of opinion in this country on the part of the people as to the conditions upon which we are prosecuting this war or what the specific objects are upon the attainment of which the present administration would be willing to conclude a peace, it becomes still more imperative each day that Congress should assert its constitutional power to define and declare the objects of this war which will afford the basis for a conference and for the establishment of permanent peace. The President has asked the German people to speak for themselves on this great world issue; why should not the American people voice their convictions through their chosen representatives in Congress?

Ever since new Russia appeared upon the map she has been holding out her hands to free America to come to her support in declaring for a clear understanding of the objects to be attained to secure peace. Shall we let this most remarkable revolution the world has ever witnessed appeal to us in vain?

We have been six months at war. We have incurred financial obligations and made expenditures of money in amounts already so large that the human mind can not comprehend them. The Government has drafted from the peaceful occupations of civil life a million of our finest young men—and more will be taken if necessary—to be transported 4,000 miles over the sea, with their equipment and supplies, to the trenches of Europe.

The first chill winds of autumn remind us that another winter is at hand. The imagination is paralyzed at the thought of the human misery, the indescribable suffering, which the winter months, with their cold and sleet and ice and snow, must bring to the war-swept lands, not alone to the soldiers at the front but the noncombatants at home.

To such excesses of cruelty has this war descended that each nation is now, as a part of its strategy, planning to starve the women and children of the enemy countries. Each warring nation is carrying out the unspeakable plan of starving noncombatants. Each nurses the hope that it may break the spirit of the men of the enemy country at the front by starving the wives and babes at home, and woe be it that we have become partners in this awful business and are even cutting off food shipments from neutral countries in order to force them to help starve women and children of the country against whom we have declared war.

There may be some necessity overpowering enough to justify these things, but the people of America should demand to know what results are expected to satisfy the sacrifice of all that civilization holds dear upon the bloody altar of a conflict which employs such desperate methods of warfare.

The question is, Are we to sacrifice millions of our young men—the very promise of the land—and spend billions and more billions, and pile up the cost of living until we starve—and for what? Shall the fearfully overburdened people of this country continue to bear the brunt of a prolonged war for any objects not openly stated and defined?

The answer, sir, rests, in my judgment, with the Congress, whose duty it is to declare our specific purposes in the present war and to state the objects upon the attainment of which we will make peace.

CAMPAIGN SHOULD BE MADE ON CONSTITUTIONAL LINES

And, sir, this is the ground on which I stand. I maintain that Congress has the right and the duty to declare the objects of the war and the people have the right and the obligation to discuss it.

American citizens may hold all shades of opinion as to the war; one citizen may glory in it, another may deplore it, each has the same right to voice his judgment. An American citizen may think and say that we are not justified in prosecuting this war for the purpose of dictating the form of government which shall be maintained by our enemy or our ally, and not be subject to punishment at law. He may pray aloud that our boys shall not be sent to fight and die on European battle fields for the annexation of territory or the maintenance of trade agreements and be within his legal rights. He may express the hope that an early peace may be secured on the terms set forth by the new Russia and by President Wilson in his speech of January 22, 1917, and he can not lawfully be sent to jail for the expression of his convictions.

It is the citizen's duty to obey the law until it is repealed or declared unconstitutional. But he has the inalienable right to fight what he deems an obnoxious law or a wrong policy in the courts and at the ballot box.

It is the suppressed emotion of the masses that breeds revolution.

If the American people are to carry on this great war, if public opinion is to be enlightened and intelligent, there must be free discussion.

Congress, as well as the people of the United States, entered the war in great confusion of mind and under feverish excitement. The President's leadership was followed in the faith that he had some big, unrevealed plan by which peace that would exalt him before all the world would soon be achieved.

Gradually, reluctantly, Congress and the country are beginning to perceive that we are in this terrific world conflict, not only to *right* our wrongs, not only to *aid* the allies, not only to *share* its awful death toll and its fearful tax burden, but perhaps, to *bear the brunt* of the war.

And so I say, if we are to forestall the danger of being drawn into years of war, perhaps finally to maintain imperialism and exploitation, the people must unite in a campaign along constitutional lines for free discussion of the policy of the war and its conclusion on a just basis.

Permit me, sir, this word in conclusion. It is said by many persons for whose opinions I have profound respect and whose motives I know to be sincere that "we are in this war and must go through to the end." That is true. But it is not true that we must go through to the end to *accomplish an undisclosed purpose, or to reach an unknown goal.*

I believe that whatever there is of honest difference of opinion concerning this war, arises precisely at this point.

There is, and of course can be, no real difference of opinion concerning the duty of the citizen to discharge to the last limit whatever obligation the war lays upon him.

Our young men are being taken by the hundreds of thousands for the purpose of waging this war on the Continent of Europe, possibly Asia or Africa, or anywhere else that they may be ordered. Nothing must be left undone for their protection. They must have the best army, ammunition, and equipment that money can buy. They must have the best training and the best officers which this great country can provide. The dependents and relatives they leave at home must be provided for, not meagerly, but generously so far as money can provide for them.

I have done some of the hardest work of my life during the last few weeks on the revenue bill to raise the largest possible amount of money from surplus incomes and war profits for this war and upon other measures to provide for the protection of the soldiers and their families. That I was not able to accomplish more along this line is a great disappointment to me. I did all that I could, and I shall continue to fight with all the power at my command until wealth is made to bear more of the burden of this war than has been laid upon it by the present Congress. Concerning these matters there can be no difference of opinion. We have not yet been able to muster the forces to conscript wealth, as we have conscripted men, but no one has ever been able to advance even a plausible argument for not doing so.

No, Mr. President; it is on the other point suggested where honest differences of opinion may arise. Shall we ask the people of this country to shut their eyes and take the entire war program on faith? There are no doubt many honest and well-meaning persons who are willing to answer that question in the affirmative rather than risk the dissensions which they fear may follow a free discussion of the issues of this war. With that position I do not—I can not agree. Have the people no intelligent contribution to make to the solution of the problems of this war? I believe that they have, and that in this matter, as in so many others, they may be wiser than their leaders, and that if left free to discuss the issues of the war they will find the correct settlement of these issues.

But it is said that Germany will fight with greater determination if her people believe that we are not in perfect agreement. Mr. President, that is the same worn-out pretext which has been used for three years to keep the plain people of Europe engaged in killing each other in this war. And, sir, as applied to this country, at least, it is a pretext with nothing to support it.

The way to paralyze the German arm, to weaken the German military force, in my opinion, is to declare our objects in this war, and show by that declaration to the German people that we are not seeking to dictate a form of government to Germany or to render more secure England's domination of the seas.

A declaration of our purposes in this war, so far from strengthening our enemy, I believe would immeasurably weaken her, for it would no longer be possible to misrepresent our purposes to the German people. Such a course on our part, so far from endangering the life of a single one of our boys, I believe would result in saving the lives of hundreds of thousands of them by bringing about an earlier and more lasting peace by intelligent negotiation, instead of securing a peace by the complete exhaustion of one or the other of the belligerents.

Such a course would also immeasurably, I believe, strengthen our military force in this country, because when the objects of this war are clearly stated and the people approve of those objects they will give to the war a popular support it will never otherwise receive.

Then, again, honest dealing with the entente allies, as well as with our own people, requires a clear statement of our objects in this war. If we do not expect to support the entente allies in the dreams of conquest we know some of them entertain, then in all fairness to them that fact should be stated now. If we do expect to support them in their plans for conquest and aggrandizement, then our people are entitled to know that vitally important fact before this war proceeds further. Common honesty and fair dealing with the people of this country and with the nations by whose side we are fighting, as well as a sound military policy at home, requires the fullest and freest discussion before the people of every issue involved in this great war and that a plain and specific declaration of our purposes in the war be speedily made by the Congress of the United States.

Labor Day Address

Radio Speech, Washington, D.C., September 1, 1924

Fellow-citizens, Men and Women of the Radio Audience:

The progressives come to you in this campaign with a constructive national program, framed in the interests and for the benefit of the mass of the people of every state and of every section. I am, therefore, grateful for this opportunity to address you in your homes and at your meeting places throughout the length and breadth of the United States.

As we are the outspoken champions of all who labor, it is fitting that we should inaugurate our campaign on Labor Day. But we recognize no narrow definition for the laboring millions of this country. The farmers, the business men who give honest service in return for righteous profits, the women who toil in the homes, the offices and the schools of the land,—all these we regard as laborers for the common good as truly as the wage-earners in the shops and mills and mines, and on the railroads.

We are in this campaign contending for the principle that every man and woman under the American flag who lives by useful and creative work of hand or brain, is entitled to an equal chance in life, to equal protection of the laws, and equal participation in the control of government with every other citizen. We believe our government, ruled by Republican and Democratic parties, has fallen under the domination and control of men and interests hostile to that principle, who subvert the great powers of the government and secure to themselves the fruits of the labor of the mass of the American people.

Abraham Lincoln foretold the condition we now face and clearly stated the principle to which all Progressives adhere when he said:

> In the early days of our race the Almighty said to the first of our race, "In the sweat of thy face shalt thou eat bread." . . . But it has so happened, in all ages of the world, that some have labored, and others have without labor enjoyed a large proportion of the fruits of that labor. This is wrong, and should not continue. To secure to each

laborer the whole product of his labor, or as nearly as possible, is a worthy object of any good government.

Such was the belief of the first President elected by the Republican party. In his time, this government, by law, made it possible—under the institution of human slavery—for a few men to live on the fruits of the labor of millions. Lincoln believed that the true object of government was to secure to the laborer the largest possible share of the product of his toil, and sustained by the common people, chiefly by the farmers and the working-men of the cities, he re-established that principle.

Since the Civil War the government has bestowed privileges and fostered through administrative favoritism a new system, under which a few men are enabled to live on the fruits of the labor of others. It is a system appearing in a form of which Lincoln never dreamed. It is a system against which I have fought continuously for the last thirty years.

When I say that the prices paid by the American people today for coal, food, light, clothing, and everything which goes to feed, warm, and shelter the human family, are fixed by great corporate combinations of wealth, I merely repeat what every intelligent man and woman within sound of my voice knows to be true. This power to fix prices, combined with the control of natural resources, of transportation and credit, has lodged in the hands of relatively few men power to amass enormous wealth by levying tribute upon the farmer, the wage-earner, and the consuming public. This system feeds on the labor of the farmer by fixing the prices he receives for his products. It feeds on the labor of the wage-earner by fixing wages below the standard found by government experts to be necessary in order to maintain the family of the laborer in health and comfort. It feeds on the labor of the consuming public by taking back in the form of extortionate profits much that rightfully belongs to wages and salaries and the reasonable profits of the farm.

This system has become so deeply rooted in American life that the two great political parties which have shared control of the government since the Civil War now recognize it as master. Under their administrations, this system has extended its power until today it not only controls the economic life of the nation, but rules the very agencies of government which the people have set up to restrain it. It has not only been left free to oppress the farmer, the wage-earner, the consuming public and legitimate business,—it has been permitted to employ the powers of the government itself to encroach upon the liberties, prosperity and happiness of all.

The Progressives have entered this campaign to convict that system which has already been indicted by public opinion. It is proper that we should come with a bill of particulars in our indictment. Exactly what do we mean by the system?

We mean the combination which rules the coal industry of this country, which fixes and exacts unjust prices from the consumer, which has baffled the Federal Trade Commission in its lawful effort to ascertain the facts regarding its profits and costs of production, and which under the last Democratic administration was aided by the Department of Justice in an attempt to crush the lawful organization of the miners in that industry.

We mean the sugar monopoly, which has its representatives on the Tariff Commission, which prevented that Commission from promptly reporting a reduction in the tariff duties on sugar and which, under the false pretense that it was protecting the sugar-beet farmers, used the tariff to increase the price of sugar to the public, with the active aid of the President, the Secretary of Commerce, and the responsible leaders of this administration in the United States Senate.

We mean the oil monopoly, which dictates prices on gasoline and oil throughout the land. It strangles independent business enterprise by cut-throat competition. It resorted to outright corruption of a member of the President's cabinet to wrest the naval oil reserves from the public domain. It has systematically defied the laws and the courts of this country for a generation, and through its agents, has for many years contributed large sums of money to both Republican and Democratic campaign funds.

We mean the banking combine, which, through its control of the Federal Reserve Board, arbitrarily fixes interest rates and controls credit in the service of the big monopoly system. It initiated four years ago a policy of "deflation," causing a shrinkage in farm prices since 1920 of more than fifteen billion dollars and a loss to the farmers in the value of their land and other property of more than twenty billion dollars.

We mean the transportation monopoly which obtained through the Department of Justice under this administration an injunction placing more than 400,000 men under the ban of the law, which dictated to Congress the terms of the Esch-Cummins Law, exacting extortionate railroad rates from the farmer, the business man and the consuming public, and which has been powerful enough with the administrations of both political parties to acquire a dominant influence over the Interstate Commerce Commission.

We mean the meat-packing combination which fixes the price on the products of the farm and the food served upon the table of the consumer, which has been powerful enough to prevent the proper enforcement in the public interests of regulatory laws enacted by Congress, and which has escaped prosecution for the flagrant violations of law through its official connections with the administrations of both the Democratic and Republican parties.

These are only a few of the combinations which constitute the Monopoly System. This system is protected by certain laws and by the failure to enforce others. Its power is so great that both of the old parties have become its abject slaves.

These monopolies, each having acquired economic control by combinations in its own field, were drawn together by common interest. They early saw the vital importance of the control of government.

They built up a perfect political System. The System controls the government at Washington. It contributes the millions expended in the national campaigns by both political parties.

It elects the President and the Congress. It makes and administers the laws. Year by year, through these laws, enacted by an obedient Congress—administered by a pliant President, and enforced by an appointed court—the System augments its power and the enormous wealth of its groups.

The Republican and Democratic parties in power term after term have not attempted to curb the exactions of this system upon the public. The Republican party asks the people to forget the admonitions of the wisest men in the history of that party,—of Lincoln, Sherman, Garfield and others. The Democratic party has repudiated the promise upon which Woodrow Wilson was elected in 1912, that he would free this government from control by private monopoly. The message of the Republican and Democratic parties today is a message of despair. In it, the American people find no ray of hope for relief from the burdens which oppress them.

The Progressive movement is the real hope of the country. We have enlisted in this campaign to restore this government to the service of the public, to secure to the laborer and producer in all lines a greater share of the product of his toil, while protecting the consumer against the trust fixed prices on all he buys, and to drive out of the government at Washington the corrupting influences now so dominant there.

I am a candidate at this time for the same reason that in the past I have been a candidate for Governor of Wisconsin and for United States Senate. I believe that if the people can once regain control of the machinery of government we can stem the tide toward economic absolutism. Although we cannot undo in a day the evil which Republican and Democratic administrations have done in a generation, I am convinced it lies within the power of a Progressive administration to achieve immediate and substantial results in the interest of all the people.

Let me say at the outset that I am not concerned by charges that the Progressive citizenship of this country is bent on radical and destructive ends, subversive of the government and the Constitution under which we live.

In a somewhat extended public career, I have observed that he who is willing to fight in the public interest is denounced a "dangerous radical," or a "foolish visionary," while he who becomes the willing servant of selfish special interests soon establishes a reputation as a sound, courageous, constructive statesman. The American people are intelligent enough to perceive the basis of this distinction. Nothing is so safe in a political campaign as to generalize about "honesty" and to treat the importance of it in public office as a new discovery, unless it be to commend as a virtue the "frugality" most of us practice as a necessity because we are the victims of the monopoly system fostered and protected by both the Democratic and Republican parties.

A quarter of a century ago, when the farmers, wage-earners, and all the unprivileged common people of Wisconsin set out to free that state from the corporate interests which then controlled it, through a corrupt political machine, we were denounced as "destructive Socialists," and "revolutionists." We drove the corporations out of politics and enacted the first general primary law adopted in this country. We collected honest taxes from the railroads and other great interests on the same basis as from farmers and home-owners. Without crippling their service or reducing their legitimate profits, we forced the railroads to reduce their rates, to give equal service to all shippers, and to base their charges on an honest valuation of their properties, without rebates and without discrimination. Each of these measures of simple justice was met, in turn, with the same charge of "radicalism" which is raised against the Progressive program today, and for the same reason. Then, as now, the Progressives offered a definite, concrete set of public policies which were thoroughly practical, which could be readily and effectively applied under the Constitution in the public interest, and which were destructive only of unjust and dishonest special privileges.

Not one of the Progressive laws which we enacted in Wisconsin has since been repealed. Most of them have served as models for similar laws in many of the state[s] of the Union. Under Progressive government, Wisconsin has preserved for its people, even in the face of the ruinous policies of Republican and Democratic national administrations, a prosperity in which all classes and all the business interests of the state have shared. Wisconsin stands today as a monument to the soundness and equity of the principles of government which we advocate, and refutes the false statement and specious arguments of those spokesmen for special interests who would deceive the American people as to the true aims and purposes of the Progressives in this campaign.

I am advocating today the same principles of government which I have defended in Wisconsin and in the United States Senate for more than a quarter of a century. If I have advanced any new or additional remedy for existing evils, it has been rendered necessary to keep pace with the ruthless encroachments of the enemies of our government. I stand today for the principles of democracy exactly where I stood in the beginning. I will not depart by the breadth of a hair from this position so long as I live.

If I am elected President of the United States, I shall proceed with the same purpose we followed in Wisconsin to enact valid, remedial, constructive legislation, and to initiate executive policies based upon sound economic principles, applied with the best expert advice obtainable.

I shall, if elected, use the appointive power of the Executive to free every department of the government from the control of the special interests. I will place the administration of the law in the hands of those who believe in enforcing the laws. I will not appoint men to office who have been repudiated by their own constituents as unworthy of public trust. I would immediately discharge from the public service in any department and especially from the Department of Justice, the Department of the Interior, and the Navy Department, and the Veterans' Bureau, any official shown to have been a party to any dishonesty or any improper conduct therein.

I would place at the head of the Department of Justice and in the office of every United States district attorney throughout the land men who would vigorously enforce all the laws. I would instruct them to bring and to prosecute criminal actions against every profiteering monopoly which violates the anti-trust laws with [the] same vigor which I would require of them in the prosecution of a boot-legger.

Without the enactment of additional federal statutes, I am convinced that great progress could be made in restoring this government to the service of the public, through honest and vigorous enforcement of existing law.

I recognize, however, that the body of our statutes is so honey-combed with special privileges to favored interests that in order to accomplish lasting benefits for the people, it would be necessary to repeal or amend many laws now on the statute books. The tariff and taxation laws must be revised in accordance with the specific pledges contained in the Progressive platform.

As an aid in curbing the power of great monopoly interests, to amass unjust profits at the expense of the public, we favor a reorganization of the Federal Trade Commission and the Tariff Commission and we would enlarge their authority and strengthen the laws, organic as well as statute laws, specifically empowering them to ascertain and make public the costs of production and profits in oil and gasoline, coal, steel, and other basic industries.

Under both Republican and Democratic administrations, private interests have wrongfully increased their control of the natural resources on the public domain. We Progressives mean to recover and conserve those resources and to make available to the people at cost, the light, heat and power which can be developed from the water power sites now owned by the government.

It is apparent to every thoughtful citizen that unjust policies of administration and the enactment of unjust laws by Republican and Democratic administrations have brought the farmers of this country face to face with an emergency which the general welfare demands should be met by emergency measures.

The farmer has been the victim of a long train of abuses extending over more than a quarter of a century of time. This unjust treatment of the farmer culminated in 1920 in the enactment of the Esch-Cummins Law, and the initiation of the policy of "deflation" by the Federal Reserve Board. No superficial, make-shift remedies will restore agriculture to the equality and independence as our basis industry to which it is entitled. The time has gone by for commissions of inquiry, without legal authority to carry their recommendations into effect. But a Progressive administration would speedily relieve the farmer from the burden unjustly laid upon him by these measures. Under the infamous Fordney-McCumber Tariff Act the price of everything he buys, including every piece of machinery on his farm, every utensil in his house, and the clothing worn by himself and his family has been greatly increased.

I intend, if elected, to summon the new Congress into extraordinary session and to recommend the repeal of the Esch-Cummins Act. The President in his first message to Congress opposed any amendment to the rate section of the present law, behind which the Interstate Commerce Commission has taken refuge in its refusal to reduce the present exorbitant railroad rates. I stand for a new rate-making provision which will enable the Commission to fix rates on the basis of the actual prudent investment of capital and to compel the railroads, under private ownership, to provide service to the public at cost, with an additional charge sufficient to insure a reasonable return to the railroad owners on capital honestly and prudently invested.

The Federal Reserve Act if it is to remain on the statute books must be so drastically dealt with by Congress and so administered by the Executive Department that never again shall the Board created under the act have power to withhold credit from the farmers and force them to throw their products on a falling market, while speculators and monopoly interests are left free to exploit the public. The present tariff must be immediately revised as an act of justice to the consuming public by reducing the present extortionate tariff rates.

When the farmer in this country receives an average of only 40 cents of the dollar paid by the city consumer for farm products, while the farmers of Denmark receive an average of 80 cents, it must be recognized that our present marketing system is indefensible. I am convinced that a Progressive administration, free from the control of the interests which unjustly profit at the expense of both the farmer and the consumer, could aid the farmers of every section in establishing a cooperative system, free from the control of the government, which would afford them every advantage in marketing their products at a fair profit above the cost of production.

I deplore the efforts which are being made in this campaign by those who would perpetuate the present inequitable conditions to provoke class prejudice between the farmers and the wage-earners of the country. I do not claim that the interests of the farmer and the industrial worker are always identical. But I do maintain that their prosperity, happiness and economic freedom are menaced by a common foe, and that they must take common political action to meet it.

Let me say to the farmers that the greatest opportunity to regain your independence that has presented itself in a generation will be lost, if you fail to grasp the hands which are extended to you today from the workshops of the cities.

The farmers, driven from the soil at the rate of more than one million a year under the present administration, can earn their bread only in competition with the wage earner. Such an enormous annual reduction in the number of producers on the farm inevitably means a decreased production of food, lower wages, higher prices, stagnant business and widespread discontent.

What have the Republican and Democratic parties to offer to remedy the evils which have arisen under their respective administrations and as a result of their policies?

They offer nothing. They evade the issue. They seek to divert the attention of the voters in this country from the domestic issues to conditions abroad. They point to Europe and say "There lies the solution." No one has greater sympathy for Europe than I. With my own eyes I have seen the conditions there and my heart has been deeply moved. No one is readier to lend aid and every moral influence in assisting stricken Europe to her feet than I, but I refuse to be deceived or to assist in deceiving the American people.

I do not intend at this time to discuss the many absurdities involved in the Democratic and Republican proposals for the revival of Europe, nor to deal now with questions of foreign policy. I merely want to call your attention to this fundamental fact. The original source of the Democratic and Republican plans respecting Europe is the same. That source is the well-known banking house of J.P. Morgan and Company. The connections of this banking house with the candidates of both old parties and with the leaders of those parties is close and intimate and confidential. The so-called Dawes plan is merely the Morgan plan. It has been hoped by our opponents to divert attention of the American people from the corruption in their own government and from the evil forces to which it is a prey, by talking about European conditions, and urging that upon conditions there, our prosperity, particularly agricultural prosperity depends. The truth is that the opportunity to stabilize American agriculture lies in the development of a home market that can absorb American products at American prices. This means a population paid well enough to consume the normal production of food and raw material. This is not true today.

Official statistics of the Department of Agriculture show that the consumption per capita of such a staple food as bread is very much less than it was a few years ago. The reason is obvious. Bread prices have remained at the level of war prices, while the price of wheat has fallen far below the cost of producing it. It means that there are many people in the United States today who are hungry for bread, and who if they had the price would buy it and thus consume the farmers['] wheat.

Development of the home market for the products of agriculture means a better, a more just, a more equitable distribution of wealth, and a better and more stable market. That is what we will have as soon as the great powers of the government are placed in the hands of men who mean to see that they are used to overthrow the system, and stop further unjust encroachments of those who are today surfeited with wealth and drunk with power.

In attaining this end we shall not trespass either upon property rights or human rights. We shall respect both.

I avail myself of this opportunity to say to the people of the country that I regard the Progressive cause as fortunate in the support which Senator Burton K. Wheeler brings to it. His ability, his integrity, and courage have been thoroughly tested. Two years ago, he came out of the West a comparatively unknown man. He did not require long service to demonstrate his great insight and his high moral courage. He saw to the very heart of our troubles and struck at the evils a swift and deadly blow. In his short term he has achieved fame as a valiant leader in the great cause for clean and honest government.

I do not doubt that the American people in November will bring to proper account the administration which has subjected Senator Wheeler to persecution under cover of the law while permitting to remain unpunished the men whose corruption he exposed.

Now, my friends, I have not sought on this occasion to discuss all the great questions which are at issue in this campaign; I have endeavored merely to indicate some of the measures we Progressives offer to meet existing domestic problems. Neither have I addressed myself solely to the interests of the men and women enrolled in the great organizations of labor.

We shall meet in this campaign the spokesmen of entrenched privilege who scoff and sneer at the aspirations of the organized workers of this country. These men, who prate of class legislation, whenever labor demands its just rights, know little of the character of the labor movement or of the true principles of our government.

No humane, Progressive law has been enacted by Congress in a generation which has not had the support of the organized workers of this country, speaking through their representatives at Washington.

It will be found, upon a fair analysis, that every special measure which has been strong enough to command the support of labor has been of the broadest public interest and benefit.

We obtained the enactment of the Seaman's Law, and now favor its strict enforcement, not alone because that law struck the shackles of involuntary servitude from the sailor, but also because, if properly administered, it promotes an American merchant marine and prevents needless loss of life on ships flying the American flag. We obtained the enactment of laws limiting the working hours of the men who run the railroads, not solely for the benefit of labor, but likewise for the safety and protection of the travelling public. Today, the Progressives alone specifically demand the ratification of the child labor amendment and pledge the enactment of a law applying its principle not only to protect the wages of adult laborers, but also because we place the health and happiness of childhood and the future of the race above the profits of exploiters of the youth of this generation.

We demand that injunctions shall not be issued by the courts in industrial disputes not only because such use of the injunction makes collective bargaining ineffective, but because it establishes a precedent which may be turned against all our citizens in the exercise of their lawful rights.

Under the leadership of men who have devoted their lives to the service of their fellows, labor has resisted, step by step, the attempts of organized wealth to reduce the worker to a condition of economic slavery and to create a permanent laboring class, against whom the door of opportunity should be forever closed.

In the hour when both of the old parties betrayed the people, you have turned to the Progressive movement, recognizing that the gains you have won at costly sacrifice cannot be maintained under Republican or Democratic control of government. You have enlisted in the Progressive movement to render secure for your children the political and economic rights which the old parties would deny you.

With your support, in the great cause in which we are engaged, there can be no defeat. The lines upon which this campaign will be fought have already been drawn. On the one side are arrayed the two old parties, serving the same masters, and seeking to preserve intact the privileges they have yielded to favored interests.

On the other, stands the Progressive Liberal citizenship of this nation. Within our ranks we welcome all who believe in orderly progress, who would use the ballot, under free speech, free press and free assemblage, to solve the problems which confront us. We would strike down special privileges enjoyed by the few, and return to the simple principle of Jefferson and Lincoln: that this government should secure to the laborer the fullest attainable portion of the product of his labor.

Our faith is in democracy. Upon that faith we enter this contest ready to meet falsehood with truth, to confront the claims of privilege with the demands of justice, to restore the government to the American people, and to establish economic freedom and justice throughout our land.

I thank you all for your kind attention.

Chronology of Major Speeches

I obtained speech texts from a variety of sources, including newspapers, magazines, pamphlets, the Appendix from the Carroll P. Lahman Ph.D. dissertation, and manuscript collections. Whenever possible, I have listed more than one reference for each speech. I have provided below abbreviations for some of the more common sources.

Assembly Journal, State of Wisconsin.	*AJ*
Congressional Record.	*CR*
La Follette's Magazine.	*LM*
Lahman, Carroll P. "Robert Marion La Follette as Public Speaker and Political Leader, 1885-1905," Appendix. Ph.D. diss., University of Wisconsin, 1939.	*LA*
Pamphlet Collection, State Historical Society of Wisconsin.	*PC*
Robert M. La Follette, Sr. Papers, Library of Congress (1906-1925).	*LPLC*
Robert M. La Follette, Sr. Papers, State Historical Society of Wisconsin (1879-1905).	*LPSHSW*
Senate Journal, State of Wisconsin.	*SJ*
Voters' Hand-Book, Pamphlet, State Historical Society of Wisconsin.	*VHB*

"Iago," Iowa City, Iowa, May 7, 1879; *PC*; *LA*, pp. 10-14; *LM*, October 1927, pp. 153, 155. Reprinted in Part II.

"Home and the State," Sun Prairie, Wis., July 4, 1879; *Sun Prairie Countryman*, 10 July 1879.

"Memorial Day Address," Madison, Wis., May 30, 1884; *Madison Daily Democrat*, 31 May 1884; *LPLC*; *LA*, pp. 258-64.

"Acceptance Speech," Dodgeville, Wis., September 9, 1884; *Wisconsin State Journal*, 12 Sept. 1884; *LA*, pp. 18-19.

Eulogy for Joseph Rankin, Washington, D. C., March 25, 1886; *LPLC*; *LA*, pp. 265-69.

On the Rivers and Harbors Bill, Washington, D.C., April 22, April 30, May 6, 1886; *CR*, April 22, 1886, pp. 3746-48; April 30, 1886, p. 4045; May 6, 1886, pp. 4243-44; Excerpt, *LA*, pp. 20-25.

"Address to Howard University Law Class," Washington, D.C., May 31, 1886; *LPLC*; *LA*, pp. 270-79.

"Oleomargarine," Washington, D.C., June 2, 1886; *CR*, June 2, 1886, Appendix, pp. 223-26. Reprinted in Part II.

"Interstate Commerce," Washington, D.C., January 20, 1887; *CR*, January 20, 1887, Appendix, pp. 184-88.

"Agricultural Experiment Stations," Washington, D.C., February 25, 1887; *CR*, February 25, 1887, Appendix, pp. 146-47.

On Republican Clubs, Madison, Wis., March 14, 1888; *Wisconsin State Journal*, 15 March 1888.

Rebuttal to Carlisle, Washington, D.C., July 14, 1888; *CR*, July 14, 1888, pp. 6307-11.

On the Tobacco Tariff, Washington, D.C., July 19, 1888; *CR*, July 19, 1888, pp. 6513-15.

On Grain Elevators, Washington, D.C., February 6, 1889; *CR*, February 6, 1889, p. 1586.

On the South Carolina Election Law, Washington, D.C., February 13, 1889; *CR*, February 13, 1889, pp. 1866-72.

On the McKinley Tariff Bill, Washington, D.C., May 10, 1890; *CR*, pp. 4473-82; Excerpt, *LA*, pp. 26-31.

"Proposed Federal Election Law," Washington, D.C., July 2, 1890; *CR*, July 2, 1890, Appendix, pp. 467-69.

"Original-Package Bill," Washington, D.C., July 19, 1890; *CR*, July 19, 1890, Appendix, pp. 517-18.

"Speech Seconding the Nomination of Henry Clay Evans of Tennessee," St. Louis, July 1, 1896; *LA*, pp. 32-33.

Campaign Speech, Milwaukee, November 2, 1896; *Milwaukee Sentinel*, 3 Nov. 1896; *LA*, pp. 34-55.

"The Menace of the Political Machine," Chicago, February 22, 1897; *Milwaukee Sentinel*, 23 Feb. 1897; *LA*, pp. 56-77. Reprinted in Part II.

Mineral Point Version of "The Dangers Threatening Representative Government," Mineral Point, Wis., July 4, 1897; *LPSHSW*.

Fern Dell Version of "The Dangers Threatening Representative Government," Fern Dell, Wis., August 26, 1897; *Sauk County Democrat*, 2 Sept. 1897.

"The Dangers Threatening Representative Government," Milwaukee, September 24, 1897; *The State*, 24 June 1898; *LA*, pp. 78-94.

"Primary Elections for the Nomination of All Candidates by Australian Ballot," Ann Arbor, Mich., March 12, 1898; *The State*, 27 July 1900; *PC*; Excerpt, *LA*, pp. 95-97.

"An Address to the Republicans of Wisconsin," Madison, Wis., July 15, 1898; *LPSHSW*.

"Acceptance Speech of 1900," Milwaukee, August 8, 1900; *LPSHSW*; *Milwaukee Sentinel*, 9 Aug. 1900; *LA*, 98-101.

Campaign Speech, Wisconsin, August 16, 1900; *LPSHSW*.

Campaign Speech, Milwaukee, September 19, 1900; *Milwaukee Sentinel*, 20 Sept. 1900; *PC*; *LA*, pp. 102-27.

Campaign Speech, Superior, Wis., October 18, 1900; *Superior Evening Telegram*, 19 Oct. 1900; *LA*, pp. 128-41.

"First Inaugural Address," Madison, January 10, 1901; *SJ*, January 10, 1901, pp. 16-56; *PC*.

"Address to the State Agricultural Society," Madison, February 5, 1901; *VHB*, pp. 105-07; *LA*, pp. 280-83.

"Dog-Tax Veto," Madison, May 2, 1901; *AJ*, May 2, 1901, pp. 1080-84; *VHB*, pp. 129-33.

"Veto Message," Madison, May 10, 1901; *SJ*, May 10, 1901, pp. 1026-35; *VHB*, pp. 133-38.

"Greeting to Dr. John Bascom," Madison, June 7, 1901; *VHB*, pp. 109-10; *LA*, pp. 284-85.

"Address to University Alumni," Madison, June 19, 1901; *VHB*, pp. 110-12; *LA*, pp. 288-90.

"Remarks to the Supervisors of Assessment," Madison, February 20, 1902; *VHB*, pp. 112-13.

"Remarks at the Funeral of Edward I. Kidd," [Madison], February 27, 1902; *Milwaukee Free Press*, 28 Feb. 1902; *LA*, pp. 291-95.

"Address of Welcome to Prince Henry," Milwaukee, March 4, 1902; *VHB*, pp. 113-14; *LA*, pp. 296-97.

"Address to Farmers' Institute," Oconomowoc, Wis., March 19, 1902; *VHB*, pp. 114-18; *LA*, pp. 142-48.

"Address at a Masonic Banquet," Milwaukee, April 10, 1902; *LA*, pp. 298-300.

Campaign Speech, Grand Rapids, Wis., June 4, 1902; *Milwaukee Free Press*, 5 June 1902; *LA*, pp. 149-58.

Campaign Speech, Blue Mounds, Wis., July 4, 1902; *Milwaukee Free Press*, 5 July 1902; *LA*, pp. 301-10.

"Governor La Follette's Speech of Acceptance," Madison, July 16, 1902; *PC*; *LPSHSW*; *LA*, pp. 159-63. Reprinted in Part II.

Campaign Speech, Milwaukee, September 30, 1902; *PC*; *LA*, pp. 164-208.

"Second Inaugural Address," Madison, January 15, 1903; *PC*.

Special Message, Madison, April 23, 1903; *SJ*, April 28, 1903, pp. 848-50.

Special Message, Madison, April 28, 1903; *PC*.

Special Message, Madison, May 7, 1903; *SJ*, May 8, 1903, pp. 1006-1009.

"Representative Government," Chautauqua, New York, July 18, 1903; *Milwaukee Free Press*, 19 July 1903; *LA*, pp. 209-18.

"Representative Government" [shorter version], Mountain Lake Park, Maryland, August 27, 1903; *LPLC*.

Campaign Speech, Plymouth, Wis., September 2, 1903; *Milwaukee Free Press*, 3 Sept. 1903; *LPSHSW*; *LA*, pp. 219-30.

Campaign Speech, Appleton, Wis., September 4, 1903; *Milwaukee Free Press*, 5 Sept. 1903; Excerpt, *LA*, pp. 231-32.

Campaign Speech, Antigo, Wis., September 9, 1903; *Milwaukee Free Press*, 9 Sept. 1903; Excerpt, *LA*, p. 233.

Campaign Speech, Sheboygan, Wis., [ca. 1903]; *LPSHSW*.

"Remarks to an Assembly of High School Students and Townspeople," Eau Claire, Wis., October 2, 1903; *Milwaukee Free Press*, 3 Oct. 1903; *LA*, pp. 311-12.

"Hamlet: The World's Greatest Tragedy," [presented throughout the United States], [ca. 1903]; *LPSHSW*; A slightly different draft can be found in *LPLC*.

"Granger Legislation and State Control of Railway Rates," Milton Junction, Wis., January 29, 1904; *PC*.

"To the Young Men's Christian Association of Milwaukee," Milwaukee, February 5, 1904; *Milwaukee Sentinel*, 6 Feb. 1904; *LPLC*; *LA*, pp. 313-14. The speech was read by John Hannan in La Follette's absence.

Campaign Speech, Milwaukee, April 22, 1904; *Milwaukee Free Press*, 23 April 1904; Excerpt, *LA*, pp. 234-41.

Campaign Speech, La Crosse, Wis., April 22, 1904; *LPSHSW*.

"Acceptance Speech," Madison, May 19, 1904; *PC*; *LA*, pp. 242-50.

Speech Delivered at the Inauguration of Charles Van Hise, Madison, June 7, 1904; *LPLC*; *LA*, pp. 315-18.

"Address at the Dedication of the Wisconsin Building at the St. Louis Exposition," St. Louis, June 29, 1904; *LPLC*; *LA*, pp. 319-22.

Campaign Speech, [Wisconsin], [ca. August, 1904]; *LPSHSW*.

Campaign Speech, Milwaukee, November 4, 1904; *Milwaukee Free Press*, 5 Nov. 1904; Excerpt, *LA*, pp. 251-57.
"Third Inaugural Address," Madison, January 12, 1905; Document Department, State Historical Society of Wisconsin.
"Speech Accepting Election to the United States Senate," Madison, January 25, 1905; *SJ*, January 25, 1905, pp. 171-74; *LA*, pp. 330-33.
"The State," [Wisconsin], February 15, 1905; *LPSHSW*.
"Remarks at the Funeral of A.R. Hall," Knapp, Wis., June 4, 1905; *Menomonie Times*, 8 June 1905; *Milwaukee Sentinel*, 5 June 1905; *LA*, pp. 323-25.
"Address of Welcome to the Elks," Madison, June 14, 1905; *Madison Democrat*, 15 June 1905; *LA*, pp. 326-27.
"Message to the Wisconsin Legislature," Madison, December 5, 1905; *LPSHSW*.
"Message Read to the Legislature Announcing Decision to Resign as Governor," Madison, December 5, 1905; *Milwaukee Free Press*, 6 Dec. 1905; *LA*, pp. 339-40.
On Mining Indian Lands, Washington, D.C., March 1, 2, 1906; *CR*, March 1, 1906, p. 3207; March 2, 1906, pp. 3254-55.
"Regulation of Railroad Rates," Washington, D.C., April 19, 20, 23, 1906; *CR*, April 23, 1906, pp. 5684-5723.
"Hours of Labor of Railroad Employees," Washington, D.C., June 29, 1906; *CR*, June 29, 1906, pp. 9683-85.
Speech Supporting Lenroot for Governor, Milwaukee, July 20, 1906; *LPLC*.
"Representative Government," Connorsville, Ind., March 12, 1907; *LPLC*.
"Amendment of National Banking Laws," Washington, D.C., March 17, 19, 24, 1908; *CR*, March 17, 1908, pp. 3434-53; March 19, 1908, pp. 3566-78; March 24, 1908, pp. 3793-3800.
Against the Aldrich-Vreeland Bill, Washington, D.C., May 29-30, 1908; *CR*, May 29, 1908, pp. 7161-7201; May 30, 1908, pp. 7221-26.
"Naval Appropriation Bill," Washington, D.C., February 11, 1909; *CR*, February 11, 1909, pp. 2199-2201.
"Civic Forum Speech," New York, March 12, 1909; *LPLC*.
On the Tariff Bill, Washington, D.C., June 9, 11, August 5, 1909; *CR*, June 9, 1909, pp. 3013-28; June 11, 1909, pp. 3126-27; August 5, 1909, p. 4954.
"Court of Commerce," Washington, D.C., April 12, 1910; *CR*, April 12, 1910, pp. 4549-64.
On Railroad Rate Regulation, Washington, D.C., April 29, 1910; *CR*, April 29, 1910, pp. 5563-66.
"Court of Commerce," Washington, D.C., May 25-26, 1910; *CR*, May 26, 1910, pp. 6896-6909.

222 Chronology of Major Speeches

On Railroad Rate Regulation, Washington, D.C., May 31, June 3, 1910; *CR*, May 31, 1910, pp. 7139-44; June 3, 1910, pp. 7372-74.
Speech at Republican State Convention, Madison, September 28, 1910; Excerpts, *LM*, 8 Oct. 1910, pp. 12-13.
"The Beginning of a Great Movement," Madison, January 25, 1911; *LM*, 4 Feb. 1911, pp. 7-9, 12.
On Organization of Senate Committees, Washington, D.C., April 28, 1911; *CR*, April 28, 1911, pp. 714-15.
On Secret Senate Meetings, Washington, D.C., May 11, 1911; *CR*, May 11, 1911, p. 1184.
"Senator from Illinois," Washington, D.C., May 22, 23, 24, 26, 1911; *CR*, May 22, 1911, pp. 1435-37; May 23, 1911, pp. 1490-95; May 24, 1911, pp. 1547-57; May 26, 1911, pp. 1600-1605.
On Canadian Reciprocity, Washington, D.C., July 21, 1911; *CR*, July 21, 1911, pp. 3139-53.
"Tariff Duties on Wool," Washington, D.C., July 27, August 15, 1911; *CR*, July 27, 1911, pp. 3264-67; August 15, 1911, pp. 3943-46, 3951-55.
"Protection of Trade and Commerce," Washington, D.C., August 19, 1911; *CR*, August 19, 1911, pp. 4183-90.
"Government Control in Alaska," Washington, D.C., August 21, 1911; *CR*, August 21, 1911, pp. 4262-67.
"The Undermining of Democracy," Philadelphia, February 2, 1912; Pamphlet, *LPLC*.
Campaign Speech, Valley City, N.D. [Auditorium], March 13, 1912; *LPLC*.
Campaign Speech, Valley City, N.D. [Normal School], March 13, 1912; *LPLC*.
Campaign Speech, Bismarck, N.D., March 14, 1912; *LPLC*.
Campaign Speech, Jamestown, N.D., March 14, 1912; *LPLC*.
Campaign Speech, Mandan, N.D., March 14, 1912; *LPLC*.
Campaign Speech, Fargo, N.D. [Agricultural College], March 16, 1912; *LPLC*.
Campaign Speech, Fargo, N.D. [Fargo College], March 16, 1912; *LPLC*.
Campaign Speech, Fargo, N.D. [Opera House], March 16, 1912; *LPLC*.
Campaign Speech, Grand Forks, N.D., March 16, 1912; *LPLC*.
Campaign Speech, Devils Lake, N.D., March 18, 1912; *LPLC*.
Campaign Speech, Minot, N.D., March 18, 1912; *LPLC*.
Campaign Speech, Rugby, N.D., March 18, 1912; *LPLC*.
On the Post Office Department, Washington, D.C., August 12, 1912; *CR*, August 12, 1912, pp. 10,728-33.
"Physical Valuation of Railroads," Washington, D.C., February 24, 1913; *CR*, February 24, 1913, pp. 3795-3801.
"The Tariff," Washington, D.C., May 16, 1913; *CR*, May 16, 1913, pp. 1596-99.

Chronology of Major Speeches 223

On Women's Suffrage, Washington, D.C., July 31, 1913; *CR*, July 31, 1913, p. 2951.

On Income Tax, Washington, D.C., August 27, 1913; *CR*, August 27, 1913, pp. 3819-21.

On the Tariff Wool Schedule, Washington, D.C., September 8, 1913; *CR*, September 8, 1913, pp. 4446-58.

On the Seamen's Bill, Washington, D.C., October 21, 23, 1913; *CR*, October 21, 1913, pp. 5714-21; October 23, 1913, pp. 5776- 83.

On Intervention in Mexico, Washington, D.C., April 21, 1914; *CR*, April 21, 1914, pp. 7007-7008.

"Proposed Increase of Railroad Rates," Washington, D.C., May 5, 1914; *CR*, May 5, 1914, pp. 7727-33.

"Proposed International Peace Conference," Washington, D.C., February 12, 1915; *CR*, February 12, 1915, pp. 3631-33.

"On Right of Petition," Washington, D.C., January 27, 1916; *CR*, January 27, 1916, p. 1619.

"Washington Birthday Message," Madison, February 22, 1916; *LPLC*.

"Armed Merchant Vessels," Washington, D.C., March 10, 1916; *CR*, March 10, 1916, pp. 3886-91.

"On Peace," Mt. Vernon, Wis., [Arbor Day, 1916]; *LPLC*.

On Military Appropriations, Washington, D.C., July 19-20, 1916; *CR*, July 20, 1916, pp. 11330-47.

On the Children's Bureau, Washington, D.C., January 22, 1917; *CR*, January 22, 1917, pp. 1738-41, 1743-50.

On the Cloture Rule, Washington, D.C., March 8, 1917; *CR*, March 8, 1917, pp. 40-45.

On American Entry Into the War, Washington, D.C., April 4, 1917; *CR*, April 4, 1917, pp. 223-34.

On Conscription, Washington, D.C., April 27, 1917; *CR*, April 27, 1917, pp. 1354-64.

On War Revenue, Washington, D.C., August 21, 23, September 1, 3, 10, 1917; *CR*, August 21, 1917, pp. 6201-10; August 23, 1917, pp. 6273-79; September 1, 1917, pp. 6503-19; September 3, 1917, pp. 6523-34; September 10, 1917, pp. 6853-61.

"St. Paul Speech," St. Paul, Minn., September 20, 1917; *LPLC*.

"Toledo Speech," Toledo, Ohio, September 23, 1917; *LPLC*.

On War Finances, Washington, D.C., October 2, 1917; *CR*, October 2, 1917, pp. 7632-33.

"Free Speech and the Right of Congress to Declare the Objects of the War," Washington, D.C., October 6, 1917; *CR*, October 6, 1917, pp. 7878-86; *LM*, November 1917, pp. 4-11, 15. Reprinted in Part II.

"Affairs in Russia," Washington, D.C., January 7, 1919; *CR*, January 7, 1919, pp. 1101-1103.
On the European Relief Bill, Washington, D.C., January 24, 1919; *CR*, January 24, 1919, pp. 1983-89.
On Government Salary Increases, Washington, D.C., February 20, 1919; *CR*, February 20, 1919, pp. 3852-56.
"Oil and Gas Lands—Conference Report," Washington, D.C., March 1, 4, 1919; *CR*, March 1, 1919, pp. 4706-16; March 4, 1919, pp. 4980-91.
"Memorial Address on the Late Senator Husting," Washington, D.C., March 2, 1919; *CR*, March 2, 1919, pp. 4811-13.
"Memorial Address on the Late Representative Davidson," Washington, D.C., March 2, 1919; *CR*, March 2, 1919, p. 4816.
On the Treaty of Peace with Germany, Washington, D.C., October 16, 29; November 6, 13, 18, 1919; *CR*, October 16, 1919, pp. 7011-12; October 29, 1919, pp. 7669-77; November 6, 1919, pp. 8006-10; November 13, 1919, pp. 8427-33; November 18, 1919, pp. 8719-28, 8748-53.
"Railroad Control," Washington, D.C., December 9-13, 20, 1919; *CR*, December 13, 1919, pp. 502-29; December 20, 1919, Appendix, pp. 8746-61.
Campaign Speech, Milwaukee, October 21, 1920; *LPLC*.
"Partial Payments of Guaranty Under the Esch-Cummins Law," Washington, D.C., February 21-22, 1921; *CR*, February 21, 1921, Appendix, pp. 4602-20.
On Ireland, Milwaukee, March 20, 1921; *The Capital Times* [Madison], 22 March 1921; *LPLC*.
"Speech to the People's Reconstruction League," Madison, March 25, 1921; Excerpts, *Wisconsin State Journal*, 26 March 1921; Excerpts, *The Capital Times* [Madison], 26 March 1921.
Speech to the People's Legislative Service, Washington, D.C. April 16, 1921; *LPLC*.
On Naval Appropriations, Washington, D.C., May 16, 17, 23, 25, 1921; *CR*, May 25, 1921, pp. 1731-57.
"The Shipping Board," Washington, D.C., July 25, 1921; *CR*, July 25, 1921, pp. 4237-44.
On Presidential Interference with the Senate, Washington, D.C., August 22, 1921; *CR*, August 22, 1921, pp. 5415-18.
On Taxation, Washington, D.C., September 29, November 5, 1921; *CR*, September 29, 1921, pp. 5868-73; November 5, 1921, pp. 7364-73.
"Michigan Senatorial Election," Washington, D.C., January 12, 1922; *CR*, January 12, 1922, Appendix, pp. 13,549-52.
Speech to the Von Steuben Club, Milwaukee, February 19, 1922; *LPLC*.

On the Four-Power Treaty, Washington, D.C., March 22, 1922; *CR*, March 22, 1922, pp. 4227-35.
"Naval Oil Reserve Leases," Washington, D.C., April 28, 1922; *CR*, April 28, 1922, pp. 6041-49.
"Address Before Annual Convention of American Federation of Labor," Cincinnati, June 14, 1922; *CR*, June 21, 1922, pp. 9076-82; *Capital Times*, 29 June 1922.
"The Tariff," Washington, D.C., July 7-8, 1922; *CR*, July 8, 1922, pp. 10,074-86.
"Congress Betrays Peoples' Interests," Milwaukee, July 17, 1922; *LM*, July 1922, pp. 100-104; *The Capital Times* [Madison], 18 July 1922; *Milwaukee Journal*, 18 July 1922.
"Address to the Conference of Progressives," Washington, D.C., December 1, 1922; *LPLC*.
"Edwin Denby, Secretary of the Navy," Washington, D.C., February 11, 1924; *CR*, February 11, 1924, pp. 2230-34.
On Election of Senate Special Committees, Washington, D.C., March 1, 1924; *CR*, March 1, 1924, pp. 3410-11.
On Relief of Distress in Germany, Washington, D.C., June 6, 1924; *CR*, June 6, 1924, pp. 10,984-86.
"Statement and Platform of Robert M. La Follette," read at Cleveland, Ohio, July 4, 1924; Pamphlet, *LPLC*.
"Labor Day Address," Radio Speech, Washington, D.C., September 1, 1924; *LPLC*. Reprinted in Part II.
"Steuben Society Speech," Washington, D.C., September 10, 1924; *LPLC*.
Campaign Speech, New York, September 18, 1924; *LPLC*; *New York Times*, 19 Sept. 1924.
"Steuben Society Speech," New York, September 21, 1924; *LPLC*.
Campaign Speech, Rochester, N.Y., October 6, 1924; *LPLC*.
Campaign Speech, Scranton, Pa., October 7, 1924; *LPLC*.
Campaign Speech, Newark, N.J., October 8, 1924; *LPLC*.
Campaign Speech, Detroit, Mich., October 9, 1924; *LPLC*.
Campaign Speech, Cincinnati, Ohio, October 10, 1924; *LPLC*.
Campaign Speech, Chicago, Ill., October 11, 1924; *LPLC*.
Campaign Speech, Kansas City, Mo., October 13, 1924; *LPLC*.
Campaign Speech, St. Louis, Mo., October 14, 1924; *LPLC*.
Campaign Speech, Des Moines, Iowa, October 15, 1924; *LPLC*.
Campaign Speech, Minneapolis, Minn., October 16, 1924; *LPLC*.
Campaign Speech, Sioux Falls, S.D., October 17, 1924; *LPLC*.
Campaign Speech, Omaha, Neb., October 20, 1924; *LPLC*.
Campaign Speech, Rock Island, Ill., October 21, 1924; *LPLC*.
Campaign Speech, Peoria, Ill., October 22, 1924; *LPLC*.

Campaign Speech, Grand Rapids, Mich., October 23, 1924; *LPLC*.
Campaign Speech, Syracuse, N.Y., October 24, 1924; *LPLC*.
Campaign Speech, Baltimore, Md., October 27, 1924; *LPLC*.
Campaign Speech, Brooklyn, N.Y., October 28, 1924; *LPLC*.
Campaign Speech, Schenectady, N.Y., October 29, 1924; *LPLC*.
Campaign Speech, Boston, October 30, 1924; *LPLC*.
Campaign Speech, Pittsburgh, October 31, 1924; *LPLC*.
Campaign Speech, Cleveland, November 1, 1924; *LPLC*.

Selected Bibliography

PRIMARY SOURCES

Publications

The Facts: La Follette-Wheeler Campaign Textbook. Chicago: La Follette-Wheeler Campaign Headquarters, 1924. Pamphlet, La Follette Papers, Library of Congress.
La Follette's Autobiography: A Personal Narrative of Political Experiences. 1913. Reprint. Madison: The University of Wisconsin Press, 1961.
La Follette's Magazine.
My Own Story. Serialized in newspapers, including *Washington Daily News*, 18-20, 22-28 Sept. 1924.
The Political Philosophy of Robert M. La Follette. Ed. Ellen Torelle. Madison, Wis.: Robert M. La Follette Co., 1920.
The Voters' Hand-Book. Milwaukee: *Milwaukee Free Press*, 1902. Pamphlet, State Historical Society of Wisconsin.

Manuscript Collections

For the period 1879 to 1905, the researcher can locate speech fragments, drafts, finished manuscripts, and printed versions of orations in the Robert M. La Follette, Sr. Papers at the State Historical Society of Wisconsin, located in Madison. These materials are also available on microfilm.

For the period 1906 to 1925, the researcher must visit in person the Robert M. La Follette, Sr. Papers at the Manuscript Division of the Library of Congress, Washington, D.C. This collection also contains drafts of La Follette's orations, completed manuscripts, and printed versions.

Unfortunately, the researcher can not rely completely upon these manuscript collections to supply all of La Follette's speech texts. Nevertheless, they contain orations that can be found nowhere else. See the Chronology of Major Speeches for specific references.

Newspapers

Capital Times (Madison)
Chippewa Herald (Chippewa Falls)
Dodgeville Star
Dunn County News (Menomonie)
Evansville Review
Madison Democrat
Milwaukee Daily News
Milwaukee Free Press
Milwaukee Journal
Milwaukee Sentinel
The Minneapolis Sunday Tribune
Monroe Sun
New York Times
New York Tribune
New York World
Sauk County Democrat (Baraboo)
The State (Madison)
Sun Prairie Countryman
Whitewater Register
University Press (Madison)
Wisconsin State Journal (Madison)
Wood County Reporter (Wisconsin Rapids)

SECONDARY SOURCES

Barton, Albert O. *La Follette's Winning of Wisconsin, 1894-1904.* Des Moines, Iowa: The Homestead Company, 1922.
_____. "Franklin Higgins, Bob's Early Teacher." *La Follette's Magazine.* February 1929, 29-30.
Black, Edwin. *Rhetorical Criticism: A Study in Method.* 1965. Reprint. Madison: The University of Wisconsin Press, 1978.
_____. "The Second Persona." *Quarterly Journal of Speech* 56 (1970): 109-19.
Bryce, James. *The American Commonwealth.* 2 vols. London: Macmillan, 1889.

Burgchardt, Carl R. "Apology as Attack: La Follette *vs.* Robinson on Freedom of Speech." In *Oratorical Encounters: Selected Studies and Sources of Twentieth-Century Political Accusations and Apologies.* Ed. Halford Ross Ryan, 1-16. Westport, Conn.: Greenwood Press, 1988.

_____. "Discovering Rhetorical Imprints: La Follette, 'Iago,' and the Melodramatic Scenario." *Quarterly Journal of Speech* 71 (1985): 441-56.

_____. "The Will, the People, and the Law: A Rhetorical Biography of Robert M. La Follette, Sr." Ph.D. diss., University of Wisconsin, 1982.

Caine, Stanley P. *The Myth of a Progressive Reform: Railroad Regulation in Wisconsin, 1903-1910.* Madison: The State Historical Society of Wisconsin, 1970.

Carpenter, Ronald H. "The Rhetorical Genesis of Style in the 'Frontier Hypothesis' of Frederick Jackson Turner." *Southern Speech Communication Journal* 37 (1972): 233-48.

Coleridge, Samuel Taylor. *Coleridge's Shakespearean Criticism.* 2 vols. Ed. Thomas Middleton Raysor. Cambridge: Harvard University Press, 1930.

Crocker, Lionel. "Robert Green Ingersoll's Influence on American Oratory." *Quarterly Journal of Speech* 24 (1938): 299-312.

Davis, Allen F. "Welfare, Reform, and World War I." *American Quarterly* 19 (1967): 516-33.

Davis, David Brion, ed. *The Fear of Conspiracy: Images of Un-American Subversion from the Revolution to the Present.* Ithaca, N.Y.: Cornell University Press, 1971.

Filene, Peter G. "An Obituary for the Progressive Movement." *American Quarterly* 22 (1970): 20-34.

Garraty, John A. *The New Commonwealth, 1877-1890.* New York: Harper Torchbooks, 1968.

Gilbert, Clinton W. *"You Takes Your Choice."* New York: G.P. Putnam's Sons, 1924.

Glad, Paul W. *McKinley, Bryan, and the People.* Philadelphia: J.B. Lippincott Company, 1964.

Grahame, Pauline. "La Follette Wins." *The Palimpsest*, May 1931, 179-88.

Greenbaum, Fred. *Robert Marion La Follette.* Boston: Twayne Publishers, 1975.

Hays, Samuel P. "The Politics of Reform in Municipal Government in the Progressive Era." *Pacific Northwest Quarterly* 55 (1964), 157-69.

_____. "The Social Analysis of American Political History." *Political Science Quarterly* 80 (1965): 373-94.

Hofstadter, Richard. *The Age of Reform.* New York: Vintage Books, 1955.

_____. *The Paranoid Style in American Politics and Other Essays.* New York: Vintage Books, 1967.

Holli, Melvin G. *Reform in Detroit: Hazen S. Pingree and Urban Politics.* New York: Oxford University Press, 1969.

Hostettler, Gordon. "The Public Speaking of Robert M. La Follette." *American Public Address: Studies in Honor of Albert Craig Baird.* Ed. Loren Reid. Columbia, Missouri: University of Missouri Press, 1961.

Ingersoll, Robert G. *Complete Lectures of Col. R.G. Ingersoll.* Published for trade, no place, no publisher, no date.

——. *The Ghosts and Other Lectures.* Peoria, Ill.: C.P. Farrell, Publisher, 1878.

——. *Great Speeches of Col. R.G. Ingersoll.* Chicago: Rhodes and McClure Publishing Co., 1885.

——. *Shakespeare: A Lecture.* New York: C.P. Farrell, 1913.

Kennedy, Padraic Colum. "La Follette's Foreign Policy: From Imperialism to Anti-Imperialism." *Wisconsin Magazine of History* 46 (Summer 1963): 287-93.

La Follette, Belle Case. "Robert M. La Follette: College Orator." *La Follette's Magazine,* October 1927, 150-52.

La Follette, Belle Case and La Follette, Fola. *Robert M. La Follette.* 2 vols. 1953. Reprint. New York: Hafner Publishing Company, 1971.

Lahman, Carroll P. "Robert M. La Follette." *A History and Criticism of American Public Address.* Vol. 2. Ed. William Norwood Brigance. New York: Russell and Russell, 1960.

——. "Robert Marion La Follette as Public Speaker and Political Leader, 1885-1905." Ph.D. diss., University of Wisconsin, 1939.

Lawler, Peter Augustine. "Robert Marion La Follette, Sr." In *American Orators of the Twentieth Century: Critical Studies and Sources.* Eds. Bernard K. Duffy and Halford R. Ryan, 277-84. Westport, Conn.: Greenwood Press, 1987.

Link, Arthur S. "What Happened to the Progressive Movement in the 1920's?" *American Historical Review* 64 (1959): 833-51.

——. *Woodrow Wilson and the Progressive Era, 1910-1917.* New York: Harper Torchbooks, 1954.

Lovejoy, Allen F. *La Follette and the Establishment of the Direct Primary in Wisconsin, 1890-1904.* New Haven: Yale University Press, 1941.

MacArthur, Robert Stuart. "Chautauqua Assemblies and Political Ambitions." *The World To-day,* October 1905, 1074-76.

MacKay, Kenneth C. *The Progressive Movement of 1924.* New York: Columbia University Press, 1947.

Manning, Eugene A. "Old Bob La Follette: Champion of the People." Ph.D. diss., University of Wisconsin, 1966.

Margulies, Herbert F. *The Decline of the Progressive Movement in Wisconsin, 1890-1928.* Madison: The State Historical Society of Wisconsin, 1968.

Maxwell, Robert S. *La Follette and the Rise of the Progressives in Wisconsin.* Madison: State Historical Society of Wisconsin, 1956.

Mowry, George E. *The California Progressives.* Berkeley: University of California Press, 1951.

_____. *The Era of Theodore Roosevelt and the Birth of a Modern America.* New York: Harper Torchbooks, 1958.

Neal, Nevin Emil. "A Biography of Joseph T. Robinson." Ph.D. diss., University of Oklahoma, 1958.

Nye, Russell B. *Midwestern Progressive Politics.* East Lansing, Mich.: Michigan State University Press, 1959.

Oliver, Robert T. *History of Public Speaking in America.* Boston: Allyn and Bacon, 1965.

Opinions of the Press: Mr. La Follette's Oratorical Victory. Madison: The Madison Democrat, [1880]. Pamphlet, State Historical Society of Wisconsin.

Peterson, H.C., and Gilbert C. Fite. *Opponents of War, 1917-1918.* Madison: University of Wisconsin Press, 1957.

Philipp, Emanuel L. *Political Reform in Wisconsin.* Eds. Stanley P. Caine and Roger E. Wyman. Madison: State Historical Society of Wisconsin, 1973.

Prather, Charles Edgar, ed. *Winning Orations of the Inter-State Oratorical Contests.* Topeka, Kansas: Charles Edgar Prather, 1891.

Ryley, Thomas W. *A Little Group of Willful Men.* Port Washington: Kennikat Press, 1975.

Thelen, David P. *The Early Life of Robert M. La Follette, 1855-1884.* Chicago: Loyola University Press, 1966.

_____. *The New Citizenship: Origins of Progressivism in Wisconsin, 1885-1900.* Columbia, Missouri: University of Missouri Press, 1972.

_____. *Robert M. La Follette and the Insurgent Spirit.* Boston: Little, Brown and Company, 1976.

_____. "Social Tensions and the Origins of Progressivism." *Journal of American History* 56 (1969): 323-41.

Vatter, Harold G. *The Drive to Industrial Maturity: The U.S. Economy, 1860-1914.* Westport, Conn.: Greenwood Press, 1975.

Ware, B.L., and Wil Linkugel. "They Spoke in Defense of Themselves: On the Generic Criticism of Apologia." *Quarterly Journal of Speech* 59 (1973): 273-83.

Weinberg, Arthur and Weinberg, Lila, eds. *The Muckrakers.* New York: Capricorn Books, 1964.

Wiebe, Robert H. *The Search for Order, 1877-1920.* New York: Hill and Wang, 1967.

Wrage, Ernest. "Public Address: A Study in Social and Intellectual History." *The Quarterly Journal of Speech* 33 (1947): 453-55.

Wyman, Roger E. "Voting Behavior in the Progressive Era: Wisconsin as a Case Study." Ph.D. diss., University of Wisconsin, 1970.

Index

Abuse, personal, 68, 70. *See* Suffering, personal
"Acceptance Speech of 1900," 45
"Acceptance Speech" (July 16, 1902), 55, 56
"Acceptance Speech" (May 19, 1904), 62
"Address to Farmers' Institute," 67-68
AFL (American Federation of Labor), 105, 111, 115. *See* Labor, organized
Agitator, 71, 122-23
"Agricultural Experiment Stations," 129
Agriculture, La Follette's defense of: in "The Dangers Threatening Representative Government," 51; in McKinley tariff debate, 26-27; in "Memorial Day Address," 31; in "Oleomargarine," 25, 31; in presidential campaign (1924), 109, 110, 113-14; in "Railroad Control," 101-2; in senatorial campaign (1916), 86
Aldrich, Nelson, 74
Aldrich bill, 74-76
Aldrich tariff bill, 77

Aldrich-Vreeland bill, 76
Ambition, 69-70
"Amendment of National Banking Laws," 74-76, 118
American entry into the war, speech on, 87, 89-90
"American Federation of Labor," 105-6
American Magazine, 79
Apology, 93, 94
Armaments, 109. *See* Munitions, manufacturers of
"Armed Merchant Vessels," 86, 88
Article X, 97
Assembly, Wisconsin, 38, 53-54, 56
Associated Press, 91, 94, 95
Athena Literary Society, 12, 14
Attack, personal, 70, 78
Austro-Hungarian empire, 97
Automobile, campaigning by, 106

Babcock, Joseph, 44
Baker, Ray Stannard, 79
Banking industry, 74-76, 83
Barrett, Lawrence, 13
Barton, Albert O., 53, 54
"Beatrice and Margaret," 16, 17
Bennett law, 28

Berger, Alexander, 12
Beveridge, Albert, 77
Black, Edwin, 5
Bonds, railroad, 74
Borah, William, 98
Braley, A.B., 14
Brandeis, Louis D., 111
Bristow, Joseph, 77
Britain, 97, 104
Bryce, James, 18
Bull Moose Party, 82
Bushnell, Allen R., 28
Butler, Nicholas Murray, 105

"Campaign Announcement of 1900," 44
Campaigns, political:
  1884 congressional, 24-25; 1886 congressional, 27-28; 1888 congressional, 27-28; 1890 congressional, 28; 1892 gubernatorial, 36-37; 1896 gubernatorial, 37-38; 1898 gubernatorial, 43-44; 1900 gubernatorial, 44-46; 1902 gubernatorial, 55-57; 1904 gubernatorial, 60-63; 1908 presidential, 79; 1910 senatorial, 78; 1912 presidential, 79-82; 1916 senatorial, 85-86; 1922 senatorial, 106-7; 1924 presidential, 108-16
Campaign speech, Milwaukee (September 30, 1902), 56
Campaign speech, Milwaukee (October 21, 1920), 103
Campaign speech, Valley City, North Dakota (March 13, 1912), 80-81
Candidate, independent, 109
Capitalism, 111
Carlisle, John, 26, 34
Carnegie Hall, 79
Carpenter, Matt, 66
Carpenter, Ronald H., 127 n.23

Caucus and convention system, 37, 39, 43-44, 49
Character, issue of, 119-20
Chautauqua speeches, 59-60, 62, 64-65, 140
Chicago, University of, 39
C.C. Washburn Grand Army Post, 24
Chapel rhetoricals, 11, 125 n.3
China, 96
Civic reform groups, 111
Civil service reform, 63, 70
Civil War, 30-31, 43, 46-47, 49
Clapp, Moses, 77, 85
Class government, 110
Cleveland, Grover, 36
Cloture, rule of, 87
Cloture rule, speech on, 87, 89
Coleridge, Samuel, 15
Committee of Forty-eight, 103
Communists, 116
Compromise, opposition to, 68, 120, 123
Congress, 87, 93, 105
Congressional Record, 89, 106
Conscription bill, 87, 102, 109
Conscription, speech on, 87, 88, 90
Conspiracy theory, 75, 88, 97, 119, 121
Constitution, United States, 33, 92
Consumers, 110
Consumption metaphor, 117-18
Contract metaphor, 68-69
Contrast, device of: in "Iago," 15, 17, 30; in McKinley tariff bill, speech on, 30, 133; in "The Menace of the Political Machine," 48; in North Dakota primary (1912), 81; throughout career, 120
Coolidge, Calvin, 109, 111, 115, 116

Corporations, 47, 98, 121. *See also* Monopolies; Trusts
Cost of living, 90
Counterattack, tactic of, 92-93, 94
County fair speeches, 39-40, 42-43, 52, 60
CPPA (Conference for Progressive Political Action), 109, 115
Crushing weight metaphor, 90
Cummins, Albert, 77
Cummins bill, 101-2
Currency, comptroller of, 38
Currency, emergency, 74, 118
Curtis, Olin A., 12, 17

Dairy industry, La Follette's support of, 25, 27, 29, 45, 121
Daly, B.J., 41, 42
"The Dangers Threatening Representative Government," 40-41, 59-60, 64-65, 78, 132
"Dante," 16, 17
Davis, John, 111, 115
Dawes, Charles, 111
Debs, Eugene, 94
DeForest, Lee, 111
Delivery, 41-42, 81
Democratic Party, 36, 44, 57, 62
Denby, Edwin, 107
Denby-Fall case, 107
Desdemona, 15, 16, 29, 118
Dewey, John, 111
Didactic rhetoric, 123
Disease metaphor, 108, 118
Dolliver, Jonathan, 77
"Dog-Tax Veto," 54

Education of the voters, 63, 70, 78, 123
Elliott, William, 26
Elliott-Smalls case, 26-27
England, 87, 97, 104

"Equation of Right," 20, 120
Emotional appeals, 90, 119, 120
Esch-Cummins Act, 103
Espionage bill, 87, 102
Europe, tour of, 107
Evans, Henry Clay, 37
Evidence, 32-33, 50, 75, 122-23. *See also* Examples; Facts; Statistics; Testimony
Evil principle, 16, 20, 117, 118
Examples, 51, 111
Expulsion petitions, 91, 92

Facts, 123
Fall, Albert, 91, 105
Filibusters, 76, 86, 122
"First Inaugural Address," 53
"Force" bill, 27
Foreign affairs, 85-86
Four Power Pact, 104
"Fourteen Points" speech, 96
Fourth of July Orations, 23
France, 104
Frankenburger, David B., 14-15, 20
Free Press, 55
"Free Speech and the Right of Congress to Declare the Objects of the War," 9, 91-96, 144
Free speech, issue of, 90-91, 93, 95

Garfield, James A., 66
German-Americans, 86, 102
Gompers, Samuel, 115
Good Government Club, 43
Gore Resolution, 85
Gorham, Christopher, 11
Grain elevators, 129 n.12
"Granger Legislation and State Control of Railway Rates," 61.
Grangers, 61, 102
Greenbaum, Fred, 82
Gronna, Asle, 85

Hagemeister bill, 54
Half-Breeds, 62, 64
Hall, Albert R., 37, 57
Hamilton, Alexander, 33
Hamlet, 59-60
"Hamlet," 59-60
Harding, Warren, 102-3
Harper, Sam, 38
Harrison, Benjamin, 36
Haugen, Nils P., 36-37
Hayes, Rutherford B., 19, 24
Henderson, David B., 28
Hepburn bill, 73-74
Higgins, Frank, 11
Hitchcock, A.N., 12
Hoard, William D., 36, 37
Hofstadter, Richard, 122
"Home and the State," 23. *See also* Tramps; Fourth of July Orations
Honor, appeal to, 50
House of Representatives, United States: Elliott-Smalls case, 26; "Force" bill, 27; McKinley tariff bill, 26-27; "Original-Package" bill, 27; Rivers and Harbors bill, 25; Tariffs, 26; taxation of oleomargarine, 25; Transportation Act of 1887, 26
Hughes, Charles Evans, 86

Iago, 15-16, 29, 47, 88, 117
"Iago": analysis of, 15-19; comparison to "Hamlet," 59; effects of, 19-20, 127; influence through subsequent career, 21, 23-24, 28, 117-18, 120-21, 127; presence of melodramatic scenario, 20; presence of rhetorical imprint, 20; relation to "The Stage," 14; resonances in rebuttal to Carlisle, 34; significance of, 6; similarities to "The Menace of the Political Machine," 47
Idée fixe, 121
Imperialism, 45, 97-98, 104, 106
Independent ticket, 109, 116
Industrialization, 121
Ingersoll, Robert G., 13-14, 126 n.9
Interior Department, 105
Interstate commerce, 26, 27, 74
"Interstate Commerce," 26
Inter-State Oratorical Contest, 14-15, 20, 127 n.14
Invisible enemy, 149
Iowa City, Iowa, 14-16, 19, 23

Jackson, Andrew, 111
Japan, 96, 104
Jefferson, Thomas, 33, 110
Johnson, Hiram, 98
Judiciary, Federal, 105, 109

Keller, Helen, 111
Kellogg, Frank, 91
Kenyon, F.L., 18
Kenyon, William, 85
Kent Theater, 39
Keyes, Elisha, 19
Knapp, Kemper, 14

Labor authority, international, 96-97
"Labor Day Address," 112
Labor, organized, 101-2, 105, 111, 114-15
Labor Party, 103
Laborers, American, 96, 111
La Follette, Belle: audience reaction (1884), 24; congressional campaign (1890), 28; direct primary proposal, 39; effects of "Iago," 20; husband's election as governor, 52; presidential campaign

(1924), 111; Special Messages (1903), 59
La Follette Peace Resolution, 85
La Follette, Phil, 106
La Follette, Robert M., Jr., 106
La Follette, Robert M., Sr.: Aldrich bill, opposition to, 74-76; American entry into the war, opposition to, 87; Athena Literary Society, participation in, 12; campaign, 1884 congressional, 24-25; campaign, 1886 congressional, 27-28; campaign, 1888 congressional, 27-28; campaign, 1890 congressional, 28; campaign, for district attorney (1880), 23-24; campaign, 1896 gubernatorial, 37-38; campaign, 1898 gubernatorial, 43-44; campaign, 1900 gubernatorial; campaign, 1902 gubernatorial, 55-57; campaign, 1904 gubernatorial, 60-63; campaign, on behalf of Harrison (1892), 36; campaign, on behalf of Hayes (1880), 24; campaign, on behalf of McKinley (1896), 38; campaign, "off-year" (1903), 59-60; campaign, 1912 presidential, 79-82; campaign, 1924 presidential, 108-16; campaign, 1910 senatorial, 78; campaign, 1916 senatorial, 85-86; campaign, 1922 senatorial, 106-7; charges of disloyalty, defense against, 91-96; Chautauqua circuit, participation in, 64-65; childhood, 11; comptroller of the currency, declined job offer, 38; Congress, election to, 25; Congress, nomination to, 24; conscription, opposition to, 87; county fair speeches (1897), 39-40; Cummins bill, opposition to, 101-2; death, 116; defeat in 1890 election, 28; delivery skills, 14; Denby, Edwin, opposition to, 107; direct primary concept, introduction of, 38-39; district attorney, reelection to, 24; district attorney, tenure as, 24; early education, 11; election of Senator Truman Newberry, opposition to, 104; elocutionist, performance as, 14; espionage bill, opposition to, 87; Europe, 1923 tour of, 107; filibuster of Armed Ship bill, 86; Four Power Pact, opposition to, 104; free speech, defense of, 91-96; governor, elected as, 46; governor, 1901 inauguration, 53; governor, 1903 inauguration, 57; governor, 1905 inauguration, 63-64; governorship, resignation of, 65; Haugen, Nils. P., support for, 36; Hepburn bill, opposition to, 73-74; "Iago," impact of, 19-20; illness in 1898, 44; illness in 1901, 55; illness in 1910, 78; illness in 1924, 108-16; Ingersoll, admiration of, 13; Inter-State Oratorical Contest, participation in, 14-15; Inter-State Oratorical Contest, victory at, 19; League of Nations, opposition to, 96-98; legal practice, begins, 23; legal practice, resumption of, 35; McKinley tariff bill, support for, 26-27; Monona Lake Assembly, role in, 36; Naval Expansion bill, opposition to, 104; oleomargarine tax bill, support for, 25; oratorical training, 11-12; "Original-Package" bill, opposition to, 27; rebuttal to Carlisle, 26; Republican National Convention, 1896 delegate to, 37; Republican

National Convention, 1920 participation in, 102-3; Rivers and Harbors bill, opposition to, 25; "St. Paul Speech," controversy over, 90-91; Sawyer affair, 35--36; Senate, U.S., election to, 64; Senate, U.S., entry into, 73; Senate, U.S., exhonerated in, 95; Senate, U.S., returned to, 78; South Carolina election law, opposition to, 26; Special Messages, use of, 58-59; Supreme Court, supported limitations of powers, 105-6; Teapot Dome scandal, role in exposing, 105; theater, interest in, 13; Transportation Act of 1887, support for, 26; Treaty of Versailles, opposition to, 96-98; *University Press*, participation in, 12; University of Wisconsin, graduation from, 19-20; vetoes, use of, 54; war revenue bill, opposition to, 87; Wilson, Woodrow, 1916 opposition to, 85; Winslow-Townsend amendment, opposition to, 103

La Follette's Autobiography, 78, 79, 82, 123, 140 n.23
La Follette Seaman's Act, 82
La Follette's Magazine, 78, 82, 107, 116
Lane, Harry, 86
Lapham, Increase, 14
Laws, banking, 74
League of Nations, 85, 95, 96-98
Leases, naval oil reserves, 105
Lewis, William, 38
Lincoln, Abraham, 111
Linkugel, Wil, 93
Literary bureau, 37, 44, 46, 52. *See also* Pamphlets, political

Literary societies, 11-12
Lobbyists, 65-66, 118
Loyalty investigations, 94-95
Loyalty, issue of, 49-50, 86, 91-93, 99, 144
Lusitania, 90, 91

MacArthur, Robert Stuart, 64-65
Machine metaphor, 48
Machines, political, 120
Madison Square Garden, 112
Madison, Wisconsin, 19, 113
"Maiden speech," 128, n.10
Marketing, national cooperative system, 110
McCullough, John, 13
McKinley, William, 36, 38, 39, 45
McKinley tariff bill, 27, 28
Melodramatic scenario: in "Amendment of National Banking Laws," 74-76; in "American Federation of Labor," 108; analysis of, 29; in Campaign Speech, Blue Mounds, July 4, 1902, 66; in "The Dangers Threatening Representative Government," 65; definition, 6; in foreign policy discourse, 87-88; in "Iago," 20; logic of, 21, 88, 119; in "The Menace of the Political Machine," 46-47; in "Oleomargarine," 29; in post-war discourse, 108; relation to evidence, 34; significance, 7, 8, 10; as unifying element, 117-22; use throughout career, 20-21, 28-29; in "Veto Message" (May 10, 1901), 65-66
"Memorial Day Address," 24, 46
"The Menace of the Political Machine," 7, 39, 46-49, 118

"Message to the Wisconsin Legislature" (December 5, 1905), 65
Metaphor, mixed, 108
Metaphors: consumption, 117-18; contract, 68-69; crushing weight, 90; disease, 108, 118; machine, 48; steam engine, 80; theatrical, 75
Michigan, University of, 43
Military appropriations, speech on, 85, 88, 90
Milton Junction Speech, 61
Milwaukee Free Press, 44
Minnesota Public Safety Commission, 91
Misquotation, danger of, 132 n.18
"Money Power" speech, 76. See "Amendment of National Banking Laws"
Money trust, 76
Monona Lake Assembly, 36
Monopolies, 108-9, 110, 113, 115. *See also* Corporations; Trusts
Moral judgments, 29-30, 34, 119
Munitions, manufacturers of, 88, 98, 104, 117, 118, 122

Narrative pattern, 47, 119
Naval appropriations bill (1916), 85
Naval Expansion bill (1921), 104
"Naval Oil Reserves," 105
Newberry, Truman, 104
New Jersey State Bar, 106
Newspapers, 80. *See also* Press
New York Board of Trade, 76
Nonpartisan League, 90-91, 102
Norris, George, 85, 106
NPRL (National Progressive Republican League), 79

Oil, naval reserves, 105
Old Guard, 36, 38, 44.

Oleo industry, 117, 118, 120
"Oleomargarine," 25, 29, 33, 117, 118
Oligarchy, judicial, 105
Olin, John M., 14
Opinions of the Press, 23, 127.
Opposition to La Follette, 61
"Original-Package" bill, 27, 29
Othello, 15, 16, 21, 118
Othello, 13, 15-16, 18, 20, 47, 118
Outrage, moral, 120. *See also* Moral judgments

Pamphlets, political, 39, 43, 46, 56, 71. *See also* Literary bureau
Panaceas, 49, 121-22
Panic of 1907, 74, 118
Paranoid style, 122
Payne-Aldrich bill, 77
Peck, George W., 1892
People, common, 89, 98
People, judgment of, 32, 73, 89-90, 98-99, 102
People, will of, 105
People's Legislative Service, 107
People's Reconstruction League, 104
Periodical Publisher's Association, 80
Philadelphia speech, 80, 82, 140 n.23
Philipp, Emanuel, 44, 55, 60
Pinchot, Gifford, 80
Plutocracy, dictatorship of, 110
Poetry reading, 11, 13, 14
Policy advocacy, 92, 94
Political machine: in "Acceptance Speech" (July 16, 1902), 55-56; and bossism, 37; in "The Dangers Threatening Representative Government," 40; in "The Menace of the Political Machine," 39, 46-49; in "Primary Elections for the Nomination of All Candidates

by Australian Ballot," 43; as villain, 117, 120-21
Pomerene, Atlee, 87
Populist movement, 122
Potter laws, 61
Pound, Roscoe, 106
Press, 86, 87, 88, 92, 94
Primary, presidential, 80-81, 82
Primary, direct: approved in referendum, 58, 60, 63; in campaign (1900), 44-45; in campaign (1902), 55; in campaign announcement (1898), 43; in "The Dangers Threatening Representative Government," 40, 51; in "First Inaugural Address," 53; introduction of, 38, 53-54; institution of, 70; in "The Menace of the Political Machine," 39, 49; precursor of, 37; "second-choice" amendment, 65; in "Second Inaugural Address," 57
"Primary Elections for the Nomination of All Candidates by Australian Ballot," 43, 51-52
Principles, moral, 120. *See also* "Equation of Right"
Profits, 88, 98
Progressives, leader of, 107, 108-9
Proletariat, dictatorship of, 110
Prophets of the past, 66-67
"Proposed Federal Election Law," 27
Protectionism, 36
Protest, voice of, 106
Public, intelligence of, 74
Public opinion, 89-90

Quarles, Joseph V., 64

Radicalism, charges of, 115
Radio, 112
"Railroad Control," 101-2

Railroads, commission for, 44, 57, 61, 70
Railroads, regulation of: consequences of, 69, 74; hearings on (1903), 58; institution of, 70; in "Interstate Commerce," 32; in North Dakota primary election, 81-82; passes, use of, 43-44; in "Railroad Control," 101-2; in "Regulation of Railroad Rates," 73-74; in "Second Inaugural Address," 57; significance of issue, 8, 32, 117; in Special Messages (1903), 58-59; status in 1903, 60-61; in "Third Inaugural Address," 64; and Transportation Act of 1887, 26
Rankin, Joseph, 128
Reading the freight rates, 8, 60, 71
Reading roll call votes, 8, 62-63, 71, 78
Record, public, 34, 77-78, 88, 95-96, 99, 104, 124
Redefinition, tactic of, 50, 69, 133 n.44
Reed, James, 98
Referenda, national, 89
Reform, causes of in Wisconsin, 42
"Regulation of Railroad Rates," 73-74
Representative government, 27, 32, 48-49, 110
Republican National Convention, 37, 82, 102, 109
Republicanism, progressive, 81, 83
Republican Party: election of 1898, 43; election of 1900, 45-46; election of 1902, 57; election of 1904, 62; election of 1912, 82; election of 1920, 102-3; election of 1924, 115; and imperialism, 45; La Follette's reputation in, 36; opposition to La Follette,

106, 111; Payne-Aldrich bill, 77; progressive faction, 78-79; Sawyer incident, 35-36; and Wisconsin, 37
Reputation, issue of, 70
Responsibility, appeals to: in "Acceptance Speech," (July 16, 1902), 68; in "Address to Farmers' Institute," 67-68; in "American Federation of Labor," 105; in "The Dangers Threatening Representative Government," 50; in "The Menace of the Political Machine," 49; throughout career, 124
Rhetorical biography, 3-5
Rhetorical imprint, 20, 128
Richard III, 15, 16
Richard III, 16
Rivers and Harbors bill, speech on, 25, 29
Robinson, Joseph, 91, 94, 96
Roosevelt, Theodore: former supporters of, 103, 111; in La Follette's Autobiography, 82; presidential election (1912), 79, 81, 82; speaker at the University of Chicago, 39; as villain, 117
Rose, David S., 56
Ryan, Edward G., 66-67

"St. Paul Speech," 90-92, 94, 103
"Satan and Mephistopheles," 16, 17
Sawyer faction, 36-38, 44-45.
Sawyer, Philetus, 7, 35-36, 44, 52
Scandals, Republican, 109
Scandinavians, 36-37, 45, 60
Schlitz Park, Milwaukee, 45
Scofield, Edward, 38, 43
Scripps, Edward W., 111
"Second Inaugural Address," 57-58
Secretary of the Interior, 105

Secretary of the Navy, 105, 107
Senate, United States: Aldrich bill debate, 74-76; *Congressional Record*, La Follette's use of, 106; conscription debate, 87; Cummins bill debate, 101-2; Denby, Edwin, debate over, 107; espionage bill debate, 87; expulsion petitions, 91; filibuster on Aldrich bill, 76; filibuster on Armed Ship bill, 86; foreign policy debates (1916), 85; Four Power Pact debate, 104; Gore Resolution debate, 85; Hepburn bill debate, 73-74; La Follette's attitude towards, 71; La Follette's election to, 64; La Follette's loyalty, debate over, 91-92; La Follette's positions in 1913, 82; League of Nations debate, 96-98; loyalty investigation, 94-95; military appropriations debate (1916), 85; Naval Expansion bill debate (1921), 104; Newberry, Truman, debate over, 104; Payne-Aldrich bill debate, 76-77; taxation bill (1921), 104; Teapot Dome investigation, 105; Treaty of Versailles debate, 96-98; war revenue debate (1917), 87; Winslow-Townsend amendment debate, 103-4; World War I debate, 87
Senate, Wisconsin, 54, 55, 56, 64
Shakespeare, William, 18, 59-60
Shantung Province, 96
Sherman Anti-Trust Law, 82
Sherman, John, 66
Ships, belligerent, 85
Ships, merchant, 86
Siebecker, Robert G., 35-36
Simpson, Jefferson B., 17
Smalls, Robert, 26

Socialist Party, 106, 111
South Carolina election law, 26
Southern Democrats, 29
Special interests, 75
Special Messages, 58-59, 64, 122
"Speech to the People's Reconstruction League," 104
Spooner, John Coit, 44-45
"The Stage," 14
Stalwarts, 45, 56, 58, 61, 63, 64, 102, 106. *See also* Old Guard; Sawyer Faction
The State, 45
"Statement and Platform" (1924), 109-10
Statistics: analysis of, 33, 67; in county fair speeches (1903), 60; in "The Dangers Threatening Representative Government," 50-51; in foreign policy discourse, 89; in post-war discourse, 108; in "Regulation of Railroad Rates," 73-74; in Winslow-Townsend amendment debate, 103-4
Steam engine metaphor, 80
Stephenson, Isaac, 44
Stevens bill, 53-54
Strikes, 114
Suffering, personal, 70. *See also* Abuse, personal
Supreme Court, United States, 33, 105-6, 108, 116-18

Taft, William Howard, 79, 81, 82
Tariff rates: in Aldrich tariff bill debate, 76-77, 139 n.13; and cotton, 77; issue in 1900 campaign, 45; La Follette's expertise on, 38; La Follette's position on (1913), 82; in McKinley tariff bill, 26-27; in North Dakota presidential primary, 80-81; in rebuttal to Carlisle, 26; and tobacco, 129 n.14; and woolens, 77; as villain, 29
Taxation, *ad valorem*, 44, 58, 60, 70, 101-2. *See* Taxation, equitable
Taxation, equitable: in county fair speeches (1897), 40; in "The Dangers Threatening Representative Government," 51; in "First Inaugural Address," 53; in gubernatorial campaign (1898), 43; in gubernatorial campaign (1900), 44, 45; in gubernatorial campaign (1902), 55; in presidential campaign (1924), 109; and railroads, 54; in "Second Inaugural Address," 57; in speech on taxation (1921), 104; and technique of redefinition, 69; in "Third Inaugural Address," 63; in war revenue bill debate, 87
Taxation, of railroads, 57, 70
Teapot Dome scandal, 105
Territorial acquisition, 87
Testimony, 32-33, 51, 66, 89, 92, 108
Theatrical metaphor, 75
Thelen, David, 19, 57, 91, 122
"Third Inaugural Address," 63-64
Third party, 109
Tobacco tariff, speech on, 129
"Toledo Speech," 143 n.18
Train, campaigning by, 46
Tramps, 23, 29, 117, 125-26 n.3
Transcendence, strategy of, 93
Transportation Act of 1887, 26
Treason, charges of, 91-92. *See also* Loyalty investigations
Treaty of peace with Germany, speech on, 96-97

Trusts, domestic, 43, 98, 108-109, 117, 120-21. *See also* Corporations; Monopolies
Trusts, international, 88, 98, 118-19
The Truth About Wisconsin Freight Rates, 61
Truth, absolute, 123
Turner, Frederick Jackson, 127 n.23

"Undermining of Democracy," 80, 82, 140 n.23
Unions, labor, 111, 114-15. *See* Workers, industrial
The University Press, 12
Upham, William H., 37
Urbanization, 31, 121

Valuation, railroad, 74. *See* Taxation, *ad valorem*
Van Hise, Charles, 12, 16
Versailles, Treaty of, 96-98, 101, 102, 104
"Veto Message" (May 10, 1901), 54-55
Vetoes, use of, 112
Victory, ultimate, 51-52, 68, 90
Vilas, William F., 19
Villain, characteristics of, 117-18
Voters, Democratic, 86
Voters, Irish, 115
Voters, Italian, 115
Votes, roll call, 77-78, 89. *See also* Reading roll call votes

Wagner, Charles L., 65
Wall Street, 51, 114, 121
War Aims Resolution, 87
War financing, issue of, 87, 90
War record, 104, 106, 108
War Revenue bill, 87
War revenue, speech on, 87, 89, 90
War, Spanish-American, 45

Ware, B.L., 93
Washington Herald, 107
Wealth, paper, 51
West Side Turn Hall, Milwaukee, 56
Wheeler, Burton K., 111
White, William Allen, 106
Wilson, Woodrow, 82, 85-88, 90, 93-94, 96-98, 117
Winslow-Townsend amendment, 103
Wisconsin, state of, 111, 115, 118, 122-23
Wisconsin, University of, 11-12, 21, 55
Women's groups, 111
Women's suffrage, 82
Workers, industrial, 114, 115. *See* Labor, organized
World War I, 87, 109, 118
Wrage, Ernest, 4, 5

About the Author

CARL R. BURGCHARDT is Associate Professor in the Department of Speech Communication at Colorado State University. He has written on the history and criticism of American public address.

Great American Orators

Defender of the Union: The Oratory of Daniel Webster
Craig R. Smith

Harry Emerson Fosdick: Persuasive Preacher
Halford R. Ryan

Eugene Talmadge: Rhetoric and Response
Calvin McLeod Logue

The Search of Self-Sovereignty: The Oratory of Elizabeth Cady Stanton
Beth M. Waggenspack

Richard Nixon: Rhetorical Strategist
Hal W. Bochin

Henry Ward Beecher: Peripatetic Preacher
Halford R. Ryan

Edward Everett: Unionist Orator
Ronald F. Reid

Theodore Roosevelt and the Rhetoric of Militant Decency
Robert V. Friedenberg

Patrick Henry, The Orator
David A. McCants

Anna Howard Shaw: Suffrage Orator and Social Reformer
Wil A. Linkugel and Martha Solomon

William Jennings Bryan: Orator of Small-Town America
Donald K. Springen